BIBLIOTHECA WIFFENIANA.

BIBLIOTHECA WIFFENIANA.

SPANISH REFORMERS
OF TWO CENTURIES
FROM 1520.

THEIR LIVES AND WRITINGS,
ACCORDING TO THE LATE BENJAMIN B. WIFFEN'S PLAN
AND WITH THE USE OF HIS MATERIALS

DESCRIBED BY

EDWARD BOEHMER.

THIRD VOLUME.

WIPF & STOCK · Eugene, Oregon

Wipf and Stock Publishers
199 W 8th Ave, Suite 3
Eugene, OR 97401

Spanish Reformers of Two Centuries from 1520, Third Volume
Their Lives and Writings, According to the Late Benjamin B. Wiffen's Plan and with the Use of His Materials
By Boehmer, Edward
Softcover ISBN-13: 978-1-6667-6220-4
Hardcover ISBN-13: 978-1-6667-6221-1
eBook ISBN-13: 978-1-6667-6222-8
Publication date 10/13/2022
Previously published by Karl J. Trubner, 1904

This edition is a scanned facsimile of the original edition published in 1904.

DEDICATED

TO

FREDERIK SEEBOHM AND JOHANNES MERCK.

Während im Riesengetriebe des britischen Reiches in Ansehn
    als Bankhalter Du wirkst, sinnest Du höheres Gut.
Glaubensgenosse der Seelen, die schlicht sich Freunde benennen,
    hast Du bedächtig erforscht, trefflich uns Allen erzählt
wie mit den weisen Gefährten getreulich Erasmus in Oxford
    gegen scholastischen Brauch biblische Lehre gepflegt.

Du, der Hapág Mitleiter, die jetzo der grössseste Reeder,
    tauchst in des Weltschrifttums heiter erfrischendes Bad.
Liebevoll suchst Du die Bücher der edlen hispanischen Geister,
    die des befangenen Volks herrschender Glaube verfehmt,
und so reihst Du die Perlen in würdiger schmuckerer Fassung,
    Freude dem prüfenden Blick, Zeugen von heiligem Rat.

Euch auch fesselte Beide das Werk, das der sorgliche Sammler,
    ledig des Eisengeschäfts, eisernes Fleisses geplant;
Ihr unternahmt was bereit nunmehr für den Leser hie vorliegt,
    reichlich ist's Euer, wohlan: nehmt es von dankender Hand.

INDEX.

Antonio del Corro . . . . P. 1
Cipriano de Valera . . . . „ 147
Pedro Galés . . . . „ 175
Melchior Roman . . . . „ 185

ANTONIO DEL CORRO.

The monks of the order of S. Hieronymus in San Isidro of Seville were induced by one of their number to open their hearts to purer religion, and the evangelical books which came from Geneva and Germany brought about a wonderful reform in the monastery. Worship of saints, fasting, horal prayers, masses for the dead, and other Roman practices were abolished; only the celebration of the daily mass was not discontinued, as this could not be done without drawing all eyes to the things going on at San Isidro. Twelve monks whose consciences could not acquiesce in such hypocrisy left the monastery and Spain in 1557 within a short time, and by different routes succeeded in meeting at Geneva, whither six or seven more from San Isidro followed them. Seven other evangelicals, men and women, had already in 1555 fled from Seville and had arrived in Geneva. Juan Perez, therefore, founded at Geneva a small Spanish congregation with a strong Sevillian element. Together with the absent fugitives, some Isidrians, who remained, appear in the next Sevillian autos, besides one who, on the way from Geneva to England, was caught while embarking from the Netherlands, and was burnt at Seville.[1]

One of the monks of San Isidro was Antonio del Corro (latinized Corranus), a Sevillian, born in the winter of 1526—7, son of a Doctor of Laws.[2] A relative of his was Inquisitor at Seville and was one

---

[1] Gonsalvius, Artes 223f. 243f. Valera, Trat. del Papa, 2ᵈ ed. 247—248. Cf. my Sp. Rf. II 73f.

[2] He matriculated at Oxford Oct. 1. 1586 as *Hispalensis LL. D. filius,* aged 59. As those entries always state the „*age last birthday*" and as he died about March 30. 1591, aged 64, which is certainly counted in the same way, it follows that he was born between beginning of October 1526 and end of March 1527. *Hispalensis* he calls himself in several publications. *Joannes de Pineda, Hispalensis,* in a passage (to be quoted below) of his commentary *in Ecclesiasten,* printed *Hispali* 1619, is sorry that the *transfuga* Corro was a *Hispalensis*. Born at Sevil, Wood, Ath. I 251; *born in Seville,* Strype, Parker II 481; *native of Seville,* Strype, Grindal 125. His

of the two by whom the process against Dr. Gil was conducted. While this lawsuit was going on during the years 1550 to 1552, the Inquisitor Corro, then about eighty, whose heart was overflowing with grief from what he had to suffer in this case, once began to talk to his young relation of the iniquities and acts of injustice occurring in the Holy Office, especially at that time with regard to Dr. Gil, whom he esteemed to be a Christian of better life than any of those who stood forth as his adversaries. Old Corro, whom as early as 1512 we find in the position of Inquisitor[3], had long ago given up the functions of that office save in the adjudication of some cases. He still retained the name and authority of an Inquisitor, but only that he might be able to assist persons who would otherwise be tyrannically treated by his colleagues whom he described to the astonished young monk as so destitute of all Christian conscience as to pass sentence of condemnation even though wholly uninformed of the accusation. „For instance we are", he said, „so utterly ignorant of this case of Dr. Gil that we cannot distinguish between error and truth and are constrained to call in monks to draw the line between heresy and truth, although we see their counsel is biassed and swayed by a wrathful, envious spirit against this worthy personage. If he be, as they say, a heretic, I am one likewise." The monk was extremely scandalized; „considering, however", he writes, „the venerableness of the man who spoke, and his personal affection to me, considering also that so distinguished a person, an eye-witness and a man of great experience, was fully entitled to judge upon such matters, I made it a subject of thorough reflection." And having done this, he begged the Inquisitor to show him the accusations and the theological

---

father is called by Wood l. c. *Ant. Corranus Doctor of the Laws.* Clark II 154: *Fil. Anthoni Corrani Doctoris Utriusque Juris. (Ath. I. 578).*

The Family was a Montañés one according to Menendez Pelayo, Heterod. II 481 f.

Antonides van der Linden, Professor of theology at Franeker, speaking in 1611, in an *epistola ad ordines Belgii,* of the first preachers of the gospel there, names some who were *ex monachis conversi,* then Feito, Antonus Corranus, Coolt *ex sacerdotibus,* then those *ex civili vita.* Miscell. Groning. t. III. fasc. 1. 1740, p. 47. But this is not a sufficient authority for believing that Corro had been priest.

3) Docum. inéditos para la hist. de España, t. X. Madrid 1847, p. 127: in Cuenca April 18. 1512 *los Señores Inquisidores licenciados Antonio del Corro y Fresneda.*

definitions given by the monks. The Inquisitor complied very readily, and showed him besides the doctor's apologies and the replies thereto.[4]

Young Corro read also some books of Luther and of other protestant doctors of Germany, which he got from Officers of the Inquisition in exchange for some present or favour.[5] To the Zurich divine Bullinger he writes in the summer of 1574: „I am one of those who by the aid of your writings, most learned sir, have acquired a purer knowledge of the Christian doctrine. For, some twenty years ago, by the providence of God, I obtained a suitable opportunity of studying your books, which the Spanish Inquisitors themselves supplied. As I perceive myself to have derived from them abundant fruit, gratitude compels me to thank you, since I cannot return the obligation." And at the end of the letter: „I pray you, most vigilant pastor, to reckon me in the number of those whom by your labours and watchings you have brought to the knowledge of Christ."

When at last he and the other Isidrians fled about the same time in 1557[6], he had been resisting the call of the Spirit for more

---

4) Corro's Letter to the king of Spain, 1567. The Inquisitor who is not named there, nor said to be the writer's relation, was Antonius Corranus, see here vol. II. p. 119. On his tombstone he is called *Licentiatus Antonius del Corro,* and *Canonicus Hispalensis.*

Also the father of the protestant Corro is called *Antonius* by Wood, see above note 2, I do not know on what authority.

Cousin, the London French minister, who always was busy to hoard up whatever might serve to cast a slur on Corro the Protestant, protocolled in the very first days of Corro's stay in London what Phares, then likewise in London, had formerly said in Geneva about Corro's parents when he had arrived there, see note 14.

5) Letter to the king [A VII].

6) On the flight of the 12 monks in 1557 cf. Valera quoted here vol. II 73. Corro says, that in 1556 he was still in Spain, Bulletin 1901 p. 214—215. That he left in 57, follows from two passages of his Letter to the king dated March 1567, fol. A iij: *depuis dix ans ença que je sortis de vostre Royaume d' Espagne,* and C iiij *me contraignirent à sortir de vostre Rogaume d'Espaigne, et par l'espace de dix ans peregriner.* A iiij he says that his departure from Spain had been *une chose grandement remarquée, tant pour la grande compaignie qui sortit au mesme temps, que pour l'occasion que nous disions nous avoir contraint,* viz. contrainte de conscience. Also Spaniards in London stated in April 1567 that Corro went to Geneva about ten years ago, see here note 14.

In lent 1558 Peter Veller (cf. here II 64) said: *De los españoles que han huido de Sevilla, los dos dellos son Antonio de el Corro é Diego de Santa Cruz, y el primero era fraile en Sant Isidro de Sevilla, é es tuerto de un ojo.* This might mean, that he was squinting with one eye, but also that he could not see with it.

than twenty months, for, as he confesses, he had recoiled from the afflictions which he foresaw would follow,[7] and had avowed his new convictions to a few persons only,[8] certainly to some of his fraternity and probably also to his relative the Inquisitor, who died in his 84th year in July 1556. Far from his country and his relatives and friends, and distressed by several bodily complaints, he writes that, if his life should end before he could explain by speech and writing the reasons for his self-banishment, his death in exile would serve to posterity as a tacit confession of faith.[9]

Even half a year after his escape, he says, the Inquisitors could hardly believe that he had fled for religion's sake,[10] so much was he in vogue.[11] And complaining of the rash judgment of Calvinists against him, he writes to the Bishop of London on July 15. 1568 that even the Spanish Inquisitors had behaved more justly. For they, when they had resolved to proceed against him, knew that he had gone to Geneva or Germany[12] in order to escape from papistry, and that he was, as they said, a Lutheran heretic; nevertheless they regarded the proper formalities, and divine and human laws, and for eighteen months summoned him with sound of trumpet and by public placards to answer in person or by proxy. He was burnt in effigy[13] as a Lutheran on April 26. 1562, together with nine other fugitives of the same monastery among whom were Cassiodoro de Reina and Cipriano de Valera.

By way of Genoa and Savoy he went to Geneva. He was the first of the Isidrians who did homage to Calvin. Others of them arrived later by way of Antwerp. Some had celebrated mass on the

7) Letter to the king [L VIII].
8) Ibid. C V.
9) Ibid. [B VI]f.
10) Ibid. C V.
11) Ibid. A iiij.

12) *à Geneve ou en Allemaigne.* Here Allemaigne means the Bernese territory which included Lausanne. — The Frenchmen, who in 1552 returning from the University of Lausanne were imprisoned at Lyon, said in the examination: *Nous sommes escholiers et venons des Alemagnes.* Hist. des martyrs 1582 fol. 204.

13) Corro says in his Epistle to the Augsburg Confessionists § 87: *les Inquisiteurs qui nous auront bannys ou bruslez en effigie, pour desployer leur rage sur la paille et papier, d'autant qu'ilz ne le peuvent pas executer sur la chair et les os des membres de Jesus Christ.*

journey in order to pass unsuspected; Corro maintains that he did not disguise his person or his religion, either then or later.

After a short stay at Geneva he went to the academy of Lausanne.[14] The academy, founded twenty years before, was flourishing as a seminary of evangelical ministers. In 1558 there were about 700 students. Geneva had no such institution as yet. The most renowned professor at Lausanne was Beza. He honoured the Spaniard, who was only 7 years younger, with his friendship.[15] As for the lectures which Corro attended, we only know that ten years later he asked Beza to get copied for him the *partition méthodique* of the epistle to the Hebrews, which he had written down according to Beza's exposition, but which had been lost.[16] At Lausanne Corro was one of the twelve pensioners, called *escoliers de Messieurs*, the Ex-

14) Letter to the king C iiij: *en Italie, Savoye, Alemaigne, France, et maintenant en vostre païs bas, Sire, je n'ay jamais dissimulé ne ma personne, ne ma religion.* Alemaigne means here Geneva and Lausanne. Geneva could still be considered as a free-town of the German empire. The birth of Philipp II, to whom Corro writes this letter, was announced by the Emperor to his Imperial City Geneva. Lausanne belonged, when Corro lived there, to the State of Berne. (That he never was at Zurich is clear from his letter to Bullinger whom he did not know personally.)

Cousin's draft of conversations held April 11.—13. 1567: *Touchant Belleriue* [i. e. Corro] *du vieil temps. Il venoit par Gennes a Geneve, et dautres venoient par Anuers. cestoit pour la Rochelle ayans crainte* [.] *et par chemin disoyent la messe pour nestre pas pris. Il y a enuiron 10 ans. Il venoit saluer Monsieur Caluin le premier, les autres en furent fasches* [faschés]. *Phares dit au marquis quil estoit vng orgueilleux filz de putain publique et dung prestre qui depuis fut inquisiteur. Apres peu de iours venoit a Lausanne ou il estudia assex bien vng an et demy, ou enuiron. escolier de Berenne* [Berne]. Phares, whom Cousin calls in the same draft also Pharesius, is the same who is called Francisco Faries in Baptista's lost will 1573 (see below in the life of Valera), Francisco Farias in the *Relacion* on the auto 1562 (Schäfer: Beiträge zur Gesch. des spanischen Protestantismus 1902 I 453, II 313), in Geneva and London (here above II 73. 171), Franc. de Farias in the list of foreigners in London 1568 (below here). The *Relacion* says: *prior que fue del monasterio de st. ysidro.* This does not mean that, when he fled, there was already another Prior; Valera says (above I 73) that the Prior fled. The Marquis is Galeazzo Caracciolo, here II 72. As for the uncontrollable gossip on Corro's parents so much is certain, that the man who became Inquisitor after Corro's birth was not that Inquisitor whom Corro venerated as we have told. The same official *Relacion* calls the heretic: *antoño del corro.*

Corro is not mentioned in the list of Spaniards at Geneva, see here II 74.

15) Corro to Beza, Sept. 3. 68. Beza epist. LIX.

16) Corro's letter just referred to.

cellencies of Berne, to whose dominion Lausanne belonged.[17] It must have been highly instructive for Corro to observe at Lausanne the evil consequences of the fatal dissensions among the evangelicals, and the failure of premature formulas of agreement. Beza, on entering office, had signed the articles drawn up at the *disputation* held in Berne in 1528; but in May 1557 he conceded so much, respecting the Lord's Supper to the Lutherans that Bullinger, Zwingli's successor, and the still more Zwinglian Bernese government were moved to indignation, and it was only with difficulty that Calvin, himself dissatisfied, contrived to appease them. In the following year Beza formulated with the help of Melanchthon another dogmatical compromise, but the influential Bullinger again remonstrated. Beza was one of the twelve members of the class of Lausanne who in June 1558 sent a protest to Berne against the order that the ministers should read from the pulpit a decree interdicting to preach on predestination, and complained against ecclesiastical maladministration; he had subscribed reluctantly, as he thought the step inopportune. They were summoned to Berne and reprimanded. Their project of an autonomous church after the Geneva model was rejected by the statesmen in power. Beza asked for his dismissal; in the autumn of 1558 he again settled at Geneva.[18]

Corro remained at Lausanne during the next winter. Then, as some liberty was to be found in Navarra nearer to his native country, he went there, with a recommendation from Calvin[19] dated May 26.

17) See note 14: escolier de Berenne.
18) Bernus: Bèze à Lausanne. Lausanne 1900.
19) *Accessit altera differendi ratio, quod hic bonus vir aliquam sibi commendationem dari rogabat. Sed dum Collonium* [Colonges] *frustra expectans tempus protrahit, literas quae ad Regem paratae erant commisi ferendas nobili tibi non incognito (Guereum vocant)... Redeo ad nuncium. Hispanus est, in quo genuinum pietatis studium deprehendimus. Quum litteris tuis certior factus essem Regem ad recipiendos ex ista gente hospites iam sponte propensum esse, commendationem meam addere non dubitavi. Abs te non aliud peto nisi ut pro solita tua humanitate in eum conferas quae absque tuo incommodo officia poteris. Quanquam hoc quoque supervacuum videtur, quia iuvare cupies non rogatus, quem scies dignum esse tuo et piorum omnium amore. Tantum sentiat testimonio meo se probatum fuisse.* Those *litterae ad Regem* are, I think, the undated letter printed as No. 2819 Cp. Rf., where we read: *Le present porteur* (Guereus), *Sire, suyvant quelques propos quon vous a deia tenu, a entrepris ce voyage pour estre mieux certifié de vostre*

1559, to La Gaucherie at Nerac, the tutor of the prince who afterwards became king Henry IV. In 1560 Corro was at Nerac when Beza was there. At that time some ministers desired that Corro should preach in French[20]; it seems he had been preaching in Spanish. In the same year he married.[21] In the next year we find him moderator of the city college at Aire. From there he visited Bordeaux, invited by fugitive Spaniards. There he wrote to Calvin on October 27., asking him to promote his work by some lines to the ministers of that region. The letter is signed *Antonius a Corro, alias Bellerive*. This second name he had probably invented in order to have a French name in France.[22] Two months later those ministers consulted Calvin about Corro. It is not known what Calvin may have answered.

There was a great lack of ministers at Toulouse. De Nort was the only one for between eight and nine thousand persons when he wrote to Calvin on February 10. 1552. On March 16. Corro was presented as *pasteur* to the *capitouls* of that town by the *procureur en parlement, au nom de l'église reformée*. But by the beginning of April the Romanists were up in arms and on May 17. the evangelicals after a valiant resistance had to leave the town. Many hundreds of them were killed in the struggle, and many hundred captives were hanged or beheaded or burnt or otherwise killed. In the first list of those against whom the parliament on May 26. ordered *prise de corps,* was Corro. He escaped.

In 1563 on July 3. the minister Merlin sent from Pau a report to Calvin in the name of the *compagnie*. Corro had complained to them that some Spaniards at Geneva had written angrily on account of bad news about him, and that he had learned that the marquis Caracciolo at that place was likewise very much scandalized. „The

---

bonne volonte et scavoir sil y auroit moyen davoir la quelque retraite pour les bons gens qui seroyent persecutez en Espaigne, a fin dy vivre sous vostre obeissance. Pour ce que iay entendu, Sire, que vous estes asses enclin desia a un tel bien, ie ninsisteray point a vous en faire longue requeste.

On many Frenchmen occurring in this my article see *La France protestante*.

20) See in Beza's epist. LIX. In 1560 Beza started from Geneva at the end of July and was back in the beginning of November. A letter of his from Nerac Aug. 25. Cp. Rf. XLVIII. Supplem.

21) See his letter of Christmas 1563.

22) Was he thinking of Bellerive opposite to Lausanne?

fact was," says Merlin, „that an ignorant man had accused him of Servetism, but his innocence had been recognized, and all bear witness to the worth of his doctrine, and of his life and conversation; his speaking and demeanour, however, appear to some very magisterial, but this is thought to come from the custom of his nation. Of one thing all judge him guilty, namely of ambition, which has caused great annoyance to the ministers, for he was never content, and was always wishing to change. His excuses will not be found quite sufficient. It is said that he exercised the ministry at Toulouse without due election; his explanation lessens the fault very much, but is not satisfactory to everyone. He was placed in a small town of this country, but he claimed the liberty to remain or to leave whenever he liked, and he importuned us so much that we could not but discharge him. He left this country, and is at present with a *gentilhomme* Mr. de Boesse."²³ This *gentilhomme* must have been Jean d'Escodeca, seigneur de Boesse (or Boisse), who was a protestant combatant in the civil wars, and governor of the ville de Pons in 1568, and in the following year was present in La Rochelle at the council of the queen of Navarra.²⁴

At the end of 1563 Corro stayed at Theobon, *maison seigneuriale* in Lot-et-Garonne, arrondissement de Duras, commune de Loube-Bernac, on the road from Clairac to Sainte Foy. Perhaps he was there at the same time as M. Boesse.²⁵ From Theobon he wrote at Christmas 1563 to his dear friend Cassiodoro de Reina who had consulted him about the proposed printing of his translation of the Bible into Spanish. Corro informs him that he had made some previous arrangements with a printer and that the queen of Navarra would allow the printing-press to be set up in a castle of hers,²⁶ and that

---

23) Beza to Corro, March 1569: Quaenam fuerit tibi cum Merlino controversia, nunquam audire memini.

24) The nobles d'Escodéca, a family of Périgord, Agenais, Quercy, were seigneurs de Boisse. Fr. protest. t. 6. col. 54. 55.

25) This is the conjecture of Bernus who also ascertained the situation of Théobon. Bulletin 1901, p. 324. — A daughter of a son of the above mentioned Jean d'Escodéca married in 1616 a marquis de Théobon. Fr. protest. t. 6 col. 58.

26) Blaise de Montluc, that persecutor of Protestants, reports to queen Catharine de Medicis that the queen of Navarra is printing in Bearn catechisms and New Testaments in Spanish, Bask and Bearnese. This report is thought to have

he ought to come. By his care Corro also wished to get some books, such as those written by Caspar Schwenkfeld and Valentin Crotvald [27] and others, who, he says, treat of the doctrine of our religion to the edification of our consciences. For, in truth, he adds, I am after all weary of Hebraisms and Hellenisms, and the prolix commentaries [28] are without savour to me. Also he desires to read Osiander's treatises on justification. And he asks for Reina's opinion on some questions. He wants to know what opinion people there hold concerning Velsius [29] and the Italian Acontius; [30] of what advantage the belief in the ubiquity of Christ's human nature might be to the Christian; how it can edify to know whether the glorified Christ is a creature or not; and so on.

From Bergerac, where he had become minister, he wrote to Reina on March 25. 1564. This was the twenty-first letter he had written during the last 8 months in order to get some positive news

been written in May 1563. Bulletin 1901, p. 557. There is no trace of the Spanish New Testament printed in Bearne about 1563.

27) On Schwenkfeld see the article in the Realencyclopädie für protestantische Theologie. On Krautwald cf. Sepp, Drie Evangeliedienaren, p. 165 f. He was a follower and friend of Schwenkfeld. Schlüsselburg the Lutheran antagonist of Schwenkfeld, says of Krautwald: vir ut videtur simplex et amans religionis.

28) *Prolixos commentarios ipse interpretatur esse commentarios Martyris, Calvini, Musculi, Gualteri et similes*, say the ministers of the foreign churches in London 1576 in their Theses and Antitheses No. 133.

29) Justus Velsius from the Hague, Doctor med. and classic philologer, admirer of Dionysius Areopagita, opponent to the principal Reformators, also to Schwenkfeld, against absolute predestination. An article on him by Sepp, Studien 91 f. On his debates in 1563 in London, where he was a member of the Dutch church, Hessels III, p. 17—29. He was charged to depart the kingdom, Strype, Grindal 91 f. Cf. Strype, Annals I 382 f.

30) Balthasar Sanchez says in his deposition against Reina, delivered with other witnesses to the commissaries of the bishop of London September 15. 1563: *il a esleu pour estre cheff de nostre consistoyre Aconcio*. (Ms. in the Archive of the French Reformed church at Frankfurt on Main.) When the Spanish church dissolved in consequence of Reina's departure, Acontius applied to the French church, but the bishop of London did not allow him to be received, nor did he afterwards admit him into the recently established Italian church. The reason was that Acontius had written a defence of Haemstede who was excommunicated from the London Dutch church, mainly on account of his tolerance for a heterodox view of Christ's incarnation. The famous Arminius calls Acontius *divinum prudentiae ac moderationis lumen*. Ramus supposes in 1567 that Acontius was living still, but perhaps he had died already in 1566. Compare on him Sepp, Polem. 165 f., Hessels, Sckickler I 117 f.

from Reina, but without success. The only letter which he had received from him for four years, arrived in September 63. There was a great opening for the Spanish Bible where Corro lived. If Reina had a better one, Corro would follow him. But at all events Reina should come. While they compared their papers, God would show them the best way for the undertaking. Corro had found some Portuguese who had business relations with Spain and were favourable to that religious work. He was staying in a place where the public preaching of the gospel was free. Without an evidently good reason he did not venture to leave, and thus give new occasion to the reproach of fickleness which he had incurred by planning from day to day to go to meet Reina. „However," he says, „when you are here, everyone will understand that, if I leave, it is because I am compelled to follow you, not because, as they now suppose, I am tired of this country." The best way for Reina's journey might be by La Rochelle where Corro's friend the minister de Nort (with whom he had worked at Toulouse [31] would receive him, and by Bordeaux where M. Le Blanc would do the same. He asks him to bring or to send soon any small treatises which he might think suitable. He could address them to the care of de Nort or of the merchant Pierre du Perrey at Bordeaux or of Mademoiselle de Saint Etienne, a Spanish lady at Toulouse, who would receive the commission through a merchant there, named Bernoye,[32] who had agents at Antwerp and London. Corro dictated this letter in French, and with his own hand he sends greetings to all, and in particular to Reina's parents. The letter was dated from his house near Bergerac.[33] This town belonged to those in the *faubourgs* of which *l'exercice de la nouvelle religion* was permitted by the royal order dated Amboise April 7. 1562 (n. st. 1563). Corro adds: „If in absence of Señor Cassiodoro some other person should receive this, I request an answer in the way which M. Jaques Fichet will indicate." Endorsed by a third hand: *Lettres pour estre adressées au Sire Jaques Fichet*

---

31) Monsieur de Nort, minister at la Rochelle, was moderator of the National Synod held there in summer 1581.

32) Hessels: Perhaps the Spanish merchant Bernui, mentioned in La France Protestante.

33) ... los señores sus padres. de .. ssa cerca de Bergerac. Hessels: The original word has been altered and it now seems to be: cassa.

Marchand de Londres pour les bailler a Monsieur Cassiodore Espagnol, ou en son absence a ses parens Londres. The letter was forwarded to Fichet by the brother of Pierre du Perrey together with a *billet* from Bordeaux, dated April 4. 1564, saying that Pierre, who had left for Spain, had charged him to entreat Fichet to get the enclosed safely delivered to Cassiodoro, as it served for the advancement of God's church *(seruent a laduancement de leglise de Dieu).*

Reina never received Corro's letters from Theobon and Bergerac. He had left England before the first one was written. It was delivered to the French Consistory on March 12. 1564 and was opened by them. They found it providential that they were thus informed of the theology of the two dangerous ex-monks. When the letter from Bergerac arrived they considered themselves even more entitled to open it as well, because Perrey had written, that it served the advancement of the church of God.[34] Although scandalized by the contents of the first letter, Cousin, the minister, did not mention it when he wrote to Corro that nobody knew where Reina was staying.

When Corro at last heard from Reina, that he was on the way to meet him, he took leave of absence from his church for six weeks and met his friend at Orleans, where he also spoke to the minister Saules (Gallasius).[35] From there both went to Bergerac.

But soon Corro was driven from this cure, as he says, by the *rigueur de l'édit du roi*,[36] the so called edict of pacification of Amboise of March 1562 (= 63) which contained the provision that all foreigners should be sent out of the kingdom as soon as possible.[37] When the Sainte Ligue urged the king to exterminate the heretics, he answered, that he had issued the edict to clear his kingdom from the strangers; he hoped to maintain his subjects in peace according to the institution of the church.[38] When subsequently the king made his tour through the south of France in 1564—5, he probably enforced that decree above all against the protestant ministers who were not French natives.

34) Capita of December 1568. Cf. below.
35) Conversation in London April 1567.
36) Corro to Beza September 3. 68.
37) Hist. eccl. Anvers 1580 II 286.
38) Serres: Inventaire de l'hist. de France. Vol. 4. Paris 1600, p. 269.

Corro, as well as his compatriot and friend Juan Perez, who had lost his position at Blois for the same reason, found a refuge at Montargis, the residence of Renée de France, Dowager Duchess of Ferrara.[39] Reina also was there with them[40] until he left for Germany, not later than early in 1565. Perez and Corro worked there together with the minister Colonges. But soon the latter was dismissed on account of his uncompromising character. Corro wrote to Beza on September 3. 1568 that Colonges and the duchess were like fire and water (the fire being of course the strict Calvinist); he does not presume to judge who was right. Admiral Coligny who had disapproved of Colonges' demeanour, changed his view and wrote to Beza in 1569 that he now realized that in such cases rigour was the best medicine.[41]

Renée had been converted in Italy to the evangelical faith, but she belonged to those who could not quite overcome their deep-rooted subservience to Rome. The Pope had in 1564 proclaimed the decrees of the council of Trent, some months before Calvin's death, but Renée to whom, as to a devoted daughter, Pius IV. had sent the apostolic benediction on July 1. 1561, was still in March and on April 13. 1566 calling Pius V. *notre Saint Pere*,[42] while she kept protestant ministers, Geneva men, and Corro, who did not like to be called a Calvinist.

---

39) Corro to Beza Sept. 3. 68. — By a letter from Orleans December 27. 1561 Renée is informed that a *gentilhomme* and *mademoiselle de Clermont*, who found difficulty in being married without the consent of the parents, are going to Montargis to ask her advice; *ils disent que vostre Excellence les cognoist et que Mr. de Belrive les a congneu et parlé à eux*. The writer, who signs *Beaumont*, is Daniel Toussain, sieur de Beaumont. As to him, cf. Cuno: Daniel Tossanus. Amsterdam 1898. 2 vols. He was in 1561 minister at Orleans. In Renée's *Livre de comptes* of that year: *a M. de Beaumont ministre 25 1. 10. s.* Jules Bonnet, Bulletin XXXVIII. 1889, p. 11. Beaumont evidently supposes in that letter that Renée appreciates Belrive i. e. Corro, perhaps from personal knowledge.

It may be mentioned that Renée who travelled and stayed in southern France at the same time as the French court, in the course of the winter 1564—5 was also at Bergerac and visited her native town Blois where she sojourned some days. Rodocanachi, Renée p. 508.

40) Sp. Rf. II 220. He stayed with Corro first at Bergerac and then at Montargis. He names the town of the duchess and the minister Perez in the first place, only because for his *Protestation* it was the more important fact, to which he subjoins the mention of his preceding stay at Bergerac.

41) Rodocanachi l. c. p. 424.

42) In the *commendatizie di messi che, andando a Roma, passano Ferrara*, Fontana: Renata III 15.

Allied to the Guises by the marriage of her daughter with the terrible duke whose murder was wrongly imputed by his own faction to admiral Coligny, she clung persistently to both these families, who were at the head of the two parties dividing France. With her personal, moral and religious feeling was blended the conception of her royalty. She felt like a sovereign, above the antagonists in her nation, ever dissatisfied with the Salic Law which deprived her of the throne, while Mary, the daughter of the sister of her son-in-law Guise, was Queen of Scotland, and Elizabeth was ruling England.

In April 1566 we find Enoch as minister of the duchess in her castle where he had arrived shortly before. He may have been called there to replace Perez who settled at Paris, supported by Renée, to get his Spanish N. T. printed. It was certainly on account of this work, to which the venerable old man dedicated his declining vitality, that the ministers of Antwerp, who on Mai 28. 1566 asked Renée to send him to them, could not have their wish. Then they asked for Corro, sending letters and deputies in the name of more than a thousand persons.[43] On August 13. 1566 the Antwerp minister du Jon[44] wrote to Corro praying him to help them. Their enemies, he said, were brewing an edict, like that issued in France, in order to drive out all ministers who were not natural subjects of the king. Corro would find a harvest so abundant that no one would think that tempest and frost had held sway. The bearer, he said, knew of the means at their disposal.

On September 2. the Prince of Orange, Burgrave of Antwerp who at that time was there as commissary of the Regent of the Netherlands Margareta, Duchess of Parma, made an *Accord* with the representatives of the new religion. Its adherents in Antwerp were allowed to preach and otherwise to exercise their religion (the Lord's Supper, marriages, baptisms) in three places assigned to them. They might have a minister for each place, and, besides, for each a vicar in case of illness or absence or other impediment. All these six ministers must be natives of the countries of His Majesty or *bourgeois* of some good town in the Netherlands and must take the oath of obedience

---

43) Lettre au roi [LVII].
44) Franciscus Junius. His biography by Cuno 1891.

and fidelity in all practical matters. All predicants of whatever religion (the papists no less than the protestants) are to abstain from inveighing and injuring and from all seditious utterances against the higher powers and the magistrate, and against persons of different religion; it is to be understood, says the document, that matters of doctrine and religious exercises and the reproof of disorderly manners shall not be considered seditious. Soon after this agreement with the Calvinists the Augsburg Confessionists likewike obtained some places for worship in the same town.[45]

On September 18. 1566 Charles de Nielle,[46] minister at Antwerp, wrote to Corro in the name of the Consistory: „Having received your answer to du Jon[47] of August 18. we write to Madame de Ferrare in order to secure you together with M. Perez;[48] or if this cannot be (as old age and his several diseases leave us little hope of getting him), that you be allowed to come to us; and if we cannot have you permanently, at least be our companion during the whole of the next winter, a request which we hope will not be refused; and we beseech you in the name of God to join us in taking it in hand, for we hope your coming will be of incalculable advantage to our poor country, as you could benefit not only the faithful who speak our language, but also the Italians and Spaniards both here and in Brussels and Bruges, some of whom have been rescued from their ignorance. Have pity on the great harvest, wholly white, which remains in the fields for want of good and faithful labourers; so much the more as in consequence of the *Accord* imposed upon us in the matter of religion, all ministers in this country must be subjects of the king either

---

45) The Prince writes to the Regent August 28. that the Augsburg confessionists have petitioned for some worship-places in the town and asks what he is to answer. Correspondance de Guillaume le Tocisturné, pbl. par Gochard. T. 2. 1850. p. 198f. On September 4. he sends her the duplicate of the accord which he could not but make two days ago. 213f. It mentions three places. That they were given to the Calvinists, one knows from other sources, from which it is also known that the Augsburghians got some other places. Cf. Gachard, ib. p. LIX.

46) See Van der Aa, Biographisch Woordenboek, and Sepp, Predikantenleven 22f.

47) Du Jon, as he tells in his autobiography, could not continue in the ministry after the September-accord, not being a native subject of the king nor a Netherlandish citizen.

48) Misprint *Pierins*. Read Pierius, cf. Sp. Rf. II 57.

by birth or by naturalisation. Come with our messenger or take another trusty companion; the expenses of the journey will be defrayed here."

As Corro aspired to nothing so eagerly as to preach the gospel in his king's dominion and to his Spaniards, the reason for his not at once accepting the invitation could only be that the Duchess, to whom he owed gratitude, was sorry to lose him. At last, the admiral and his brother the cardinal and several ministers, who had assembled to deliberate the question, decided in favour of Antwerp.[49] In the testimonial drawn up by the class of Montargis and Chatillon are these words: *Le frere Monsieur de Bellerive, autrement appellé Corranus, present porteur, a longuement conversé en ce quartier avec toute approbation et de sa vie et de sa doctrine entre gens de bien, y ayant fidelement servy a l'eglise du Seigneur comme homme doué de parties necessaires en l'estat du ministere, autant que le pouvez requerir dun homme mortel. Iceluy mesme est de present en pleine liberté de sa personne ayant eu congé de son eglise de Bergerac ainsy que [ic]elle nous en a escrit.* And soon after: *il a servy en ce pays en la maison de madame la Duchesse de Ferrare [.] celle ayant ses ministres ordinaires, ç'a esté sans y estre [en] aucune precise obligation que l'ayt icy attaché. quoy consideré vous prions ne faire scrupule ou difficulté de l'empescher entre vous en l'œuvre du Seigneur.* Dated *12. d'Octobre 1566. A Chastillon sur Loing ... de nostre seigneur l'admiral.*[50]

When he departed, the Duchess charged him to write her from Paris news of Perez, who was very ill. Corro only just arrived in time to see him die and to receive his last commissions for the Duchess: he entreated her to carry out the printing of his N. T. and of certain tracts, and to take care of his two Spanish assistants[51] to whom he

49) Corro to Beza Sept. 3. 68.

50) I have added the complements, have put a comma instead of a full-stop before *ç'a* which I have written instead of *ca*. Besides, I have written *attaché. quoy consideré, vous* instead of *attaché quon considere. vous.*

51) I have conjectured in my *Romanische Studien* IV 484, that these two assistants are the two friars whom king Philip in April 1568 wishes his ambassador in France to get away. Menendez, Heterod. II 472 thought that one of these friars is certainly Corro, the other perhaps Diego de Santa Cruz; he has been misled by the notice reprinted here above note 6. Corro never left England, and there remains no reason for supposing Diego de Santa Cruz to have been one of the two. I should think, that one of the assistants was Bartolomé Gomez whom Reina, as he says in

entrusted the manuscripts. Corro reported this to Renée on October 20. and he also caused the Consistory at Paris to oblige the two Spaniards to render account, when the printing would be finished, to the Spanish Reformed church which in the meantime would be established somewhere.[52]

In November Corro was at Antwerp. — The Prince of Orange, son of Protestant parents, had lived at the court of the Emperor who loved the youth, and being in the King's service under the Regent of the Netherlands he attended mass and even wrote submissively to the Pope in the summer of 1566, although clinging to his evangelical sentiment. His political aim was the liberty of religious confession and meeting. Before leaving Antwerp on October 12. he recommended to the canons to combine the exercise of their own divine service with peace with the dissenters. He said, that in one of his towns in Germany both parties lived so much in accord that they exercised their religion in the same church. The diversity of opinions, he added, concerned the sense of words, the substance *(rem)* being one and the same.[53]

On October 17. 1566 Count Hoogstraten, the representative of the prince, received at Antwerp a petition for tolerance to be sent to the king, signed by Marcos Perez and others in the name of the Reformed churches and the Augsburg Confessionists in the Netherlands. They referred also to the fact that the Pope allowed the Jews to exercise their religion even in Rome. And in order to prove their readiness to do whatever they could for the King's service, they offered to present him with thirty tons of gold when he granted their petition.[54] The Prince of Orange said in November in a memoir: The Netherlands, **le marché de toute la Chrestienté,** would be ruined by the present policy of Spain.[55] On November 5. he wrote to the Land-

his letter of September 27. 1567, believed to be corrector of the press for the N. T. then printing at Paris. Diego Perez, to whom that letter of Reina is directed, *était il l'un des deux?* asks Bernus: Marc Perez 1895, p. 46.

52) Corro to the Bishop July 15. 1568.

53) On this speech the prévôt Morillon writes to the cardinal Granvella from Brussels Nov. 15 1566. Correspondence du card. Granvella 1565—86, pbl. par Poullet 1880, p. 88.

54) Bor: Nederlandsche Oorloghen, boek 3 1621f. 86f.

55) Archives de la maison Orange-Nassau. Pbl. p. Groen van Prinsterer. T. II. Leide 1835, p. 438.

grave William of Hesse: To declare publicly his adherence to the Augsburg confession would not be opportune. He apprehended that, if he did so, the Calvinists would claim and obtain foreign assistance and have recourse to violence which would provoke the King to repression.[56] The Landgrave answered him on November .27.: The Calvinists ought to accommodate themselves to the Augsburg confession. St. Paul, although teaching that the observance of the Jewish law was unnecessary for salvation, still on the recommendation of James underwent a legal custom, and he also circumcised Timotheus, and he called himself a Pharisee (Act. 21. 16. 23). If the Calvinists could not forbear making a remark on the question of the Lord's supper, they might express their agreement with the declaration in the preface which the princes, who were assembled in Naumburg in 1561, had added when they subscribed to the Augsburg confession; even the Elector Palatine (who was of the type of the Heidelberg catechism which he got published in 1563) had subscribed to that preface.[57] The Prince was of the same opinion; only under that condition could he hope for an intervention from the empire.

Corro declared his readiness to subscribe to the confession of the church which had called him, but when the minister Jean Taffin exhibited it to him together with the additional summary of principal heresies, such as Anabaptists, Arians, Libertines, Schwenkfeldians, partisans of Castalio etc., the condemnation of which was required of each minister, he refused, saying he would subscribe to the word of God, not to the opinions of men.[58] They yielded. It seems to have been shortly after his arrival that he took part in a discussion between Calvinists and Martinists (Lutherans) on the one side and Romanists on the other on the subject of the eucharist. Porthaise boasts that on that occasion he had routed Taffin and discomfited the Germans so completely that they offered to give a written answer. We have no report from the other side.[59] In the last week of November the

---

56) Ibd. p. 454 f.

57) Ibd. p. 492 f.

58) Taffin in a letter of 1583 in Sepp: Drie Evangeliedienaren 56 f. Taffin is one of the three; supplements on him in Sepp's Polem. 81 f. and in his Verboden lectuur 207. An article on him by Rahlenbeck with portrait in the Bulletin de la commission pour l'histoire des églises wallonnes. La Haye T. 2. 1887, p. 117—179.

59) Rahlenbeck in the just quoted article on Taffin p. 151 reports from the

Walloon church asked the Count Hoogstraten, and the Magistrate of Antwerp, to allow Corro to preach. The petitioners received the answer that they must await the decision of the Prince who was absent. But the church authorities being in a difficulty because Taffin was unwell, were so confident as to make Corro, who was a native of the King's dominions and was ready to take the oath, deliver a French sermon on Sunday December 1.[60] Soon afterwards Hoogstraten received a letter from the Regent, dated Brussels November 30., with postscript of December 1., who wrote[61] that she had learnt that three Martinists[62] and a Sevillian apostate to Calvinism had lately arrived at Antwerp. The dogmatizing foreigners were not to be allowed in the town, and above all, care must be taken that the Spanish apostate should not preach,

---

Belgian archive that *Quelques jours aupararant le banquier anrersois Marc Perez, membre du consistoire des Gueux... donna dans ses salons un banquet auquel il convia Me Sébastien Baerts, „le grand curé de Notre Dame", afin de lui offrir l'occasion d'amuser ses convires en essayant ses forces contre les ministres réformés. Le Conseil des troubles reprocha plus tard a l'échevin Jean Rubens et au secrétaire de la ville, Henry de Moy, d'avoir assisté à ce prélude inconvenant d'un tournoi théologique.* And Flacius speaking of the sermons of a *monachus Gallus* at Antwerp on the eucharist, adds: *Idem etiam contra me in quodam convivio praesentibus pluribus vehementissime contendit.* P. 197 of *Defensio Confessionis ministrorum Jesu Christi, ecclesiae Antuerpiensis, quae Augustanae Confessioni adsentitur, contra Judoci Tiletani varia sophismata. Basileae 1567.* The *Prologus* and the *Adhortatio* appended to the book are subscribed by *M. Fl. Illyricus* and *Balthazar Houwaert* only. Colophon: 1567 *Mense Augusto.* In the *Adhortatio* the departure of the ministers from Antwerp (which happened in April) is mentioned. I think that the *monachus Gallus* is the Franciscan Jean Porthaise, of whom Rahlenbeck says: *accouru tout exprès de Paris* for this discussion, and that the *convivium* is the banquet of Perez. What Porthaise might call a *publique disput* may have taken place in the house of Perez. The doubts of Sepp, Naspor. 153 are not tenable. I cannot suppress the query: was perhaps the discussion at the convivium the only one? There are strange blunders in Rahlenbeck's article p. 149.

60) Bor: Nederlandsche Oorloghen 1621, fol. 88. Corro preached in the *Temple rond*, but in the open air. After the *accord*, still in September, the Walloons grounded their churchbuilding which from its form was called the *Temple rond*, and Ysbrand Balck laid the first stone to the Dutch Calvinist church. Sepp, Predikantenleven 23. At Christmas the walls were not yet under roof. Ricardus Hilles Henrico Bullingero. Antuerpiae Dec. 23. 1566 Zurich letters, Cambridge 1842, p. 103f.

61) I give extracts from the correspondence between the Regent and Hoogstraeten, appended by Gachard to La defense de messire Antoine de Lalaing, comte de Hocstrate. Mons 1838.

62) Hamelmann, Spangenberg, Wolf arrived towards the end of November. Preger: Flacius II 1861, p. 291.

or His Majesty would be greatly offended and the majority of the Spaniards residing there would be scandalized. On December 5. having learned that Corro had preached, the Regent urged his capture and punishment. On the 7th the Count answered that he had not preached again and should not do so, pending the decision of the Prince. To arrest the man was not expedient on account of his great reputation with those of the new religion; there would be a risk of a dangerous commotion. The church authorities had begged to be excused and had stated that they had stopped Corro's preaching.[63] On the 13th the Regent wrote to the Count: Command him to leave the town, or at least not to leave his lodging, and not to preach even secretly. The Count was anxious to avoid such a step; on the next day he dissuaded the Regent from using, contrary to the *Accord,* any violence against the protestants. Margaret complained to the King on the 18th: „Antwerp is our principal trouble, for no other places do anything without the advice of the ministers of that corrupt town".[64] On January 1. 1567 the Count reported that, the day before, those of the new religion had asked him to administer the oath to Corro, as they had reason to hope that he would be permitted to preach. The Count awaited the Regent's decision, but he begged to remark humbly, that the *Accord* which maintained the peace would loose all its efficacy if the Spaniard was not allowed to preach. Nevertheless the permission was not granted.

In the meantime Corro had enough to do with the Martinists. In October Flacius Illyricus had arrived at Antwerp. This renowned scholar had been summoned together with some others by the Augsburg confessionists in order to help in the organisation and extension of their community. Corro called on Flacius and was received kindly. Both had left the tyranny of Rome, but peace could not last between the sharp-edged characters of these two hot-blooded men of southern climates, the Sevillian and the Istrian; no union was practicable between the Ultra-Lutheran and the Latitudinarian. Flacius proposed a *disputation* on the question of the Lord's Supper. Corro's

---

63) Bor. l. c.
64) Gachard Corresp. de Guill. le Tacit. XXXIII. Morillon writes in November 66 l. c., p. 91 that the Antwerp Calvinists said they were 50000, while the whole population of the town was about 86000.

advice was to point out in a confession of faith the articles on which all evangelicals agreed. „Well," replied Flacius, „then take the confession of Augsburg, subscribe to the articles you accept, and interpret the others according to your intelligence." „We did that," says Corro at the beginning of the year, „and we are going to make it known". (This seems to have been prevented by subsequent events). „Flacius, who is said to be the superintendent, so to speak, of your church, did appear disposed to agree to my entreaties, but has nevertheless been the author or instigator of a confession of faith which you have brought before this church of Antwerp, the main object of which would seem to be to bring trouble upon it."[65]

This report of the controversy with Flacius is taken from Corro's printed epistle to the Augsburg Confessionists (9.—11. 38) whom he adresses *Messieurs et Freres en Jesus Christ*. It is a document of lasting importance. Corro writes: „We call each other Martinists, Calvinists, Osiandrians, Melanchthonians, Brentians etc. and we are right in doing so as long as we do not fix our eyes upon the advancement of the glory of Christ and his church, which is catholic and universal, and upon that alone (6). Some take their confessions, catechisms, commentaries and traditions, for something like a fifth gospel (8). Luther and Melanchthon were good servants of God, but after all were men, and, as such, liable to ignorance of many things. In presence of the great opposition to the pure doctrine, they may have thought it preferable to gain hearts by mild methods and not to alienate them by dogmatizing on the sacraments, but to wait a more convenient time for fully establishing the true exercise and meaning of those holy ceremonies. No one can deny that Luther in the beginning of his preaching was ignorant of many things which were afterwards revealed to him, so that at last he came to the conclusion that mass must be abolished. In the Augsburg confession Melanchthon protested that they still celebrated it (12. 13). According to

---

[65] That they had brought forth *(mis en avant)* the Confession, does not necessarily imply that it was already printed. It was printed in Latin and French with the date 1567 (I know both editions, not the Dutch one) which year, however, may have been anticipated. In another place in the Epistle (11) Corro says that after his conference with Flacius the Martinists printed some libels in which they called certain ministers *tison d'enfer ou chose semblable*. By *Hellbrand* they meant Ysbrand, Sepp Naspor. III. 115.

my conviction, the sense of the Lord's Supper is that we are incorporated in the celestial Adam as his members, and nourished by his virtues (20. 21). Christ said also: I am the vine, ye are the branches (and this cannot be taken literally. 26). Flacius and his companions believe that Christ's body and blood are really received with bread and wine, externally, not only by faith, or spiritually, and are taken by unworthy as well as by worthy; and they say: „Those who teach the contrary we condemn by virtue of the Augsburg confession." It would be against common sense to leave the tyranny of papistry in order to undergo another tyranny almost equal to it. Read Rom. 14. What reformation of life is there in our churches? They are full of vices and we let them pass, swallowing camels and straining at gnats by pronouncing condemnation against such as do not penetrate the subtilities of our interpretations of the Lord's Supper. Who can understand so many kinds of communications of Christ: the physical, the mystical, the spiritual, the sacramental? (46—49). There is even a difference between your confession of Augsburg and what you call the corrupt edition (51 f). The Augsburg confessionists are not in accordance with one another on the words of the eucharist. Flacius, whom I believe to be the author of your confession, disagrees with Melanchthon (58f). If we adhered to you, we should fall into disfavour with many of the Protestant Princes of Germany, where Illyricus, your superintendent or the author of your confession, is hated in the most illustrions churches and universities (74). We have not been baptized in the name of Martin, Zwingli or Calvin, but in the name of the Father and the Son and the Holy Ghost,[66] and therefore we detest and hold in abomination all those names and surnames of sects: Martinists, Zwinglians, Calvinists and the like.[67] If the doctors who have taught heretofore, and to-day are preaching the gospel, were more sage and modest and purely devoted to looking to the glory

---

66) as Christ commanded to his apostles, says Corro in the letter to the king E VII.

67) *Defensio Confessionis* of the Antwerp Augsburghians p. 183f.: *si quis nos Lutheranos vocet, injuriam nobis facit, cum tali nomine nos non jactemus: neque Lutherum aliter sequimur nisi quatenus nobis verbo Dei unicum illum Dei agnum peccata mundi tollentem monstrat. At isti non solum gaudent vocari Mariani, Augustiniani, Benedictini, Franciscani, Dominicani, etc. sed etiam ponunt spem salutis in suos illos patronos eorumque mediationem ac merita.*

of the Lord and noways to their own, the people would have greater liberty of conscience, and would be worshippers of one God only, and not of mortal, ignorant and blind men, who want to raise themselves up as idols in order to be followed and held in admiration (56). Let us be diligent by our preaching to lead the people to Jesus Christ, our sovereign doctor,[68] and not to follow either the Augsburg confession or the catechism of Martin or the interpretations of John or Peter.[69] Let us make known to the princes and potentates of Germany that all these questions are discarded, and that we wish to live in perfect harmony and friendship (80). As to the Romanists, in uncovering their abuses, let us proceed with such modesty, soberness and gravity, that they may understand that we are not prompted by any hatred of their persons, but by spiritual zeal for the glory of God." Corro cannot, however, abstain from saying: „Being ravenous wolves, they called themselves shepherds of God's flock." Nevertheless he continues: „In conclusion, let us try to live in peace with one another, be we of the Roman or of the reformed religion." „Let us love all, help all, and bear the ignorance and infirmities of all. For it is better to err in this direction, if error there be, than to set ourselves up as judges of conscience and pass sentence of condemnation against those who are not in accordance with us. By the consciousness of our ignorance we are urged to the desire to learn, and not to be inquisitors and censors of the belief of others. (89. 90) The Epistle is dated January 2. 1567.

As the Augsburghians had repeatedly proposed a *disputation*, the others at last on January 10. sent to Flacius some articles to be observed by both parties, if a public discussion under competent moderators and judges should be ordained by the magistrate. The next day the Licentiate Hamelmann, sent by Flacius, notified that the dispute on the Lord's Supper must begin with the question of the omnipresence of the body of Jesus Christ, and if they did not believe this, an understanding with them was impossible. In consequence of this, a discussion was not found practicable.[70]

68) § 11: *le souverain Docteur gradué non point à Paris, mais en Paradis.*
69) Jean Calvin and Pietro Martyr Vermigli.
70) This annotation is appended on p. 77.

Corro is said to have been earnestly admonished by Antwerp ministers not to print several passages of the above epistle.[71] Certain is it that his church wished him to be allowed to preach and that for that purpose they sent a deputation in January to the Prince of Orange at Amsterdam. On the 21st the Prince wrote to the Regent that since his arrival there on December 20. he had not seen any deputy or sectarian except a minister of Antwerp with three or four bourgeois who came to ask permission for Francisco Correa (a slip of memory, instead of Antonius Corranus), a Spaniard, to preach there (at Antwerp) in French, „as Your Highness will have learnt more amply by my letter of the 18th of this month".[72] That letter is missing, as also the answer of the Regent on this matter. It was impossible for Corro's publication to please the Prince,[73] as it practically put well nigh an end to the hope he had been entertaining for some months[74] of inducing the Calvinists, in consideration of the menacing condition of public affairs, to conform to the Augsburg confession, in which case he hoped to be aided by German Princes to establish in the Netherlands an arrangement like that of the Augsburg Peace of 1555, by which the rights of the Augsburg confessionists and the Roman Catholics were settled. He was too prudent however, to give way to his displeasure and refuse their request which was founded on the *Accord* of September. But though he gave a conditional permission, the Regent certainly did not consent.[75] On

71) See below the document of March. 23. 71.

72) Gachard, Corresp. de Guill. II 339. That Correa means Corro has been noticed also by Sepp, Naspor. III 106. In the letters of the Prince of January 12. there is not as yet anything about the deputation.

73) Porthaise says: *Anthoine Coran, Espagnol, ministre du Prince d'Orange à Breda.* But neither has he been minister of the church of Breda, nor would the Prince, partial for the Augsburg confession, have appointed him his own minister. Sepp, Naspor. 153. 102 f. Besides, he could not take as his or his wife's private chaplain just the Spanish apostate whom the Regent especially detested. However, if the Prince, as probably he did, admitted Corro to an audience in Antwerp in February or March, he certainly shewed his esteem for the man whom Renée de France had distinguished. And after all, the political trend of the prince was the same as that of Corro, both wishing for religious liberty of evangelicals and Romanists to be protected by the civil government. After his return to the Netherlands the prince joined the prevalent Reformed party. Taffin and Loiseleur Villiers became his chaplains.

74) Poullet l. c. 376—77. Cf. 633. 647.

75) Compare her letter of February 8., Gachard l. c. 401 f.

February 2. the Prince wrote to his brother John and to the Saxon Elector: The German Princes of the Augsburg confession ought to ask the King for liberty for the followers of that confession in the Netherlands, and they ought to declare that, if their fellow-believers there were persecuted for their religion, they would not, as Christians, leave them without assistance. On February 5. he returned to Antwerp and tried, in obedience to the commands of the Regent, to do away with the public sermons.[76]

In March Corro published a letter to the King of Spain. He details the experiences which led him to leave his country and to wander about for ten years. In order to live with foreign people, he was constrained, like an infant, to learn to speak. He had to endure poverty and indigence,[77] but God had protected him. The spies who pursued him did not recognise him, or became so confused that they did not know what to say or to do, and after leaving Spain he had never hid himself in any corner. On the contrary, he says, as would be testified by a hundred thousand persons, „I have preached the gospel in great and celebrated towns and in presence of Princes and Seigneurs ranked amongst the most illustrious of Europe. I well know that I am of the fallen race of Adam, and that my works shall in the face of God be abominations, but before man, Sire, I need not disguise myself.[78] When I arrived in your town of Antwerp, it struck some as incredible that a native Spaniard should have embraced the pure doctrine of the gospel so entirely as to come forward as preacher of it."[79] Of course Corro condemns the outrages perpetrated by some mischievous persons in the Low Countries not long before his arrival, the smashing of images and altars, and other acts of violence, which the Protestants had neither plotted nor known of beforehand.[80] He praises highly the population of the Netherlands: they are full of humanity and surpass in hospitality all nations of the

---

76) Archives de la maison Orange-Nassau. T. III. Leide 1836.

77) C iiij ... d'apprendre des langues estranges. Besides the French he must mean the *langue d'oc* and perhaps the Basque.

78) C V.

79) A iiij.

80) [C VII]. M ij. In Antwerp the populace had on Oktober 17. 1566 begun the devastation of a Roman church, count Hoogstraten had, however, stopped it and had hanged six of the malefactors.

world. „Where," he exclaims „except in Flanders did the Spaniards find people who gave them their daughters in marriage, and made such as had nothing but cape and sword rich persons of influence? And at present what a worse than brutal ingratitude!" Corro describes the massacre near the ramparts of the town which he witnessed two days before he finished this letter.[81] He sketches the Roman doctrine and practices, for which he repeatedly refers to a treatise dedicated to King Philip by Ruard Tapper[82] (compare the way in which the man is characterized in the Memoirs of Enzinas), and contrasts with it the Protestant faith as set forth in the Bible, which he wishes[83] to be translated into all languages. „But the Scripture is a dead letter to the reader, if the Spirit does not teach him.[84] The true penitent is no longer considered as a child of Adam, but as a brother of Jesus Christ, who is joined and united with him by faith and by the bond of the Holy Spirit, so that the Christian and Christ, and Christ and the Christian, are but one (John 17).[85] Corro points out that not only in Constantinople are three religions allowed to be professed, but that even in Rome the Pope tolerates the Jews, and the exercise of their religion.[86]

81) L ij foll.
82) [C VIII].
83) D iij. Already Erasmus had wished in his Paraclesis that the gospel and Paul's epistles were translated into all languages.
84) See below the extract, docum 2.
85) G iiij.
86) M ij foll. Under the Grand Turk lived Mahometans, Persians, Jews, many varieties of Christians; if such diversities of religions must cause seditions and tumults, he could not have grown so mighty. These remarks, certainly known to Corro, are made towards the end of the *Brief discours envoyé au roy Philippe* .. *pour le bien & profit de sa Majesté, et singulierement de ses pays bas* .. 1565 (Rahlenbeck in the *Bulletin* ... *des églises wallonnes* T. 2, p. 138). Reprinted in the *Recueil des Choses memorables* ... *pour le fait de la Religion* ... *depuis la maiorité du Roy, 1563: jusques en l'an 1565*. Vol. III. Strasbourg 1566, p. 869f. (Known to Wiffen). Also in *Memoires de Condé. Londres. T. cinquiéme*. 1743, p. 374f.; on the margin of each page the year 1565. Translation: *Ein kurtz Christlichs Bedencken* .. 1566. (A copy in Merck's collection). That even in Rome the excercise of the Jewish religion is permitted by the pope, is emphasized in 1563 in the *Apologie de l'Edit du Roy sur la Pacification de son Royaume*. Of course permission is not approbation, says this apologist; one permits brothels. *Mem. de Condé*. Londres. T. 4, 1743, p. 426. — Cf. above p. 18.

With great difficulty the Prince had succeeded in quelling the armed rebellion of the Antwerp Calvinists aroused by the massacre of Austruweel on the 13th. On the next day the Government, to avoid defeat, called up the Augsburghians to assist in bearing arms, which they did obediently; on the 15th the excitement, strained to the highest pitch, was happily appeased without bloodshed.[87] On April 7. at Brussels the Regent declared to the deputies from Antwerp that she pardoned only persons domiciled in the town since before August, but no ministers, predicants, apostates, or certain other classes which she named. On April 10. the ministers and predicants in the city-hall of Antwerp received the communication that the Regent commanded them to leave the town in twenty-four hours and the Netherlands in three days, under penalty of hanging. A general exodus followed. The prince himself left on the 11th for Breda, and thence for Germany.[88] Deputies from the German Augsburghian Princes arrived at Antwerp, where Margaret resided, on May 19. and left on the 22., after receiving her answer that she would send the document, which they had handed her, to the King, though they had already written to him.[89] The intercession pleaded only for the smaller party of the Netherlandish Protestants, and even for them was too weak and too late, for the bloody government of Alba was at hand.

As early as April 8. Corro was in London. His first idea was only to stay some months in England, and then to return to his station,[90] but eventually he remained there for life. England was at that time becoming more and more the asylum of all the worst people, —

---

[87] Schultz Jacobi in Nederlandsch Archief. Door Kist en Royoards. Leiden 1844, p. 129 f.

[88] Gachard, Corresp. de Guill. le Tac., Préface.

[89] Archives de la maison Orange-Nassau. T. III. 1836, p. 80 f.

[90] Corro to Humfrey, March 20. 76. The *station* means that in the Antwerp community to whom he felt still obliged to serve if they should reassemble safely somewhere else. See Capita of 1568, Confirmatio primi capitis. What he says in 1574 in the dedication of his Dialogue theologicus: *decennio quo in Galliis Gallico sermone docui,* and in that letter to Humfrey 1576: *Gallicanae ecclesiae (cui decennium in ministerio Evangelii inservivi,* is inexact. His French ministry which in fact endend in 1567, had not yet begun in 1557. On the other hand when he said in a letter from England (see Beza's epist. LIX) that he served a full *quinquennium* to *Gallia,* which seems to mean Navarra and France, he gives rather a short measure.

this is the Pope's lament in 1569, but bishop Jewel, preaching in 1570 against the *seditious bull*, bore testimony to the work of the Christian refugees. „They are our brethren," he said, „they live not idly. If they have houses of us, they pay rent for them. They hold not our grounds, but by making due recompense. They beg not in our streets, nor crave anything at our hands, but to breathe our air and to see our sun." Even Andalusians preferred the sunshine of Elizabeth to that of Philip. „They labour truly, they live sparefully. They are good examples of virtue, travail, faith and patience. The towns in which they abide are happy, for God doth follow them with his blessings."[91]

On April 16. Cousin and eleven Elders deliberated on a remonstrance to be made to Corro. „Let us tell him the reasons why we do not show him such a *bon visage* as he would like. Has he not doubts about the three states of Christ? Why does he meddle with writers whose bad doctrines are known? (See his letter to Reina). Nor has he shown a testimonial from his first church. That of the class of Montargis and Chatillon rouses suspicion by the excessive eulogy it contains. Also he is said to have published a book at Antwerp unauthorised, and to have preached at the same hour as the public service."

Accordingly an inquisitorial paper was sent to the Netherlands. Among many questions were these: Had Corro signed the confession of the churches of the Netherlands? Had he preached or taught secretly at the hours of public sermons? Did they consent to his writing a book against the Martinists which had troubled the peace between the two churches, and consequently violated the *Accord* made between them and the Magistrates? And, seeing that the book had irritated the Prince of Orange and had discontented many persons, how had the publication of it been permitted? Were they not informed that when the troubles at Antwerp increased, he said he would leave with or without the consent of the church? Had the contents of the

---

91) Jewel's works, vol. VII 1848, p. 265. Beza in his dedication of his *Tractationes theologicae*, III Cal. Mart. 1570, speaking of the persecuted evangelicals: *ut jam plane videatur Anglia comitatis etiam et humanitatis singularis palmam populis omnibus praeripuisse.*

letter of the Consistory, which he brought here opened, been made known to him?

Bishop Grindal of London reporting to the State's secretary Cecil on the beginning of the controversy between the London French church and Corro, writes (Sept. 20. 1569): „The Consistory called him before them and burdened him with his said letter, which ministered great occasion of suspicion (as they thought) that the said Corranus did not think well in some principal articles of Christian religion. He answered that his letter was written by the way of questioning and not of affirmation. They replied that such kind of questioning was not meet in these times for a minister of God's church, but in the end offered that, if he would subscribe the true doctrine and acknowledge that the letter was *imprudenter scripta*, he should be received into the church. Corranus answered that the letter was written in good and lawful manner, and that he did not repent the writing of it, and that he would (if need were) set it out in print with a defense or apology annexed. Whereupon the ministers and seniors of the French church would not receive him."

At this time a countryman of Corro, Baltasar Sanchez, a fugitive in England, who had borne witness against Reina in 1563, urged the two disciples of Perez who lived at Paris to bring forward their complaints against Corro, and recommended Cousin to ask the Consistory of Paris to inquire into Corro's doctrine and person.[92]

Cousin wrote on May 7. 1567 to the Reformed church at Paris: „Although Corro is very much renowned among the people as a very excellent preacher, we have not given him permission to preach, principally because in a letter of his which we had a just reason to open,

---

[92] The depositions of Balthasar Sanchez against Reina are in the archive of the French Reformed church at Frankfurt o. M. It is my conjecture, that he is the same whom Corro in his letter of Juli 15. 1568 calls only Baltasar, and also the same who in the first colloquy with Corro in London is only mentioned by this Christian name. Balthazar Sanchie in the list of strangers in London in 1568, see below here p. 33 f. Balthazar Sanchez signed among the diacres the letter of the Consistory to the bishop November 22. 69 (Hessels III, p. 97. Sauchez, misprint). February 15. 83 (= March 1. 84) Balthazar Sanche an elder of the London French (in the French text of the same document Balth. Sens). Febr. 25. (= March 7.) 89 Balthasar Sancio of the London French church among the contributors towards the cost of a company of Dutch soldiers under the command of Sir John Norris and Sir Francis Drake. (Hessels).

we found some propositions which to our judgment savoured of the dreams of Servet, Osiander and others. We send you a copy translated from Spanish into French. We warned him to acknowledge that such a letter was bad and imprudent, chiefly because he who has to teach ought not to indulge in idle questionings *(ne se doit amuser a faire telles questions)*. He, however, threatens to have it printed, to which we object. He has also shown us several testimonials, among which is one from the class of Montargis and Chatillon." Cousin quotes from it as referred to above, and continues: „Please ascertain if they did give him this testimonial, for we are in doubt about it, as the man does not at all seem to us to verify such high praise." As to the answer of the Parisians, dated June 3., we only learn that they reported some heterodox expressions of Corro who was said to have gone so far as to deny that children, as they had no faith, participated of the baptismal grace. Cousin also sent a copy of Corro's incriminated letter to Saules at Orleans.[93]

On the 5th of June 1567, Bishop Grindal gave the following jugdment: „Whereas it has been reported to sundry persons, as we have heard, that some, on account of a certain letter privately written, have conceived suspicions concerning master Antonius Bellerivus Corranus, a Spaniard, lately minister of the church of Montargis in France and afterwards called by the church of Antwerp, which suspicions, after arrival of the said master Antonius among us, being talked of by many in our own as well as in the churches beyond sea, have considerably increased. We, moved with the disire of preserving the concord and peace of the church and of defending the good fame of the said master Antonius, have cited him before us and have diligently conferred with him, in the presence of some pious and learned men, on those points of the Christian religion, concerning which he had fallen under some suspicion, and, from the conference had with him, we have plainly understood that the said master Corranus is averse from all impious opinions and that he entertains right and pious sentiments concerning Christian religion, and embraces from his heart the pure doctrine of the gospel, which our own and other reformed churches profess. And since he has abundantly satisfied us, that all others also may be satisfied and that his character

---

93) Corro to St. Pol, June 16.

may remain unimpeached, and the suspicions which had been conceived may be removed from the minds of all, we wish these things to be testified by this writing unto all who may read or hear it."

On June 16. 1567, Cousin writes to François Hotman, sieur de Villiers Saint-Paul: „Corro's letters of Christmas 63 *sentent à pleine gorge les reveries de Servet et d'Osiander, item l'ubiquité de Brence.* When he was remonstrated with in presence of the elders for such scandalous imprudence, he did not by any means confess it. He has presented himself once at our Lord's Supper without speaking, although he heard the admonition to the people, and three days before had used rough words against us. Since the first of May he has not entered our temple, and when afterwards he was summoned before our Consistory on account of a brawl with another person of our church, he did not come to be reconciled. Lately he has been called before the Bishop, where he has declared that he would not sustain the propositions of his letter, and thus he has obtained a written word of justification, as the Bishop told me. He himself has not deigned to speak to us of it. God be praised that he has delivered us of such a man."

The Bishop on July 18. writes to Cousin that Bellerive had called lately on him complaining of members of the French church of London who allege that he is in France condemned of Servetian heresy, that he is a false prophet and that Cousin boasts of having received letters about this from France. The Bishop advised him not to care for it, and told him he wondered that six men had requested from the Consistory what he, the Bishop, had already refused (evidently, to let him preach in the French church. That indeed would have been stirring the fire of combat.) Corro replied that he did not himself desire, under existing circumstances, to preach in the French Church, even if a large prize were offered him. Whereupon Cousin remarks: the fox did not wish what he could not reach. The letters from France, said Cousin, had been read in the Consistory in presence of the Seniors and Deacons. „If I find anyone to upbraid him with such proceedings, I shall admonish him to desist."

After the Bishop's testimonial for Corro, the preacher of the London Italian church, Girolamo Jerlito,[94] had no objection to receiv-

94) *Jeremino Jerlito, a Preacher of contynuance ij yeares,* from a list of

ing Corro into his church, and to allowing him to preach in Spanish to the Spaniards who were members of it. When Reina had left four years before, his Spanish church had dissolved itself, some going to the Italian church, some to the French. A certificate of the Lord Mayor on the strangers in London in 1568 gives interesting particulars as to their numbers, and also mentions Corro. „Anthony Coran in Cripplegate ward, preacher in the Italian church, born in Spain; tenant to the duchess of Suffolk; Mary his wife; John and James, their children; David de Dieu and Joan Leveresse, their servants; and they go to the Italian church." „The whole number of strangers, as well denisons as not denisons, dwelling and remaining within the exempt jurisdiction and liberties adjoining to the city, together with the city of Westminster, 2598. Whereof... Spaniards 24, Italians 28. The whole number of strangers, as well within the city of London, as within the exempt liberties, and places aforesaid, near adjoining to the same, was 6704. Whereof... Venetians and Italians 83, Spaniards 95." „Whereof of the English church 1815. Of the Dutch Church 1910. Of the French church 1810. Of the Italian church 161. Of no church 1008." (Sum the above 6704). The following Spaniards are mentioned as associating with the Italians: „Francis de Farias, Spaniard, and Jacomina his wife, his children, and Nicolas Duprey, his servants, silk-weavers, go to the Italian church. Fernando Almarez, Spaniard, a buttonmaker, goeth to the Italian church." Other Spaniards associated with the French; the certificate names; „Balthazar

1567, Lansdown ms. X 5, quoted by Southerden Burn p. 6 of *Foreign Protestant Refugees*, 1846. *Hieronymus Jerlitus appears to have arrived in London 1565*, ibid. p. 229, where also it is mentioned that a Latin letter of his on behalf of a painter is in the Lansdown mss. The *Calendar of State Papers, Domestic*, 1547 to 1580, p. 312 records that on July 22. 1568 Hieronymus Jerlitus, minister of the Italian church, recommended to Cecil Raphael van den Putte to be appointed postmaster for the foreigners, and that on the same day Jean Cousin did the same. Jerlitus sends to Cecil on August 7 a confection of Saccarum solaceum with directions how it is to be taken. In that list of strangers in London in 1568: Jeronomo, the Italian preacher, and Loweraie, his wife, with her maiden and a boy, all go to the Italian church. About the end of 1568 Hieronymus Jerlitus is mentioned as Italian minister, Strype, Grindal 135. My copyist wrote in Corro's Apologia ad Italos 85, 86 Jeronymus Ferlitus and Jeronimo Ferlito, and in the letter of the London foreign churches March 23. 1571 Jeronimi Ferliti. Hieronymi Jerlini *cujus memoria est in benedictione*, in the letter of the same churches 1576, Sepp Polem. 26; probably mistake for Jerlitti.

Sanchie [correct Sanchez], denison, born in Spain, hath an English woman to his wife; John Lewis his servant, born in Valentian de Aragon, and is a comfit-maker; they both go to the French church, as they say; hath two tenements; the one he bought, and the other he payeth rent for." There may be mentioned here also: „Angel Victorys, Sardinian, denison, schoolmaster, and his wife, came for religion, and are of the French church." Moreover: „Mr. Gasperin, a Spaniard, one of the queen's servants."[95]

Corro was happy to have found at last what he had longed for in vain for so many years: a Spanish evangelical audience. Living with his very poor countrymen as their minister, very poor himself, he experienced, he writes,[96] heavenly rejoicing. But a new blow fell upon him. The National Synod of the Reformed Churches of France held at Vertueil in Angoumois from the 1st to the 7th of September 1567 concluded: „The churches shall be advertised that they do not admit Corro Bellerive unto functions of the ministry till he have cleared himself of those crimes for which he stands impeached by the church of London." One cannot disapprove of this decree; the fault is Cousin's and his stubborn helpers'.

On December 8. 1567 Cousin, somewhat to his surprise, received a visit from four ministers who were alarmed by the news that Corro intended to publish an Apology which he had already communicated to somebody, probably to the Italian minister. He had, however, said that he would not proceed without being advised, and those four ministers might see to the matter. Jaques Touillet dit des Roches blamed the zeal of some in allowing a man to preach without being

---

95) *En 1564 les Espagnols étant retirés dans l'Église française, la compagnie de cette Église demanda des cotisations en leur faveur à des marchands anglais qui avaient précédemment contribué aux frais de leur culte.* Actes. Schickler I 124. In the *catalogus municipum Gallorum qui nomen dederunt ecclesiae Gallicae quae hic collects est Londini*, of the year 1564, occurs one Spaniard: Franciscus Courtois, Hispanus, fimbriarius. Schickler III 58. Courtois is Cortés, *frenchified*.

The Spaniards of the Italian church who assembled to attend sermons in their language, dit not form a body, recognized by the English ecclesiastical authority. Nevertheless Corro could call himself in a letter to the bishop July 15. 1568: *ministre pour le présent de l'Église Espagnole de Londres*. In the title of the Acta published 1571: *Hispanorum peregrinorum concionatorem*.

96) In the dedication of his Dialogus theol. **1574.**

received by the church government (the Bishop), and suggested that Corro had wished to thrust himself forward, as the letter of the Bishop showed. He ought to be induced to promise to follow the advice, which he asks for, and to acknowledge his fault, and purge himself. Antoine Robert dit de Blesi agrees. „Corro should do nothing to stir up the people against Cousin, and should purge himself, especially from what has been reported in the letter of the Paris church. He does not seem to think much of de Saules; I do not know if anything particular has happened between them." (He had brought the case of Corro before the synod, as Corro writes to the Bishop July 15. 1568 and to Beza Sept. 3. 1568). „Give nothing in writing, lest he run to the Bishop, but talk to him. I do not know if it would be expedient to make much remonstrance against that letter (of Dec. 24. 1563) of which the Bishop has taken cognizance; it would irritate him still more." It was replied that the Bishop had not justified the letter. Blezi went on to beg M. Cousin to give notice to the elders to try and stop people saying that the Italian church was a receptacle of good-for-nothing fellows. Cousin answered that he did not like such language, but neither did he like the baptism of children of persons who did not bring themselves into line with the churches of their own nation. In a case mentioned by Cousin, Blezi defended the Italian minister. Pierre Mayence judged: „The worst is to leave the truth in suspense. In procuring the good and quiet of the church we do not encroach upon the Bishop's authority. We only wish that Bellerive purge himself in doctrine and in life, so far as he may be found in fault; and our action is so much the less odious as he himself asked for it, as he has openly said to two of the brethren. Then his book of apology will not come to light." Laurens Bourgignon said: „To show him the letter for which we reproach him, cannot be prejudicial, I do not, however, advise leaving a copy in his hands. But those who will be charged to report to him ought to have a summary of the letter to help their memory. His book should remain unpublished. If he gets justified or reconciled with the church, Cousin should hold him as a brother and companion. I do not say that he ought to admit him into his church, but he ought to hold him in esteem as his vocation demands *(selon sa vocation)*. We do not touch the preeminence of the Bishop, who can only be very glad that we should negotiate for peace. Some brethren should go to Bellerive; you, M. Cousin, it seems to me, would do well to be reserved, with your Consistory, and not advance anything to exasperate the feelings; the synods of France might be consulted. And let us keep peace with the Italian church." Cousin was confident enough to say that he had tried to put a stop to this affair *(mettre le pied sur cest affair)*, foreseeing that only confusion and trouble for the church of God could follow from it, but Bellerive on the contrary had taken pleasure in divulging it, threatening the whole Consistory to get his letter printed. On December 9. the same ministers assembled again at Cousin's house. The letter of the church of Paris was read. Cousin was commissioned to write down the chief points concerning Corro's life and doctrine, to be communicated to him orally, not in writing. Corro is to be required to follow the advice of the brethren, which he asked for, as far as he reasonably may *(en ce qui sera de raison)*, principally to purge himself and not to print an apology nor to spread rumours.

As for the result of the negotiation, we only know that the apology remained unprinted. If the deputies told him they could not allow him a copy of the fatal letter, they must have been painfully surprised by his dry remark: „I have already got one from the Bishop."

In January 1568 Corro sent his two French Antwerp publications to the Archbishop of Canterbury, Matthew Parker, for his two sons who, he understood, were studying French. He continues: „Lately I waited on the Bishop of London, and he, with his usual kindness towards me and other foreigners, granted me a quarterly fee *(aliquot coronatos)*. I should like to serve you and your kingdom in some way, but if there is no opportunity, you will take the will for the deed."

In order to silence the opposition which still continued, Corro, printed Grindal's favorable judgment of June 1567 in the Latin original with a French translation, and distributed copies of the leaf, together with a short manuscript report, in which he said that the Bishop had considered the iniquity of the proceeding and had by his testimonial *manifested* the malice of Corro's adversaries. After Corro on July 21. had given a copy to one of the French ministers, these and the elders and the deacons remonstrated in a letter to the Bishop against that *libelle diffamatoire* which had been spread through the whole town and of which they had heard rumours long ago. As a matter of fact Grindal had only declared in that testimonial that the suspicions against Corro's orthodoxy were unfounded and had abstained from any expression of blame against Cousin and his followers. But whilst they refused Corro to read his letter to Reina and so give him a chance of answering the accusations derived from it, the Bishop had, by the fact of allowing him a copy of it, shewn his disapproval of the proceedings of the French.

Some days before Corro handed that libel, as they called it, to one of the ministers, he had on July 15. presented to the Bishop a complaint against Cousin and his adherents.

On August 31. he wrote to the French Consistory: „Last Friday morning M. Cousin called on the Bishop, who two hours later informed me that I was accused before him of having preached in French to my Spanish congregation, with the purpose of drawing hearers away from your congregation to mine, and, as far as I can conjecture, Cousin is my accuser. As during the last fifteen months he has waged an atrocious war against me by tongue and pen, in this kingdom and abroad, professing to have the Consistory's authority for so doing, I should like to know whether the present accusation is made with your approval. The accusation is false and full of calumny. I never preached in French to my few Spaniards. I have this year, in my sermons on eight chapters of the epistle to the Romans, endeavoured to explain to my hearers the method of the apostle, and the connexion and order of his arguments, without the amplifications and prolix exhortations usual in sermons; but, because some of my church of Antwerp are not fully acquainted with the Spanish idiom, I interpret some of the more important things in Latin or French, merely in order to assist those who wish to understand the epistle. I am not desirous of drawing away or alienating anyone from his congregation. I think that without distinction of language or parochy all ministers ought to be mindful of our being one body to whatsoever congregation we may belong. I have not accused you of retaining several persons of my nationality in your church, some against their wish, nor of enjoining them in the examination before the Lord's Supper to speak in Spanish, which language your minister does not understand sufficiently to judge whether what they say is right or wrong. Moreover I do not deliver those repetitions from the pulpit or seated, but while walking about, in order not to give a handle to envy; and they are held three hours after dinner *(tertia a prandio)*, at which time you have no preaching nor convention *(coetus)*. It is therefore calumny to say that I want to withdraw hearers from you. If Cousin wishes to reserve his language to himself so that no one may declare in French what he means, unless the minister vouchsafe it, he must exhibit his privileges, which finally would deprive us of the use of that language even in our homes and bedchambers." (I think Corro's wife was French.) „If he apprehends that I draw his hearers to myself, and consequently remunerations and stipends, he is greatly mistaken, for I want nothing from those I teach except docility for embracing the gospel. I am not of those who compose catalogues (of members) in order to fish in their purses, but, following the apostle's word: ‚I seek not yours, but you.' 2 Cor. 12. Is he afraid lest my hearers should learn the purity and sincerity of my doctrine, and the detractions, fallacies and calumnies of those who discredit it should become notorious? I trust in God that men of probity hereafter will understand the facts, and, even tough I may not speak in French, the very stones will cry aloud and testify the truth of God *(licet Gallice non loquar, lapides tamen clamabunt et veritati Dei ferent testimonium)*. Brethren, let us live in peace, and not like dogs and cats. As regards the Articles which I presented to the Bishop on the 15th of last month and to which Cousin is preparing an answer, I desire them to be read to you. As he says that whatsoever he has undertaken against me he has done in your name, I could not but complain of the action of the Consistory. If he abuses your authority, the fault is his."

The Consistory wrote to the Bishop, on September 2.: „You have seen the libels full of injuries, which were spread abroad clandestinely. We have not yet seen the accusations which, as you said, scent of gall and venom. Two days ago he sent us this letter (dated August 31.) in which there is scarcely a word undeserving of blame. It is useless to answer; he is desirous of nothing more than of a new opportunity to trouble us. We pray you urgently, as you know our piety and modesty, both before and after Corro went to London, not to leave us exposed to so many libels. J. Cousin.

J. Desroches. [Estienne] Mermier. [The three ministers]. In the name of all."

These accusations seem to be the same on which the Bishop writes to Cecil in the above quoted report. He says: „Corro, thinking himself injured by the refusal of the French church to receive him, and offended with certain speeches uttered by some of that church in Lumbardstreet and at tables in London, which I always advised him to contemn, wrote a pamphlet which he called an Apology, but indeed a sharp invective containing many slanders against the ministers and seniors of the French church, and also sundry untruths of my own knowledge."

On Sept. 3. Corro sent transcripts to Beza, asking him to lay the whole matter before the Genevan church. This, however, Beza did not think opportune.

On November 28. the ministers, elders and deacons signed *Les articles que l'Eglise française met en avant contre Ant. Corran.* A Latin translation was sent to the Bishop, probably in December. The accusation is summed up in four chapters: ambition, calumnies, lies, mockeries; many probatory documents were appended. The Bishop gave the chapters to Corro who answered them in French, the church replied, and the Bishop named, as judges, royal commissioners and six ministers of churches of France: Loiseleur, Le Chevalier, de la Faye, Robert, Bourgignon, Feugeray. The sentence was pronounced by the Bishop on March 17. 1569, to the effect that, on account of evil speaking and unshakable obstinacy Corro was interdicted from preaching and public reading or interpreting of God's word and suspended from all ecclesiastical functions. In the course of the trial Corro got so much off his balance as to exclaim: „It is evident that Englishmen do not only wage civil war against the Spaniards, but ecclesiastical also; civil in taking their ships and money, ecclesiastical in my person." It is easily conceivable that Corro did not keep his temper in view of some of the articles, for instance of what was said about opening his letters to Reina. Cousin, whose autograph of the articles is extant, says there that Corro is a calumniator if he does not prove that several of his letters have been intercepted by theft, and he calls it a lie of Corro to say that they would not show the cover of his scandalous letter, on which cover they pretended to have read that the enclosed was important for the church of God. But, alas, Cousin has been unfortunate enough to prove with his own hand the facts he denied. He states in these articles that the Consistory received that letter on March 12. (the same date in the Latin text), and he adjoins the original cover which contains the words referred to by him in the articles, namely „that the enclosed serves *à l'avancement de l'église de Dieu.*" He only overlooked the fact that it is dated April 4. and belongs to Corro's letter of March 25. He probably had made the same mistake when he wrote to St. Pol on June 16. 1567 speaking of the same letter of Corro from Theobon: „There was a notice *que c'estoyent lettres d'importance pour l'église de Dieu.*" At all events Cousin could not produce a cover of the Theobon letter and it remains undeniable that in more than one case they appropriated and kept what was not theirs.

On March 11. Beza had despatched three letters to London, one for Bishop Grindal, to whose decision he referred the whole Corro business, another letter to Cousin, and a third to Corro. In the latter he criticizes Corro's letter to Reina. As for Reina himself (who was at that time at Basle engaged in finishing the printing of the Spanish Bible), the Geneva authority declared that he could not receive him as a brother until he (Reina) had changed his opinion on the Lord's Supper. Corro's desire to get Schwenkfeld's and Osiander's writings had likewise made a most unfavorable impression on the Calvinistic divine who thought those theologians execrable. Corro had asked Reina what was thought of Velsius and Acontius; Beza answers: „the one is insane, the other full of paradoxes." Besides, Beza cavils at the questions proposed by Corro in his private letter. Corro had asked, in what substance the Word, promised by God to men, had shown itself to the fathers of the ancient covenant. „If you deny", says Beza, „that this is a Servetian question, you are denying the sunshine at noon. It is true, the matter has been questioned by the Church Fathers of old. Why then not acquiesce in their decision? And why propose it even to a man who is (possibly wrongly), accused of Servetism?" Nothing, he exclaims, could be more imprudent than the testimonial of Montargis for Corro, and nothing more inconsiderate than his making use of it.

The small Spanish congregation was now dissolved, — by the stratagems of Satan, as Corro says some years later,[97] using the title words of the book of Acontius: *Satanae stratagemata.*

On August 6. Corro delivered a speech before the French Consistory; they praised his candour and asked him to write down the summary of it. He could not well refuse, although foreseeing new debates. In the summary which was sent on Aug. 11. he says: „If someone of you feels himself offended by me, I pray him to believe that I did not act out of malice, but in human weakness, and that God has uprooted all hatred and all seed of enmity in me. May it be the same to everyone of you." He also wished for a written declaration. They answered on the 18th that as he by his libels had grievously offended not only the Consistory, but many in England and beyond the sea and had created a public scandal, a document of repentance was necessary. It ought to contain the following three articles, which they submitted, however, to the ecclesiastical authority. First, that he approved the tenor of the sentence of the Bishop and the royal commissaries. Secondly, that he retracted all libels published in London and elsewhere, and expressly declared his regret for having written that he had found less humanity and hospitality in their church than he could have got among Turks and heathens, and that their church had used him with greater iniquity and tyranny than the Spanish Inquisitors. Thirdly, that he promised to keep peace with them. They expected his answer in a few days. The letter is signed in the name of the whole senate by Jaques Taffin. Two elders handed it to Corro on the 20th. He answered on the 24th. „The sentence of the judges does not require to be approved by the parties, but to be respected and obeyed. I retract whatever I may have said or written exceeding the bounds of Christian moderation. I regret to have used the comparison with Turks and heathens and Spanish In-

---

97) Dedication of Dialogus theologicus 1574: *Sathan suis usus solitis stratagematis et coetum illum peregrinorum Hispanorum . . . . dissolvit prorsusque pessum dedit . . .* The ministers of the foreign churches in London say in 1576 in their antithesis 131: *coetus ille Hispanicus dissolutus non est. Solus D. Corranus ejectus est a suis conterraneis et fratribus Italis, qui unum corpus Ecclesiae constituunt.* But indeed it was dissolved into the Italian church. And he was not ejected from the Italian church, but excluded from the Lord's Supper, and most likely the accusers were not his Spaniards, but the Italians, instigated by the French.

quisitors, when I rightly felt offended by a certain want of hospitable kindness and further by tyrannous treatment of me. Many fascicles of letters which I sent in the course of four years to friends in London have been opened and kept by your minister and not delivered to those to whom they were addressed. By such a violation of the right of all nations, even the most patient man can be inflamed with anger. I entreat the brother with whom those letters still remain to restore them to me, especially those written to me by a merchant of Bordeaux on very serious matters. One of my private letters to an intimate friend of mine, containing questions in dispute in those churches which are freed from the yoke of Antichrist, has been translated into several languages with distortions and omissions, and distributed in England in many copies. And when, while I lived in France, Cousin wrote to me saying that Cassiodoro had left England and no one knew where he was, he did not mention his suspicions against me, although he had already censured me in England and Flanders and France on account of that letter and of what he said he learned from France. On a complaint being made with reference to that letter by an elder who was sent to Antwerp, I completely satisfied that church; but, although this fact must have been known, as soon as I arrived in London the pureness of my doctrine was openly attacked before I was privately admonished, and that too after they had approved it when they heard me explaining it in their coetus. It was asserted also that I had intruded myself into the Lord's Supper, but the fact is that one of the elders introduced me and ceded me his place, the which he would not have done if my partaking had been interdicted by the Consistory. My wife was not admitted to the Lord's Supper, because the minister lacked a testimonial with regard to her from France. Excerpts from a book of Brenz were shown to many with the rumour that I had edited the book. When the works which I had published at Antwerp were called heretical here, I durst not remain silent, especially as orthodox doctors and churches, including Beza, as his letter shows, did not disapprove of them. In spite of the autograph testimony of the Antwerp church which may be certified by elders and deacons of that church living here, there was a hint of some accusation proceeding from the same church, but no trace of such a one has hitherto appeared. As for the comparison with Spanish Inquisitors, it must be considered in what connection it was made. I had ardently besought you to show me my letter by which you were scandalized, that I might acknowledge it. Nothing, however, was exhibited except a French translation made by a man who was so much my enemy that some days later he pursued me to my home with floods of abuses and injuries. When I asked to be permitted to compare that translation with the original, I was frustrated. When at last the translation had been read in my hearing, I supplicated to be allowed to have either my letter or the translation, to enable me to answer, and I added that, if I did not satisfy you, I would submit to the judgment of the Consistory. All in vain. Your minister threatened even to send copies to many quarters. It was when relating these proceedings, that I exclaimed: ‚I adjure the church of God to shew any equal to this iniquity and tyranny, the like of which has never been seen to this day, not even in the case of the Spanish Inquisition which they regard as the most cruel of all tribunals.‘ These are my words in art. 22. I acknowledge that the comparison is odious and ungrateful, but if an enquiry be instituted as to whether I said it rightly or wrongly, I shall not refuse you yourselves as my judges after our quarrel is over. I know that the Inquisitors would not have refused to allow me to read and inspect my letter, and would have given me an authenticated copy, as the Bishop afterwards did not disdain to do. Of my apology containing those complaints nobody has received a copy except the Bishop and Beza, and I have read it only to some intimate friends. I shall strive for peace to the last. At present let them judge whose concern it is." On September 8. Nicolaus Fontanus wrote to him in the name of the whole ecclesiastical senate: that the letter of Aug. 18. ought to have been sufficient for him by reason of its fairness and submission to the church authority. They now left the case to the judgment of the Bishop. Nic. de la Fontaine is the same to whom Calvin had given the role of public accuser of the captured Serveto.

To a letter of the Secretary of State, Sir W. Cecil, Bishop Grindal answered on September 20.: „Acknowledging myself always most bounden unto you, I will, according to the request of your late letters, labour to compound and finish the controversy between the Spanish and French preachers so soon as possibly I can. There are some impediments of expedition at this present; partly because I cannot well finish this matter, except I myself remained at London two or three days, whither I am somewhat loath to go hastily, for that the plague is most stirring near my house there, and partly because the French preacher buried one out of his house of the plague, the 15th of this month. I will send for Corranus and talk with him first, and after with the other parties. If anything be offered to Corranus on my part that is too hard, I am well contented to refer the moderation thereof to your judgment. True it is that Corranus hath good learning, but I have no good liking of his spirit and of his dealings, whereof I have had good experience. And because I perceive ye have not been informed where the original fault was, so soon as I can, I purpose to send you some notes of the beginning and process thereof; thus much only signifying in the mean time, that upon sundry judicial hearings of the matter the fault was by sentence pronounced to be in Corranus. For restitution of Corranus to his preaching or reading there is now lately a new difficulty arisen. Corranus of late hath caused a table which he wrote in the French tongue, intituled *de operibus Dei*, to be printed at Norwich, not offering the same to be examined here before it were printed. The minister and seniors of the Italian church in London (whereof Corranus is a member) mislike the doctrine contained in the said table, and therefore have monished the said Corranus to answer for the same before them. Thus much Hieronymus, the Italian preacher, told me sithence the receipt of your letters. If the controversy with the French (which is only about offence in manner) be compounded, I cannot see but his restitution in reading or preaching must be deferred, till he have cleared himself before the governors of his own church in matters of doctrine, which is a matter of far greater moment. I do not yet know the particular matters, but I have willed Hieronymus to translate the said table into Latin, and to send me a copy, that some conference may be used in it." The promised notes of the „beginning and process" were sent, probably in October; we have above made use of them for some particulars.

On November 7. the Bishop wrote to Cousin: „About two months ago one of my principal friends who is a patron of your churches [Cecil] wrote to me asking me to find some means of reconciling Corro with you. Corro himself has, more humbly than is his wont, submitted entirely to my judgment. I have directed him to write down a very short form of acknowledgment of his fault in charging you with Turkish and Inquisitorial cruelty, and to promise to live peaceably henceforth; these two things you yourselves have required in your letter to him. The third postulate, namely that he should acquiesce in the sentence, is the concern of us commissioners. We will take care that he makes this submission to us, and apologizes for the language which he used against us, thereby showing want of proper respect. Only the two first mentioned points concern your church. Accordingly, he has sent me the formula which I enclose to you. In this formula the word ‚submission' did not please me; it will, however, be replied that you used the same word in the same sense in a writing of yours. I do not quite understand your phrases. If you wish to have something emended in this formula, please note it on a separate paper and send it together with the formula as soon as you conveniently can. I also pray you to show goodwill in accepting the reconciliation and to solicit others to do the same; nothing you can do would be more agreeable to me. He has now for fully eight months been suspended from the ministry for offence, not in doctrine, but in conduct, which punishment has indeed not been a small one. As regards the controversy which he now has with his church about doctrine, it is another affair, and he will not be restored to the public ministry before that has been settled. At present I only plead this, that, when he shall have acknowledged his trespass in a short document read in your Consistory and delivered to you signed by his hand, you forgive him all the past." Cousin answered on November 12.: that on the following Sunday the Consistory would decide, and then two or three would call on him on a day chosen by him, or, if he preferred, the decision would be sent him in writing. Further, they expressed the wish to look over the papers of Corro which Beza had recently sent to the Bishop, for they did not like to demand anything from Corro without having seen his writings, as he had reproached them with doing a similar thing in the session at which the Bishop and the Royal Commissioners gave the sentence upon him. — The Bishop had hoped they would relent to some extent, but they remained invincibly obstinate. They answered on November 22. that they proposed a new formula. The document signed by him they intended to read to their people who had been offended by him." If he does not agree with us in doctrine, what accord can we have with him? S. John says (2nd epistle): ‚If there come any unto you and bring not the doctrine of Christ, receive him not unto your house neither bid him God speed.' We learn that he has printed a *Tableau,* and do not know whether he has submitted it before printing to the persons authorized by the laws of the country. He has a quarrel with one of our brethren, the minister of Norwich, who found something objectionable in the doctrine (of the Tableau)." Signed by the ministers Cousin, Desroches, Mermier, seven elders (including Fichet), eight deacons (among whom was Balthasar Sanchez). The proposed formula is the following: „By this document signed with my hand I confess to have given just occasions to the French Consistory of London for doubting with good right of my doctrine on account of a certain letter written by me to a friend of mine which was delivered, according to God's will, *(comme Dieu le voulut)* into the hands of the Consistory in 1564. And although I have hitherto maintained that letter to be good and Christian, I now retract it as scandalous and imprudently written. Item, I confess that in a little book composed by me at Antwerp are several things worthy of censure as well in doctrine as because I much prejudiced the writings and the renown of faithful servants of God who in our time have done great work for the restoring of God's church. I am sorry to have thereby opened the way for adversaries to mock at the pure religion of the reformed churches. Item, as to certain libels prohibited by divine and human laws, or apologies injuring the French church of London, which I have spread even oversea, without ever consenting to communicate them to the attacked persons," [In the letter, the Consistory complains: ‚when we desired to see them, he refused, at least at any rate as regards the great apology, till to day.'] — „I retract all of them entirely as scandalous, mendacious and unworthy of a Christian. Especially I regret to have written: ‚I would have found more humanity or hospitality among Turks and heathens, than I received from them; that their cruelty and tyranny towards me was greater than that of the Spanish Inquisitors; that I call them children of the devil and led by the spirit of Cain; and other similar outrages. I supplicate all to whose hearing these things have come, to pardon me in the name of God. Burying the doubts expressed in my letter regarding the person of Christ, I recognize that in his divinity he is the true Son of God, equal to the Father, having the same essence since all eternity, and in his humanity true man, before and after his resurrection, at present in heaven and not on earth. Before Whom, I solemnly promise to live in future in Christian spirit, and to edify my neighbours by pure doctrine."

To such a recantation Corro could not subscribe.

At the same time he was involved in great difficulties with the Italians. But he had plenty of courage. The controversy hinged on his *Tableau de l'œuvre de Dieu*. The Tableau occupies only the inner side of an open folio sheet, and gives in short sentences a summary of the Christian doctrine. A page with the same title without the name of the author had been printed in 1556, and a manuscript copy of it was given to Corro when at Antwerp, with the request, that he would retouch it. This he did thoroughly, and he allowed manuscript copies to be taken of it. A merchant, who had obtained one, printed it a couple of years later at his own cost in Norwich; the publication is dated July 15. 1569. Corro sent the first copy of the edition to the Cardinal of Chatillon, another to the Vidame de Chartres,[98] others to Sieur de Jumelles and some more French noblemen, then refugees in England. A French minister at Norwich noted 25 censures against the Tableau, and Corro was denounced to the Italian Consistory. The Italian minister translated the Tableau into Latin at the Bishop's wish, and added criticisms, making use of the French censures. Copies were sent to the Bishop and to Corro. The accused gave to the Italians the French dialogue he had com-

98) Strype, Grindal 139, under the year 1569: The vidame of Chartres, a great nobleman of France, and of chief account among the Protestants, a learned and a very good man, was now in August here, upon some business relating to religion. Strype adds that the Bishop of London and some other favourers procured him a habitation until Michaelmas. A year later we meet him again in England as Corro's adviser, see below, p. 53. After the Bartholomew massacre he fled to England in September, Strype, Parker 355; his letter written shortly after his arrival to the Lord Treasurer Burghley ibd. Appd. 112f. Cf. also Parker 483. And Annals II 168. IV. Suppl. 9. In the despatches of the Spanish London ambassy he is mentioned sometimes in 1572 and 75 and 79, Coleccion de docum. inéd. p. la hist. de Esp. T. 91 p. 59. 67. 87. 312.

posed against the French censures, but they wished for a Latin answer. So he brought a new *Apologia* to the Consistory on December 9., and as they found it very bulky, an Epitome in the same month. By this exposition of his doctrine the feeling against it was only increased, and it was said that the virulence of his pen against the minister and the elders, his mocking tone, insults, evil speaking and lies were intolerable. An answer to the Apologia was written, but they did not give it to Corro. They admonished him several times, and on January 7. 1570 in presence of the congregation, which on the next day was to celebrate the Lord's Supper, to which it had been resolved not to admit him. He said he had not intended to offend and was ready to revoke what might be found injurious and to satisfy them concerning his doctrine. At last on January 30. he submitted to the sentence on doctrine and offences to be pronounced by the assembly of that day, consisting of the Consistory, seven other members of the church, two French ministers and two English ministers, those four being invited with the consent of Corro who was present in the assembly. On the next day, however, he wrote that, as the Italian minister and the elders were the accusers, the right of judgment belonged only to the four other ministers, to whom he also prescribed the procedure and the law. This is the report from the Italian side; any observation on it by Corro is wanting, but it is possible that, having consented to the common inquiry and promised submission to the sentence, he found it necessary to reiterate what he had often said before, that the Italians were, like himself, parties to this action. Nevertheless he is said to have been convicted of lying in his narration of the conflict, and on account of his pertinacity and contempt of church-discipline, and his many private and public quarrels with the brethren, it was proposed to interdict him the Lord's Supper as long as the doubt concerning his doctrine lasted and he showed no repentance for his outbursts against the Minister and Elders. The proposal was made by six of the church members, two Englishmen, one of them a *domesticus* of the Archbishop of Canterbury, and Magister de Feugeray (who, in spite of the fact that in March 1569 he had been one of the judges who condemned Corro, was on this occasion accepted by him as a judge), and the Consistory decreed accordingly. In the name of the Consistory Antonio Giustiniano,

Elder and Lector, sent a report to the Bishop and begged that he would protect them in their opposition against such writings as the Tableau (also a Dutch translation, made by a disciple of Corro, of the Tableau and of the Consistory's animadversions on it, was circulating), and as his Spanish dialogue (which he also translated into Latin) on the Epistle to the Romans; in both works they find that he treats on justification in a new, strange and perplexing way.

A Dutch translation of the Tableau was, shortly after the publication of the French, read to the Minister of the London Dutch, Joris Wybo Sylvanus. He was ill at that time and could not give a judgment on the whole work; he thought that in some places the translator had not exactly given the meaning of the author, but it seemed that the latter attributed too much to human power; Wybo expressed, however, his satisfaction regarding the article on Christ's ascension, on which he recollected having read the same in Calvin's Institution.[99]

As a New Year's present for 1570 (I think it was the English New Year, the 25th of March) Corro sent a revised edition of his French Tableau to Madame de Stafford,[100] and the first edition of his Latin translation to Queen Elizabeth, both with a printed dedication. He had translated the Tableau into Latin in order to give it to the Bishop of London.[101] It was certainly the same Latin which he sent to the Archbishop of Canterbury, Parker, who added some articles and licensed its publication.[102] The same Archbishop had also permitted to publish the English translation of the Antwerp epistle to the Augsburghians[103]; it appeared *cum privilegio*, with the translator's dedication of December 10. 1569.

In Spring 1570 Corro had the honour to be received in king Philip's *Appendix* to the Pope's *Index* among the first class heretics whose writings, edited already and all future ones, are prohibited.

99) Sepp, Naspor. III 166f.
100) According to Sepp, Naspor. III 165, probably the widow of the translator into English of some letters of Erasmus and of Fox's book de differentia regiae potestatis et ecclesiasticae.
101) Epitome December 1569, extract below.
102) Corro to Huntingdon, below. The statement cannot be doubted, otherwise Cousin would not be silent about it in his remarks on Corro's letter to Huntingdon.
103) Epitome ad Italos, secundum praejudicium.

August saw the beginning of a new negotiation with the London French. The first stage is told in a letter, which therefore we place here, although it starts from a preceding letter which we shall translate below. An Italian captain, Franciotto,[104] doubtless a member of the Italian London church, writes to the Earl of Huntingdon, London January 27. 1571: „Having seen a copy of the letter to the Earl, in which Corro says that, invited and suborned by partial and factious persons, he had entered into a conference with the French ministers, I feel bound in honour to tell your Excellency the truth in opposition to such an impudent lie." (It seems Franciotto thought that Corro had alluded to him, for which idea there cannot be discovered the slightest reason in Corro's letter.) „Corro called on me on August 20. or 25., complaining of the French ministers and chiefly of the minister of the Cardinal de Chatillon, M. de Villiers, who talked of him as a heretic. Corro beseeched me urgently to ask Villiers to abstain from such language. He should like a friendly conference with Villiers. Apprehensive of Corro's inconstancy I refused several times, saying: ‚Monsieur Antoine, if you should fail to keep your promise, we could not be friends any longer.' As he, however, swore by God to submit to the judgment of the deputies of the Universal Company and of all the ministers, I yielded, soliciting him to write to Villiers. He sent me the minute to correct if it should be considered too vehement, and I made some cancellations and additions. The next day I went to Shene [near London] to the Cardinal, who not only asked but commanded Villiers to undertake this. On the Monday Villiers went to London [this must have been August 28.] and ‚I sent a message to Corro by Agostino Bovazo the Genovese. They met and appointed a convention for Tuesday. On Tuesday I was invited to be present at the dispute in the house of a Fleming, L'Empereur, where, thirthy-six Ministers being assembled, the arbiters and the president were chosen, and Corro signed a promise to acquiesce in

---

[104] Cecil manuscripts, Part I: „1568 Aug. 20. Walsingham's report from Franchiotto, the Italian. Franchiotto regrets that his faithfulness, which for forty years has been manifested before all the world in many transactions of the greatest importance, should now require the testimony of France, and professes his devotion to Her Majesty's service". He warns her against poison and sends a list of suspicious persons.

whatever conclusions were arrrived at in the conference." [This promise was signed on August 30., which was a Wednesday.] „During the dispute in my presence the articles of the Tableau were examined; to some objections he yielded, for many others he submitted himself to the arbiters. Two entire days were employed in the conference." [I think August 30. and 31.] „For the third session no day was appointed and I was not summoned to it. I am told that Corro heard the sentence and the ratification thereof by the general assembly, and humbly consented and promised to sign it, protesting that it was his intention to be in union with the French church and their doctrine, but that when he was actually requested to sign he arrogantly refused."

The protocol and the adjoined notices give more particulars. Pierre Loiseleur, seigneur de Villiers, had said that the Tableau contained erroneous and heretical propositions. Corro complained of this to some *particuliers notables personnages.* These requested the Compagnie of thirty-six ministers of France, who had assembled in London on behalf of their churches, to examine the Tableau, and Corro consented thereto. One of these *personnages* was doubtless the Cardinal de Chatillon. He wrote to the ministers and elders of the Dutch and Walloon (= French) churches from Shene on August 16. 1570: „I send you M. de Villiers to make known to you some particulars which I think deserve careful and prompt consideration." We do not know what these particulars were, but they probably concerned the Corro affair. The assembly of ministers deputed six of their number, with Alexandre Gaudieu de Lestang as their president, and besides two secretaries, and decided that M. Guill. Feugeray should with Loiseleur take part in the discussion with Corro. These three on August 30. signed the promise of submission to the decision of the deputies, without prejudice to the inquiry already moved before the Anglican church. The protocol of the discussion and the sentence of the committee being approved by the whole assembly, the judgment was pronounced on September 4.: „The Tableau" (they had compared also Corro's Latin translation)[105] „and Corro's declaration contain some erroneous and heretical propositions, and some suspected, obscure, confuse, and contradictious statements; passages of Scripture are

---

105) P. 111: *la seconde version Latine,* viz. not the former made by Jerlito, but Corro's own which had been printed. It is also mentioned p. 114. 122.

corrupted or badly interpreted, and there are also omissions which are of dangerous consequence, and many improper and strange phrases." From the Latin record of the discussions they made a condensed extract in French to be handed to Corro, the main points of which are the following: Corro confounds the eternal Word with the preached word received in the hearts, and so falls into the heresy of Osiander's essential justice and destroys the deity of Christ. He teaches free will and derives a part of our justification from our works. He maintains an eventual election.[106] Adam's persuasion that God was against him he attributes to blindness of a perverted mind, not to the impression made by the law. He never names Christ nor the Holy Spirit God.[107] He does not openly speak of Christ as Redeemer. Not Christ, but his manifestation, is called mystery *(sacramentum)* 1. Tim. 3.[108] The sentence and the extract were read to Corro in presence of the whole company on September 5. He owned to errors and faults with which he was charged (some objections he had already accepted in the course of the discussion), saying he preferred to be found ignorant than obstinate, he asked them, however, to have regard to his reputation for the sake of his nation. It was answered that he himself might inform the persons to whom he had distributed copies of the Tableau. If he did not do this duty, the ministers of the foreign churches in London with their Consistories must communicate the facts to their flocks. The company of the ministers, who were on the eve of returning to France, desired Corro to sign a paper containing the retractation which he had made orally and the promise to remain in union with the whole company according to the pureness of the word of God; to which he consented in the evening, but when the next morning a paper was brought him

106) P. 122: In Tabula recitatur (see the third division), inobedientibus mortem aeternam paratam, ac homines sibi accersere interitum sponte sua, ut Latina continet versio. Cui objectum est, si damnatio illis tantum destinatur qui non obediunt, sed propria voluntate sese agunt praecipites, inde sequeretur Deum injustum qui Esau odit antequam bonum aut malum fecisset.

107) In the Latin it is reported that in the discussion Corro *Christum asseruit verum λόγον ὑφιστάμενον sicut Athanasii explicatur symbolo.* And *coetus probat confessionem expressam a Corrano de S. Spiritus deitate.*

108) *Ita Sebastianus Francus, magnus vineae Domini vastator, Christum vocat Sacramentum,* had said the Italians in the *Responsio ad prolixam Apologiam.* Cf. Antithesis 13 *of* 1576.

by the president of the conference he refused to sign, and although summoned by the other deputies to keep his word, he did not do so. Then ensued disputes about this affair in the three churches, so that their ministers and elders agreed on January 8. 1571 that it was necessary to give a short exposition of the facts and to exhort everyone to keep peace and avoid useless disputes and false doctrine. And this conclusion was carried out. Such is the report on the occurrences of September 5. and foll. as written by the hand of Cousin,[109] who concludes by mentioning a letter of January 18. to a peer of England in which Corro declares himself ready to justify his doctrine before all European churches.

This letter was written to the Earl of Huntingdon. Some months before Corro had sent him his *Tabula de divinis operibus*, with regard to which a fresh disturbance was brought about by Cousin and other French ministers. „I have sent the same", he says, „to many bishops and other scholars of this country, and no one of them has as yet told me either verbally or in writing that he has discovered anything therein wanting in purity of doctrine or in orthodoxy; on the contrary many have wondered at the carping propensity of these Frenchmen. When others arose in favor of my detractors, I sent more than a hundred copies to scholars of Germany. I like to be taught, but with fraternal charity. How could I trust the man, who two years ago passed me off as the author of a book printed fifteen years before under the name of Brenz? To tell the truth, I doubt their candor. They even condemned their own confession of faith because it was written by my hand. If I had not experienced this in my own person,[110] I should scarcely have believed it on the evidence of a thousand witnesses. It happened thus. Some of them, feigning friendship, asked me to let the whole controversy be settled by their *coetus*, who only wished to pacify me and to restore my reputation weakened by Cousin. After having in long disputes endeavoured to get the affair committed to free arbiters, I at last left it wholly to them, against the wish of the Vidame (de Chartres) and other friends of mine who know that kind of man. So I went to the French ministers.

---

109) Substantially the same regarding September 5. and 6. is said in Cousin's Annotation to Corro's letter to Huntingdon.

110) Read: *Quod ni* (not *in*) *praesens adessem*.

But the discussions turned out to be sophistical and hostile. I saw this at once and expostulated with those who had drawn me into the arena by their fallacious persuasions. They excused themselves by saying, it happened because the *coetus* of ministers suspected me concerning the three main articles of our religion, viz. predestination, free will and justification by faith alone; they advised me to write and deliver a very short expression of my belief regarding those questions. On my return home I found the paper formerly exhibited to the bishop of London, on which I had copied word for word those three articles from the *Confessio Helveticarum ecclesiarum* [Bullinger's work, printed 1566], only changing the plural into the singular: — I, instead of we, believe, trust, confess. I joined a verbal transcript from Nicolaus Hemmingius' explanation of St. Paul's passage: ‚I have loved Jacob and hated Esau.' When the candid censors had looked at these papers, they called the confession on predestination delirious while the articles on free will and justification they found derived from the school of Melanchthon and therefore not altogether pleasing, and the interpretations of Hemmingius [the Melanchthonian Dane [111]] they deemed to be of Castalio and upbraided my audacity in bringing them the words of such a vaporous heretic. I sent for the books, and at the public lecture and the comparison with my papers they were stupefied, and they rebuked me for neglecting the duty of charity by giving them only my manuscripts, which I had done three days before [on September 1. or 2.], and not the books. As if there were more charity in condemning the truth merely because written and signed by me! The debate ended thus: I was to avow myself in a short writing as their brother and fellow-minister *(symmysta)* and to declare that I embraced the articles of the Helvetic Confession [to which also the ministers of the church of Geneva had given their assent] and detested all heresies and errors against the evangelical doctrine. This I promised to perform. So we parted shaking hands and embracing, with the applause of all. I intended to execute the writing myself, but the next day [September 6.] they sent a formulary of palinode to which they asked me to subscribe, that they might

---

111) In 1569 there had come forth translated into English Hemming's Postil or exposition of the gospels usually read upon sundays and feast-days of saints. Strype, Annals I 577.

proclaim from the pulpit my condemnation of the Tableau as being full of many errors. I rejected it, not at all conscious of impure or perverse doctrine. Im am ready to defend myself before all European churches. The calumniators now have the audacity to call me a heretic, a schismatic, a seducer, in spite of the fact that the Archbishop of Canterbury examined the Tableau, added some articles to it, and allowed me to print it. Let them whose authority is thus slighted see whether such a thing is to be tolerated. Shall I recant what I never said or wrote? It is iniquitous that the accusers should be also the judges. Besides this, they show a letter which they say Beza has written to me. The writer calls me his friend and himself a Christian monitor, but they obtrude the admonitions as accusations. May I believe the letter a stratagem? I do not recognize the handwriting of Beza; I see no seal.[112] The unrestrained rating proves that the letter does not come from a moderate man. While professing to admonish me in a friendly way, he affronts the whole Spanish nation. Wherefore does he mention Servetians, Valdesians and Jesuits? Am I to account for all my compatriots? But enough. Neither can Beza by his letters render me heretic, nor can I, howsoever officious, make him, the Frenchman, a friend of Spaniards. May Christ's gospel, which the Eternal Son of God brought for all nations, make us coalesce in one flock, where there is neither French nor Spaniard, but all in Christ, the Saviour and Redeemer of all men. I leave it to your Lordship and to the other chief men and magnates to perpend whether it is adequate to Christian charity and in accordance with the laws of this kingdom that I should be defamed in public sermons. From my museum on January 18. 1571. I intended to call on you personally, but a letter from the Bishop of Chichester summons me to fulfil my duty. The necessity of writing has this advantage, that you may hand on my letter to the Bishop of London."

Probably the Earl did so, and the Bishop sent the copy to Cousin who has endorsed it and made some annotations upon it. He sneeringly says: „Corro is absolved by the silence of the bishops." He reports:

---

[112] Beza sent the letter destined for Corro open to the Archbishop *ut iis utaris prout expedire censueris*. The Archbishop must have sent it to Cousin, and Cousin must have exhibited it to Corro. It was, no doubt, written by an amanuensis and Beza had not even signed it.

„The ministers dealt with the controversy on the request of Franciotto and Augustine Bovazo, the Italian, whom Corro had interposed, and afterwards of Corro himself. Corro speaks of ‚our protestant churches', though he does not himself belong to any church, and there are many persons in London so dependant on him that they rather prefer to live unruly lives or, so to say, as libertines, than taking the yoke of Christ upon them to profess the faith with the foreign churches. Whether this be not furthering sects may be judged by those whose concern it is. Corro says that he could not have believed on the evidence of a thousand witnesses that the French ministry had condemned their own Confession; is one, therefore, to credit the single Corro against so many ministers? Paul prescribes 1. Tim. 5.: ‚against a presbyter receive not an accusation, but before two or three witnesses.' Is that impudent lie to be admitted? He exhibited his papers in order to interrupt the examination and the judgment of the whole dispute, but no new action was to be undertaken, and by consensus of all, the papers did not come into the question. Anything that may have been said by one or two *(ab uno aut altero)* of the assembly is referred to by Corro as representing the conclusions of the whole." It appears, however, from the report of Corro, which is not invalidated by Cousin, that his opponents could not be silenced by their colleagues without collating the printed books. „That lastly he was to declare his consent to the Helvetic Confession cannot possibly approximate to the truth *(ne verisimile quidem esse potest)*, for the dispute had not been instituted on that confession, but on Corro's Tableau. As for Beza's letter, the present Archbishop of York received, read and delivered it." Cousin's draft is certainly the substance of a report to the Bishop of London. Grindal had been transferred to the see of York, on May 1. 1570, and his successor in London was Edwin Sandys. The Bishop of Chichester, Richard Curteys, was appointed president of a commission to finish the Corro quarrel. It was certainly in order to be heard on this business that Corro was summoned by the Bishop of Chichester, as he says in the letter to Huntingdon.

To a letter from Cousin of December 31. 1570 Beza answered on February 14. 1571: As regards Corro, God be praised that he remains confounded *(qu'il est demeuré confus)*. Beza had learned the news already from another correspondent who had also sent him Corro's writing (certainly the Tableau) which Beza calls trash *(fatras)*, adding: „I hold that he should be avoided und that if he does not, as he promised, detest his doings and does subscribe without any conditions to the sound doctrine, he should be excommunicated."

A friend of Corro printed, with a postscript dated March 1. 1571, under the title *Acta consistorii ecclesiae Londinogallicae cum responso Corrani,* the correspondence of both parties from August 11. to September 8. 1569, together with Corro's letter to Reina of Christmas 1563 in the original and in a Latin translation, and the testimonial of the Bishop for Corro of June 5. 1567.[113] He relates that a French nobleman of great authority (certainly the Cardinal) who had been against Corro, after better information had asked the Bishop of London to impose an end to the controversy.

When on March 19. 1571 the French and Italian ministers received the invitation of the Bishop of Chichester and his assistants, to send them in writing their articles against Corro, they answered that they begged first to know in whose name and to what end this was asked of them. They could not have written in this way if they had been duly told by their Bishop of London of the nomination of that committee. On the 23rd they sent their report to the commissioners entrusted with the *information in this cause,* — essentially the old stories with new declamations against that *spiritus immundus* and *versipellis.*[114]

From April 2. to 11. a National Synod of the Reformed church of France was held in La Rochelle. Beza was elected Moderator, and Nicholas des Gallars, sieur de Saules (who had been minister of the London French church 1560—1563), and another, were chosen as Scribes. Beza acquainted the assembly with the heresies dispersed in Poland and Transylvania by divers persons (the English translator names on the margin Davidis, Gentilis, Blandrata, Socinus, adding an *&c.*) against the unity, divinity and human nature of our Lord

---

113) This is the publication hinted at in the letter of the three London churches in 1576: *edito aliquo scripto et evulgato famam nostram lacerasset.* Sepp, Polem. 23.

114) It seems therefore to be an error of the editor of the *Acta consistorii* etc. saying that on March 1. 71 both parties had already been heard by the commissaries.

Jesus Christ, receiving the errors of ancient heretics, particularly of Samosatenus, Arius, Photinus, Nestorius, Eutyches and many others, and of Mahomet himself also. Whereupon the Synod unanimously voted their detestation of all those abominable errors and heresies. Information was also given concerning the errors of Corranus by the minister of Normandy, and de Chandieu and de l'Estrange were ordered to examine the Tableau of Corranus and to bring in a report of it, and finally it was rejected and voted detestable. The English Bishops were to be desired to forbid the reading of the books of the said heretics, if they could not hinder their being brought into and sold in their dioceses. The minister of Normandy, Jean de Lescourre, M. Secours, representing Normandy in this synod, and Alexandre Gaudion, dit de Lestang, had been, in September of the last year, among the six arbiters on Corro's Tableau. There were present at the Synod the queen of Navarre with her son Henri, and the admiral Coligny and other seigneurs.

On July 3. Cousin received a declaration from Corro who says that he desires to join a Christian *coetus*, and to remove all doubts of the brethren about his belief. „I acknowledge that the divine word is expressed in the Holy Scriptures, which fully contain all doctrine necessary for salvation, and that what is contained in the creeds of Nicea and of Athanasius and in what is commonly called the Apostolic creed, is catholic, founded on the authority of sacred writings and therefore to be considered by all Christians as trustworthy decrees on our belief.[115] And I profess that what is prescribed in this kingdom about faith and religion, and that the views which are held on the same subjects by the strangers who are permitted to have their churches here, are orthodox, and entirely in agreement with the Holy Scripture. I always abhorred and I do now abhor unscriptural opinions, such as the dogmas of Arius and Pelagius and of Osiander, Servet, Schwenkfeld, the Anabaptists and the Papists, as my printed confession of faith and my other writings testify. At no time or place have I ever disputed with or differed from the reformed churches on the question of the purity of their doctrine *(re-*

---

[115] The *Defensio* of the Antwerp Confession of the Augsburghians 1567 says p. 303: *Fatemur sane et nos ad scripturam non extremae necessitatis sed pusillorum Christi confirmationis gratia adjungenda esse tria symbola.*

formatis ecclesiis cum quibus nullam habui unquam aut usquam controversiam neque dissidium de doctrinae puritate). In a private letter in Spanish to a Spanish friend I had asked him to buy and send me books of Caspar Schwenkfeld, Valentin Crotoaldus and Andreas Osiander who in reformed churches have got an ill name and are deemed heretics; I added a request to send also other books which treated of the doctrine of our Christian religion to the edification of our consciences. From these words which they incautiously connected *(contexerunt)* with the foregoing petition, some suspected me to have been a disciple of those men (whom I never saw or knew), or at any rate to have approved of their writings, and others supposed that I wanted those writings in order to strengthen my inclination to glide off *(animum jam tum labantem confirmare)*. From all this I stood and stand aloof, as my only Master is Christ and I intend to conform my mind only to the divine word, avoiding all the heretical opinions of men. To the ministers of the church it is free to read the books of heretics in order to weigh the arguments of either party and confute the errors. My Table of the works of God contained unusual phrases and many obscure and perplexing things, and did not shew sufficiently clearly that the sense was orthodox, so that some suspected me of the errors of Arius, Pelagius, Servet, Osiander. But, as I never intended at all to join them, I beseech the brethren to interpret candidly that Table as many most learned men of the European churches have done hitherto, and if anything is missed or desired to be expressed more clearly, I shall take pains to render it quite plain and obvious, when public authority permits or commands me to do so. Concerning other actions of my life, with regard to which I was once blamed for evil-speaking by the very revd. father in Christ, the Archbishop of York, and which have often offended the feeling of my brethren, and chiefly concerning my separation from the French church, I confess that in my complaints I often gave somehow more vent to private woe than perhaps was decent for a Christian or expedient for the Church. Nevertheless my complaints were directed rather towards freeing myself from suspicion than towards impairing their authority or the esteem in which they were held. Conscious of my human frailty and little confident where my own glory and fame are concerned, I urgently pray all the pious to forgive me in so far as hitherto I have failed in the duty of a peaceful man desirous of the church's tranquillity; and I beg them to believe, what I now spontaneously promise, that whatever *coetus* I may belong to from this time forth, my moderation will be such as to administer everything soberly and, so far as lies in my power, to edification.

The copy of this sent to Cousin is not written by the hand of Corro, who only signed it. The original had certainly been laid before the Bishop of London, Edwin Sandys, who appears to have been satisfied by it, for he gave his assent when Corro was called upon by the two London Temples to deliver them theological lectures in Latin. This shows so much the more the reliance people had on him, as shortly before Archbishop Parker of Canterbury had taken steps that in the London Inns of Court the overbold speeches and doings touching religion should be controlled and better order be established. In 1574 Corro published his Dialogue on the Epistle to the Romans which he had explained in those lectures and dedicated it *Generosis viris utriusque Templi qui legibus municipalibus Angliae operam dant,* whom he thankfully assures that he has led a happy life full of keen study since, with the Bishop's approval, he became doctor in their community, three years ago. The Dedication is dated May 31. 1574. Corro represents the apostle in lively conversation with a Roman who visits him in the prison.[116]

The French National Synod held at Nimes on May 6.—8. 1572, resolved: „Upon reading the letters sent us from our brethren, the English ministers, it was ordered that the two books written by Corranus and dedicated to some members in the church of Bordeaux and brought unto the present Synod, should be put in the hands of monsieur Beza" (who was present), „who should report of their contents to us, and an answer should be returned to our brethren of England". And towards the end of the protocol it is said: „As to the business of Corranus before mentioned, monsieur de Saules shall be entreated by the assembly to answer our English brethren and to send them Corranus' books and the remarks made upon them." De Saules was by the same Synod granted for one year more to the

---

[116] In Merck's copy a former possessor has written: *De Apollinari Juniore commemorat Socrates, cum Evangelia et Apostolorum scripta redegisse in formam dialogorum.*

queen of Navarre. Those books seem to be the two Antwerp publications.

Strype writes [117], that in 1573 Corro read upon the Epistle to the Romans, and in 1574 he contracted these lectures into a theological dialogue wherein the Epistle was explained, and then printed them, so that there might remain some public writing among them as a record of the pureness of the doctrine which he taught in their company, and how much he abhorred the opinion of sectaries which troubled the churches now-a-days with their errors. And he called them for his witnesses after what manner he confounded the forward opinions of the Pelagians and selfjustifiers in the discourse of justification. They knew also with how great diligence he had in the discourse of predestination or of the calling of the gentiles unfolded and confuted both the madness of the Stoics and chiefly the horrible blasphemies of the Manichees. The poor man (Strype continues) had undergone great troubles, not only from papists in Spain, in France and Flanders, but by the officers of the French church in London, complaining of him to Bishop Grindal and Beza before the time he was chosen reader at the Temple, having been cast out of other places upon suspicion of his doctrine. But under these afflictions he seemed to carry himself very Christianly. And for his better vindication of himself he set forth this year with his Dialogue articles of his faith, which he did, as he said, to disprove such as slandered him with Pelagianism without any just cause, only because he exhorted his hearers to good works; which he denied not, but owned that he did so very diligently-Howbeit, not for that he thought the children of Adam to be able to attain salvation by their own strength without the grace of God. For I impute, said he, the beginning, the increase and the accomplishment of our salvation and happiness to the only free favour and grace of God. But forasmuch as I see man's nature forward enough of itself to embrace vain carelessness and fleshly liberty, I minded that my saying should rather hold them in awe and lead them away from the pleasures and delights of this world, as it were by casting a bridle upon them, than putting spurs to them running already of their own accord to do evil.

117) Parker 482.

On sending a copy of the Dialogue of 1574, Corro writes to Henry Bullinger on July 7. of that year: „The appended articles are taken from your Confession; when they were only in ms., they were condemned because they were thought my product." And on the same occasion he asks Rudolf Gualther to include the letters to him in covers addressed to the Bishop of London, „that I may receive them by his hand and they be not intercepted by my adversaries as has happened sometimes."

On March 4. 1575 Archbishop Grindal of York writes to Archbishop Parker of Canterbury: There is a great talk here of new sects and heresies sprung up about London, of Judaism, Arianism, &c. I would be glad to understand the truth. Parker answered from Lambeth on March 17.: Concerning these sectaries, Mr. Alvey came unto me to have my counsel how to deal with Corranus, reader in the Temple, whom his auditory doth mislike for affirming free will, and speaking not wisely of predestination, and suspiciously uttering his judgment of Arianism, for the which I hear some wise of his said auditory to forsake him; and more than this, saving for the common precisianship in London, I hear of no sects.

In 1575 the English translation of Corro's Dialogue on the Epistle to the Romans was published, and Beza supplied in the second edition of his theological epistles the name Corranus, where he had suppressed it when he printed in the first edition, in 1573, the three letters of March 11. 1569 on the Corro affair.

William Barlow, son of a Bishop and afterwards himself Bishop, wrote from Eton to Josia Simler at Zurich on January 25. 1575: „Two famous divines are now lecturing in London, the one a Frenchman, the other a Spaniard. The Frenchman's name is Villiers, a man of great learning and piety, the Spaniard's is Corranus, learned and eloquent, but some worthy men entertain great doubts whether in respect of piety he is to be compared with Villiers. He is wont to disparage the authority of some individuals who have deserved exceedingly well of the church; he is a great admirer of Castalio, of whose version of the Bible he declares his opinion that he is a very bad interpreter, for he has given anything rather than a literal translation, but if you speak of a paraphrase, then, says he, Castalio excels all other translators by many leagues." [The edition of 1551 has a dedication to King Edward VI]. „I know also that he (Corro) made earnest inquiry of a person of my acquaintance whether or not he had some dialogues on the Trinity by an anonymous individual, printed at Basle, but Castalio, he said, is thought to have been the author of them; and he added that he was very anxious to procure them." [The author was Ochino whose *Dialogi, in duos libros divisi, secundus potissimum de Trinitate*, appeared at Basle 1563, edited and perhaps translated by Castalio]. „I have only been present at one lecture[118] of his, in which he inveighed against the men of our age, some of whom wished to be called Lutherans, others Calvinists, &c., though neither Calvin nor Luther died for us; ‚but we are saved', he said, ‚by the blood of the Lamb slain for the sins of the world', whereas in the text it is: ‚from the beginning of the world'. [Apoc. 13, 8. But cf. Joh. 1, 29. 1. Petr. 1, 18f.]. But that I may not seem to strain at a gnat and perhaps swallow a camel, I will here conclude, though indeed I am afraid of being a gnat to a camel.[119] I wish he had staid at Compostela!"[120]

Loiseleur Villiers had been elected in the assembly of the three London foreign churches on December 3. 1572, to a theological professorship, and on October 15. 1574 he became minister of the French church. In this same year he published at London his annotations to the N. T.

The antagonism between Villiers and Corro rose to a competition for an academical degree of theology. Corro had informed himself about the two English Universities by a trip to Oxford, and the next year (probably 1575) to the *comitia* of Cambridge. Now at the end of 1575 or in the beginning of 1576 he applied to Cambridge to obtain the degree of D. D., thinking to get it confirmed by Oxford where the *comitia* were held later in the year. But Cambridge answered that the statutes did not allow them without a royal dispensation to confer the highest honour to a scholar who had not obtained the lower degrees, but, if he succeeded at Oxford, they would confirm him as doctor. So he sent his petition on March 20. 1576 to the

[118] *Lectioni unicae.* Hastings Robinson translates: at an excellent lecture.
[119] *quanquam sane camelo culicem esse metuo.*
[120] Barlow seems to think, Corro's proper place was rather among the partisans of meritorious works.

Vice-chancellor of Oxford, Lawrence Humfrey D. D., together with a letter of recommendation by the Chancellor, the Earl of Leicester. To him Corro had dedicated last year the English translation of his dialogue on the Epistle to the Romans with the annexed articles of faith. The Chancellor wrote to the convocation: „He is fit for the degree, but he has not much money, and the degree is costly, especially if he take the inferior degrees. Pray excuse him taking the degrees in order and remit the fees of the doctorate." On April 2. the grace was conceded, only he had to purge himself of heretical opinions. For this purpose he should by lecturing or preaching declare his faith, and free himself by disputation from suspicion. Corro wrote thankfully. In the mean time a copy of his petition was sent by an Oxford man to Villiers. Corro had therein expressed his wish by this step to provoke his detractors and calumniators into a legitimate arena. On April 20. the University received the supplication of Villiers, Doctor of Civil Law and Professor of Theology, to incept in theology, without payment, as he, an exile for religion, could not afford it. The candidate for the degree of D. D. ought to be a B. D., but by dispensation both degrees could be taken together, and this accumulation was the commonest way of taking the D. D. degree.[121] Corro's supplication for the highest degree without having obtained the lower implied the wish to accumulate both, but Villiers, by simply supplicating for graduation in theology discreetly aspired to the bachelorship only. On May 1. Humfrey wrote to Villiers that the degree of D. D. was spontaneously and free of charge bestowed upon him. Villiers, who had not been ambitious for this honour, accepted it only after consulting his brethren and colleagues. In the debates at Oxford concerning Corro a member had said: „Before promoting him one ought to obtain the opinion of Archbishop Grindal, lest his judgment on Corro, whom he, when Bishop of London, had prohibited from reading, should seem to be disregarded." This incident was mentioned in a letter to Villiers on April 10. The adversaries of Corro in London followed that hint. The ministers of the three foreign churches wrote to the Archbishop and to the Bishop of London, and annexed a great many phrases extracted from Corro's writings with their own anti-

---

121) Clark I 139.

theses. The extracts were taken from the *Tableau de l'œuvre de Dieu*, from the *Magnum responsum* and its two epitomes, Corro's own and another one, approved by him, made by Launoy, formerly minister in France, now deposed as heretic by the Synod of Guienne,[122] and from the *Monas Theologica*[123] which he sent to Longastre,[124] who was his assistant against the French church, and was now a papist. All this had been written by Corro before his peaceful declaration of July 1571, and before the Bishop of London, who still continued in the same office, had licenced him to lecture. The only later work was the dialogue on the Epistle to the Romans, printed by privilege in 1574; they excerpt much from it. Moreover, they note six questions from the ominous letter to Reina, some sentences from his sermons and Temple lectures, and even two from private conversations. They find his doctrine contrary to the Scripture and to the Anglican and the Helvetic Confessions to which he constantly refers „in order to deceive those who are less prudent." Thesis 2.: „Many have heard from Franciotto that Corro said in a sermon: If thou art a Turk, do well; if thou art a Jew, do well; if thou art a Christian, do well; and thou shalt be saved!"[125] Thesis 35: „I will not have such a cruel God who condemns men before they are

122) The National Synod held at La Rochelle in summer 1581 names in the *Role des apostats et des coureurs: De Launoy, ci-devant Ministre de la Province de l'Isle de France.* Cf. as to him, Sepp, Drie Evangeliedien. 44f. Polem. 62f.

123) about February 1570, as it would seem. It is a short somewhat aphoristical chapter of mystical monism. That there is no mention of the eternal Trinity does not prove antitrinitarianism. Neither Melanchthon's Loci nor Farel's Sommaire speak of that Trinity; it was not a requisite to the primary instruction. Corro shows himself soon after as a follower of the Helvetic and the Anglican Confessions.

124) Corro may have made his acquaintance at Antwerp. In the *Note sur la situation d'Anvers,* first published by Groen van Prinsterer in the *Archives de la maison Orange-Nassau,* t. II. 1835, p. 332 Longastre is named among *Les Gueus qui favorisent aux sectaires de la ville d'Anvers.* The *Note* is undated, but as it names also the Lutheran deputies from Germany and states where each of them is lodged in Antwerp, it was not written earlier than the end of November 1566, when Hamelmann and Spangenberg had just arrived (Preger: Flacius II 291), nor later than February 1567, for Flacius, who on February 24 was still at Antwerp, on March 5. was already at Frankfort (ibd. 293).

Corro is not mentioned in that *Note*; as *Les predicants Calvinistes* are named six, *au temple rond Taphin* and *Charles* [de Nielle].

On Longastre cf. Sepp, Polem. 68—69.

125) Is it at all credible that Corro preached this?

born."[126] Theses 134—135: „The magistrate ought not to use the sword against heretics, but ought to leave to everyone free religion, as religion cannot be forced."[127] Thesis 128, complaining that in the church only one speaks and all the others must sit silent, is stigmatized as anabaptistic and against the established order of all churches. But it is the Roman who makes that statement in Corro's Dialogue of 1574 (XII 6), and the apostle answers there: „In other churches two or three prophets speak and hearers give their judgment (1. Cor. 14, 29 f.); everything must be done decently and in order; he who has got a ministry, may he be incumbent in it, &c." (In the London French church, prophesying, as the expounding of a proposed portion of holy scripture was called, was used only in certain conferences of ministers, and only ministers prophesied there, several such in each conference, other hearers being admitted. In the Anglican church the Queen had early in 1574 desired the Archbishop of Canterbury to suppress the vain prophesyings, and as this had been interpreted somewhere in favor of new instructions for the practise, she ordered, soon after the confirmation of the new Archbishop Grindal in 1576, the entire suppression of those exercises, which were deemed apt to be abused for sectarian purposes; Grindal did not comply, considering that they might be made subservient to true religion, and was thereupon sequestrated, and never afterwards fully reconciled to the Queen). From a Temple-lecture of Corro the accusers report these words: „You ought not to inveigh against the Roman church, for most of you have been born and baptized in it."

A copy of those Theses and Antitheses and of the letter to the prelates was sent by the authors to Oxford University with a new letter. Corro had said in his first letter to Oxford that the reason why he had not applied before for a lower degree was that the French Reformed churches did not greatly care for it.[128] The Londoners reply

---

126) The Lutheran Concordia of 1580 calls it a blasphemous doctrine that God destines some persons to damnation, not in consideration of their sins.

127) In England Thomas More had proclaimed in his *Utopia* that no man is to be punished for his religion.

128) *gradus istos non putat magnopere expetendos.* — Clark I 380 among the „Students and Graduates of (unnamed) Foreign Universities": „2nd April 1576, Corrano (Corano), Anthony, LL. D. of a foreign University, suppl. D. D. (See pp. 153 foll.)" But neither there nor in that supplication nor anywhere else is he

in their letter to Oxford that Corro shows himself very ignorant of French affairs; the Protestants there had repeatedly claimed equal right in the academies, but it had been refused unless they took the oath to the Pope. The fact remains that, after all, the French evangelicals did not think it indispensable for a minister to be graduated by a University. The Londoners continue: „What he there says concerning himself is altogether alien from the truth, for when he went to us he was of an age in which usually every one, who is not unworthy or incapable of mastership, has already attained that honour in his own country; but he had been educated where no one attains mastership, and in conformity with the religious order in which he lived he could not attain it.[129] We would not have mentioned these things if we did not wish to confute the charge unjustly brought against us; he ought rather to have remembered the answer he gave not long ago to the Cambridge men, that he had always neglected those trifles." It is evident both that, if the Isidrians were not allowed to take a degree, he shewed his want of concern for these matters by the fact of entering that order, and also that he has been received minister in several Reformed churches of France, although an undergraduate. At present, as he writes in his petition to Oxford, he very much desires to receive the degree of doctor in order to prove to his adversaries his agreement with the Anglican churches.

Wood tells us in his Athenae Oxonienses:[130] „I have seen a copy of a letter written by Jo. Rainolds of Corpus Christi College to Dr. Laur. Humphrey, then Vice-Chancellor, dated June 7., wherein several things being said of Corrano and his doctrine, you shall have the contents only. (1) That if Corrano be settled in the University, it is to be feared that it will raise such flames therein that they will not easily be quenched. (2) 'T is requisite that it be really known whether he be able to shew that he be lawfully called to the ministry of the gospel and charge of teaching publicly, either by the order of any Christian church beyond the sea or by the authority of the church

---

called LLD. He had no academical degree whatever when he supplicated for D. D. He was son of a LLD, see above here p. 3. 4.

129) I do not know if really the rule of the order forbade to take a degree. See what is to be related in the Life of Valera on the nostrification at Cambridge.

130) I 251.

5*

of England, or whether ordained by a bishop, of which matters there be some that doubt. And if he be not, how can he read? And if he be, it would be well if it be known. (3) That he is evilly thought of for heresy of the French church and others, and Beza doth publicly charge him of it in an epistle of his that is extant. (4) That he is supposed to be tainted with Pelagianism which partly appears from certain Tables which he brought with him and afterwards scattered abroad. On which a certain person of sound judgment made such notes that from thence one may evidently perceive that Corrano's obscure speeches in the said Tables do give just suspicion of very great heresies about predestination and justification by faith, two of the chief points of Christian religion, &c. And therefore it is hoped that as you were a means to remove Franc. Puccius[131], so you will endeavour to stop Corrano from coming among us, who is thought to be a master of Puccius &c. Thus in brief from Joh. Rainolds."

On June 13. 1576 the convocation at Oxford debated whether it were possible without the greatest discredit and infamy of the whole University to grant the doctorate to Corro whom very learned and very worthy men of subtle and sincere judgment and longtime much versed in theology incriminated as a person who was inflated by some of the grossest errors and had imbibed certain vain opinions abhorrent from the true piety of pure religion and defended them without a blush not only with audacity, but with obstinacy and petulance. It was ordered that Corro be not allowed to proceed to his degree till he bring letters testimonial from Archbishop Grindal and Bishop Sandys that he had not been imbued with any depraved and impious opinions since he arrived in England, or that if for some time he had been rashly susceptive of influence remote from piety and Christian religion, he had been led at last by the goodness of the cause to detest what was false and discard it totally. He has to purge himself fully of all and every impious and perverse opinion, error, and superstition, in presence of the Vice-Chancellor and the

---

[131] Francesco Pucci, of the Florentine family, disciple of Corro. See Wood Ath. I 587. 580. III 290. Clark I 379: „18. May 1574 Puccius, Francis, of Florence, was lic. M. A." (graduated). Documents in Hessels III n° 313. 328. 333. January 22. to May 3. 1575. Pucci entered also into some connexion with F. Socinus, but at last he returned to the church of Rome.

Council of the theologians of the University before the next *comitia*. Wood says: „This they did for this cause that the Chancellor had designed him to read divinity in the University and to allot him a catechist lecture, upon some consultation (as 't was pretended) for the utter extirpation of the Catholic religion from the University. This being the seeming design, as it was afterwards the real intention of the Queen's Council and High Commissioners, to plant him among the academicians, you cannot imagine, what fear and jealousies were raised in the heads of the old puritanical doctors and others who were fully bent to root out the dregs of popery in the University, lest that which they laboured in should be frustrated by a stranger."

Such an order could not but displease Leicester, and this may have been the decisive reason why Humfrey, Vice-Chancellor since April 2. 1571, did not continue in the office longer than June 23. 1576, when the Chancellor wrote indicating Humfrey's resignation. He added that in future he would „distribute the travail by the yearly change." He then nominated Dr. Herbert Westfayling as Vice-Chancellor.[132]

On July 4. the University register relates: Villiers, whom Corro by letter to the Vice-Chancellor accused with acerbity, though perhaps wrongly, of heresy and false opinions quite full of errors, was called before Convocation and asked to repel these accusations, which he did with so great gravity and piety, that his defence was lauded by the Vice-Chancellor and approved by the majority of the convocation. This speech of his was allowed to stand instead of his responding *in comitiis* (which were to be held on July 9). On July 6. he was dispensed from presenting himself, as the statute required, in D. D. habits of his own within 15 days. And on December 15. 1576 he was allowed to defer his *lectiones*.

When Guillame Bogaert wrote on March 7. 1578 from Ghent to the ministers and elders of the Dutch community in London, he mentioned their peril connected with the Corro-case which was at present again on the tapis.[133]

The Oxford register of July 7. 1578 runs as follows: In letters from the minister of the Dutch church, from the French church and

---

132) Clark I 243.
133) de perijculen der seluer ontrent der saken (nu wederom vernuewet) Corani.

the Italian church, the single churches traduce [134] M. Corranus for various crimes, not without several stains *(labeculis)* of heresies. But because he has been commended to this University, both by the royal general Commissioners who examined him, and by the Earl of Leicester, the Chancellor of the University, and he himself has not only by several public lectures abundantly declared his opinion, but has desired to be by some means purged of such stigmas, it has appeared to the convocation equitable to appoint a committee, consisting of Dr. Laurence Humfrey, Dr. Arthur Yeldard, Dr. Lloyd, Mr. Brown, Mr. Chamberlayn, Mr. Reynolds, Corp., in order to confer with Corro about the letters sent to the convocation together with the book, and about the articles from the same writings *(de litteris cum libro ad convocationem missis et articulis ex eisdem scriptis.* The book was most likely the dialogue on the epistle to the Romans, the articles are the Theses). On July 10. Corro was brought into congregation and gave a declaration of his opinions. He undertook to stay six, five or four months in the University, to confer with all who desired to do so. He did not doubt that he would satisfy them if they would candidly hear him; if, however, he should be justly convicted, he would readily recant. He also promised to abide by the judgment of the royal Commissioners in ecclesiastical matters or of the majority of the doctors of this University.

That his character was acknowledged as honorable and his doctrine as correct, is proved by the fact that in the next year he was in office in the University as teacher of theology. The committee, instructed on December 20. 1578 to correct and enlarge the statute on the caution against heretical pravity, and consisting of Dr. Laur. Humfrey, Dr. Thomas Bickley, and Mr. Bartholomew Chamberlayn B. D., on January 27. 1578/9 presented the statute as amended by them. For instructing the youth, the greater catechism or the Elements of Christian religion by Andr. Hyperius or the Heidelberg catechism are to be used. For adults Bullinger's catechesis and Calvin's Institutions may be jointly used or the Apology of the Anglican church or the 39 Articles. For each college and for each hall the principal of it

---

[134] Clark I 155: *Litterae missae a ministris ecclesiae Belgicae, ab ecclesia Gallica et ecclesia Hispanica, in quibus singulae ecclesiae perstringunt* ... But *Hispanica* must be a mistake for *Italica*. I have translated accordingly.

had to nominate a catechist to read and to interpret the books he selected from among the above mentioned. On February 23. it was urged that no one should be admitted to the degree of B. A. without being sufficiently instructed in catechism. On May 2. 1579 all principals of halls or their deputies were called before the Vice-Chancellor to state the number under their charge; the figures were as follows: in three halls, Glocester with six commoners, S. Mary with sixty-eight, Hart with fifthy-four, making together 128, Corro was the *lector catechismi*, while three other such lectors in three other halls had together 142 commoners, and one hall had not yet a catechist.

Corro's paraphrase of Ecclesiastes upon which book he had lectured in the Temple in 1572, was on May 16. 1579 licensed „under the hands of the Bishop of London and the wardens" and published in the same year, at the authors expense, and dedicated to the Lord Chancellor, Thomas Bromley. It has been reprinted several times and esteemed by Protestants and Roman catholics.[135] In the dedicatory epistle he says: „the best reformation would be the renascence by which Christians should set aside their differences."

On November 22. writing from Oxford to the secretary of the Earl of Leicester, Corro speaks of a letter favorable to himself addressed to the Earl by doctors of the University and asks the secretary, as a promotion of Bishops was now going on, to remind the Earl of his promise. Leicester must have promised him a prebend, at some future vacancy.[136] In 1579 negotiations took place to transfer the Bishop of

---

135) *Joannis de Pineda Hispalensis e societate Jesu in Ecclesiasten commentariorum liber unus. Hispali* 1619. (Palermo Comunale). *Praefatio*, cp. XIII § II p. 38: *Scio suam quoque peculiarem* [translationem] *huius libri* [Ecclesiastae] *confecisse Antonium Corranum, quem noluisse*[m] *vel Hi*[s]*palensem, vel Hispanum; quippe antiquae et Catholicae Religionis transfugam. Suam quoque Tremellius, et Junius, ac suam Mercerus. Sed in his nullum magnum pretium operae, quod ex superioribus illis, quas recensuimus, facile comparare non possimus, praesertim cum hostium et Haereticorum dona suspecta nobis esse debeant.* § III, p. 39: *Paraphrasis vero Antonii Corrani quamquam per se neque inculta, neque inelaborata: sed quia hominis haeretici, et excucullati, prorsus reijcienda.* In the appendix to the *Catena Graecorum patrum in Proverbia Salomonis* with a preface by Juan de Pineda of 1614, p. 476 among those who *In Ecclesiasten scripsere: Antonius Corranus Hispalensis (salua censura).* (Palermo Comun. without title). Corro's Ecclesiastes was reprinted in 1619 by Abr. Scultetus, then professor at Heidelberg, whose irenic endeavours were constantly disfavoured by the Lutherans.

136) Menendez II 489 says: *promesa de darle una mitra.* But Leicester

Norwich to the see of Ely, the Bishop of which was to have resigned, but after all he held the Bishopric to his death in 1581.[137]

Wood says of Corro that he lived as a student in Christ's church in 1579, if not before, of which house he occurs *censor theologicus* in 1581, 82, 83, 84 and 85.[138]

Dr. Pierre Baron, Margaret Professor at Cambridge, wrote to Guillaume de Laune, minister of the London French Church, on September 14. 1580 that from his (Baron's) intercourse with Corro, and especially from the fact that Corro praised him, they ought not to conclude that he completely agreed with Corro. And he assured them that it was not true that he had joined the Family of love, as Corro was, wrongly, he thought, suspected to have done. Three weeks after this letter, on October 3., a proclamation was issued against the sectaries of the Family of love, followers of Henry Nicolas, a Dutch mystic. As for predestination Corro and Baron indeed fairly agreed with the so called Familists. These said: „predestined unto preservation is Christ and all his incorporated members, predestined unto condemnation is the man of sin, the Antichrist, and all his incorporated members; we know not of any other predestination."[139] Baron was against Calvinian fatalism; he distinguished between an antecedent and a subsequent will of God, and believed that the universality of

---

cannot have thought to procure a bishopric for a foreigner who raised so much opposition in the English church.

137) Strype, Annals II 580f.

138) Ath. I 252. Wood says there also: „In 1579 he stirred again for the degree of doctor of divinity, but I cannot yet find that he was admitted (notwithstanding he stiles himself doctor of that faculty, in his dialogus theologicus an. 1574.)" But when, two years before he applied to get the academical degree of doctor, in the dedication of that book to the gentlemen, who had called him to be reader of divinity in the Temple, he wrote: *ab eo tempore quo in vestro coetu doctoris fungi munere coepi,* he of course took the word doctor according to classical Latinity in the sense of teacher. On the title of the same book he calls himself with equal right *theologiae professor.*

139) Strype, Annals II 378. On that Family ib. 375f. 508. 584. 595f. 606f. 628. III 45f. 184. The Libertines also were said to be derived from that Family; see on them ib. II 598f. III 44f. 69f. What Corro's opponents reported of his sayings about the Turks and for not inveighing against the Roman church, above here p. 65. 66, was certainly meant to caracterize him as a follower of the mystical indifferentism of the Familists, with whom they group him also in Antithesis 100. 101. See on the F. of love Nippold 1862 and after others Loofs in the Realencyklopädie für Protestant. Theol. 1898. Cf. Sepp, Polem. 71, Verbod. lectuur 187.

salvation was made impossible by sin. He was convinced that the thirty-nine articles were not opposed to this view. After all, however, as the heads of the University complained of his doctrine to their Chancellor Burghley in 1596, he gave up his professorship.[140]

In 1581 Corro edited a second work on Paul's epistle to the Romans with a prefatory letter to the youths of Oxford University.

In March 1582 the prebend of Harleston, a dependency of S. Paul's of London, was conferred on him by Bishop Aylmer.[141]

On May 7. 1582 the Chancellor wrote from Court: „Rumours have been spread that Mr. Corrano is detained prisoner. They are a mere slander. Corrano wishes to purge himself of any charges against his doctrine or life, and I intend to hear him on 17. May, having with me some of the French church and others. Send here any charges you have against him, or any person who is willing to bring charges against him. If there is no clear accusation, let them bring even the cause why they suspect him. Send two or three of your body to hear his defense with me." To this letter Dr. Withington, Vice-Chancellor, replied: „As regards Corano's doctrine, I never attended his lectures or disputations and so have nothing to say. As regards his life and conversation, I know of no crime which can be charged against him or any of his family. On the advice of the heads of houses I called a convocation, read your letter, and asked any accuser or suspecter to come forward. Neither then nor since has anyone appeared." — Wood says:[142] „In the year 1582 in April he lay under the censure of heresy again, upon which arose some trouble, but soon after quieted and he restored to the good opinion of the generality of scholars and others."

On January 2. 1583 he wrote from Oxford to Jean Hotman, sieur de Villiers Saint Paul, who had become doctor there in March 1581, and about the end of 1582 secretary to Leicester. Corro asked

---

140) See on him Strype, Annals II 383. III 47f. IV 229f.; Whitgift, book IV. France prot.². I 1877. Letters of his Cambridge Aug. 19. and 25. and Oct. 7. 1579 and Sept. 14. 1580. Hessels II.

141) So, rightly, says Schickler I 178. Wood does not give the date nor the name of the bishop. Hessels II 989: „On March 29. 1582 bishop Grindal appointed him to the prebend of Harleston". But the Bishop of London was at that time Aylmer, Grindal being Archbishop.

142) Ath. I 252.

him to give the enclosed Italian letter to the Earl before he met the Oxford doctors to whom Corro wished to be recommended by him. He would like to know how the letter was received; it was possible that old calumnies might be renewed. He greets Sir Philip Sidney. This is Leicester's nephew, „the common rendezvous of worth in his time", the famous writer who admired Spanish literature and fought against the Spaniards, was wounded and died some days later in 1586.

In 1584 Corro made a new edition of his *Tabula divinorum operum* with an admiring and thankful dedication to queen Elizabeth.

Jean Castol, minister of the French at London, writes to Beza on August 26. 1584: „We are not yet persecuted; we only learn that our open adversaries, for instance Corro, are in credit with the Queen and the Archbishop, wherefore one thinks that something is brewing. We are even told that Her Majesty has entertained great suspicion and displeasure against us from the false reports of certain flatterers. If those who have hitherto favored us should give way, as we have occasion to apprehend, still we shall not lose courage, for our strength is not founded on men."

Travers, the author of the *Disciplina ecclesiae sacra ex Dei verbo descripta*, published at Geneva in 1573, which had become a standard book of the English presbyterian party, in 1586 charged the learned divine Richard Hooker with teaching „certain things concerning predestination not unlike that wherewith Corranus sometime troubled the church." Hooker said: „Predestination is not the absolute will of God, but conditional." When Master of the Temple he preached in the morning, and Travers, who was lecturer there, used to confute him in the same pulpit in the afternoon, so that it was said: „the forenoon's sermon spake Canterbury, the afternoon's Geneva."[143]

In 1586 Corro published at Oxford a comparative grammar of Spanish and French, which was rendered into English and enlarged in 1590 by John Thorie.

On October 1. 1586 were matriculated in Christ church Anthonio Corrano, aged 59, and John Thorie, aged 18.[144]

---

143) Hooker's works, Oxford 1841, vol. 2, p. 662, vol. I, p. 48. Strype, Whitgift 173 f. 235 f. 249 f.; Annals III 243 f. 339 f. 429 f.

144) Mr. Hessels wrote me: „In 1581 Corro was appointed, as a foreign refugee, to the post of Censor theologicus, which gave him a locus standi in the University

July 12. 1587 Corro wrote at Oxford in the album of a friend the words of Croesus: Sufferings are lessons. He had already placed the same Greek words on the back of the title-leaf of his Cohelet 1579.

In 1588 Corro published in Latin a treatise of Faustus Socinus on the authority of the holy scripture with a preface by himself. He did not, however, mention the author's name nor his own, but said on the title-page: *Per R. P. Dominicum Lopez, societatis Jesu,* and as printing place he gave Seville. Why this concealment? The little book appeared in the year of the destruction of the huge Spanish armada, against which Catholics as well as Protestants had armed themselves for the defense of England. Now it must have been favorable to the cause of peace between all Christians that a Jesuit, without speaking of popery, should go so far as to prove the necessity of receiving the Bible as the foundation of belief. How cleverly Corro played at hide-and-seek is seen by the fact that the Jesuits were not crafty enough to detect his contrivance, but catalogued the work among their productions, and confessed the mistake only in 1872, although the book had already been printed with the real author's name in 1611. The editor of that reprint observed also that the preface of 1588 contradicted to some extent the opinion of the author. And in 1650 Trigland said that the first editor, and the man who wrote the preface, was Corro. The convincing proof of Trigland's simple assertion I discovered in the perfect agreement between the preface and some striking conceptions in Corro's letter to the King of Spain. And why Seville? It is Corro's native town. Although heartily thankful for the hospitality of the island which had become his definite refuge, still how often amid the fogs of England must the old man have longed for the sunny banks of his Guadalquivir! and how fervently prayed that the holy scripture should shine forth there!

On June 13. 1590 he wrote from Oxford to Jean Hotman. The latter, in 1584 Professor of law at Caen, had on account of the new civil war returned to England, whence Leicester took him to the Netherlands where for some months in 1586 and 87 he was political agent of Queen Elizabeth. Since 1587 he was accredited at the courts

and (I suppose) a salary. But this post did not make him an ordinary member of the University; these always become so by matriculation (signing their name in a register and paying some fee)."

of England and Scotland by the King of Navarra, who in 1589 inherited the crown of France as Henry IV. At present Hotman was on the point of joining his sovereign in the siege of Paris. Corro thanked Hotman for having sent him spectacles. As for the Theses of Villiers on the church,[145] on which Hotman had asked his opinion, he answered that he had never seen them, but he should like to get them. Lastly he wishes to receive his friend's news from France. Hotman left in the same month. He was afterwards again diplomatic agent of France. He did not cease to strive, in writing also, to reconcile the Christian parties with each other.[146]

Corro died in London about the end of March 1591 and was interred in St. Andrew's church by the Wardrobe in the City on April 3.[147] He left behind him his wife and a daughter.[148]

When some years later a movement was going on against Pierre Baron, chiefly on account of his uncalvinistic views on predestination, his adversaries „could not be beaten out of it, that they thought that as a certain Spaniard, named Ant. Corranus, was brought to and settled in Oxon, purposely to corrupt the true doctrine, so Pet. Baro, a Frenchman, was for Cambridge; which last is nevertheless reported in the following age by a high church of England man, that tho' he was a foreigner by birth, yet he better understood the doctrines of the church of England than many of the natives, his contemporaries in the University of Cambridge."[149]

Corro is named among the friends of Drusius, the great orientalist, who was twenty-three years younger.[150] They may have had

145) Probably the *Theses* which Sepp has printed, Polem. 77 f.

146) On Hotman see Schickler I 244—5 and the articles on the same in Bulletin XVII, 1868. On three letters of his to Archibald Douglas, Oxford Sept. 15. 1583, Wanstead July 15. 1588, Edinburgh July 29. 1589 see Cecil Mss. Part. III, 1889.

147) Wood Ath. I 252 said: „that he dying at London March. 30. or thereabouts in 1591, aged 64, was buried in the church of St. Andrew; but whether in that in Holbourn or in that by the Wardrobe, I know not (perhaps in the last)". Wiffen, according to an extract made for him from the Register of the burials in the parish of St. Andrew by the Wardrobe in the city: „Aprill 3. Antony Corrano a Spanyard." Hessels II 989: died March 30, interred in St. A. by the W. April 3., „as appears by an entry in the register of that parish." 148) Wood ibid.

149) Wood Ath. I, Fasti 114. On Baron compare Strype's Whitgift. Cooper's Ath. Cantabrig. II. 1861. And Schickler.

150) In Drusius' Life by his son-in-law Curiander 1616, see Sepp, Naspor. III 182. An article on Drusius in the Realencycl. f. prot. Theol. 1898.

some personal intercourse in the years that Drusius lived in England. From 1576 he remained in the Netherlands where Arminius and Uytenbogaert were his friends. Uytenbogaert praises Corro on account of the letter to the Augsburghians as a very moderate divine, and reporting from his dialogue that the apostle in the epistle to the Romans taught but the predestination of the believer for happiness and of the unbeliever for damnation, he adds: „which is also the opinion of the Remonstrants,"[151] whose protagonist was Arminius. Drusius said: „I am not a theologian, I am a Christian, and I submit my opinions to the judgment of the catholic church." Of course he does not mean the Roman church, any more than Corro when he uses that term.[152]

[151] Uytenbogaert: Kerckelicke historie. 1646, p. 157 f.
[152] For instance in his letter to the Augsburghians and Rom. XVI 18. Cf. Sp. Rf. II p. 176.

70) Hist. des martyrs 1582, fol. 668. One of the Augsburghians is said there to have uttered: *Jesus Christ pend encore en Anvers à la croix entre deux brigans: entendant les Papistes et les Gueux.* (A kind of Protestant pendant to the Papist's sentence related Sp. Rf. II, p. 373 at the end.) Jean Crespin, the author of the *Hist. des martyrs*, was at Antwerp in 1567. Taffin writing in the name of the French church there to the syndics of Geneva March 7. 1567 regrets that Crespin departs to return home. Rahlenbeck, Bulletin du bibliophile belge, t. XV, Bruxelles 1859, p. 363. — Flavius writes November 23., he insisted upon a discussion, Dec. 7. the other side hold on some hope of its taking place, January 18.: it is hindered by them. Preger: Flacius II. 1861, p. 292 f.

The Regent, who already on Sept. 13. 66 had reported to the king that in Antwerp they were trying an accord between the Lutherans and the Calvinists *pour estre plus forts,* Gachard, Corresp. de Guill. II 382, on January 11. 67 wrote to the Prince of Orange: At Vianen has *nagueres* been printed a book *contenant la concordance, faicte en la ville d'Anvers, de la confession d'Auguste et de la religion calvinisticque* and a great many copies are distributed at Amsterdam and perhaps also in other places of Holland. Gachard, Corresp. de Guill. II 426 f. And on the 13th to the Prince: „at Christmas and later was sold and distributed at Antwerp a book printed at Vianen in the nature of an agreement of the errors of Calvin with the Augsburg confession". The Prince answered that he knew nothing of a heretical press at Vianen and could not discover a trace of such a book. Gachard l. c., 328 f. 338. It probably was the Augsburg confession printed in 1566 together with a treatise of Zanchi on the needless disunion of the reformed churches on the Lord's Supper, both in Dutch translation. See the title in Sepp's Naspor. III, 138. (The *Confutatie* licensed on Oct. 12. 66, ibid., has nothing to do with that book. Sepp, Mededeel. 45 f.). — Corro's letter to the Augsburghians, dated January 2. 1567, cannot have been sold in Christmas 66.

DOCUMENTS.

[I have revised the orthography and the punctuation of the Latin texts].

1.

From the Acta Consistorii, *printed* 1571.

Antonii Corrani epistola ad Cassiodorum missa ex Aquitania anno 1563.

Eam tibi opto pacem et consolationem, quam Jesus Christus, noster solus Redemptor relinquere voluit et revera reliquit veris suis discipulis quamdiu viverent in hoc mundo.

Domine ac dilecte frater, hactenus arbitrabar crebras meas litteras in causa fore ut aliquod saltem epistolium a te acciperem, sed, cum jam quattuor menses frustra responsum expectaverim, nil aliud conjicere possum quam aut meas litteras tibi non esse datas aut tua responsa nequaquam facile ad me pervenire posse. Interea loci, eam fidem adhibeo divinae providentiae ut credam ipsius Majestatem consulturam huic negotio eumque in modum facturam ut animi nostri sensa aperire possimus, si non verbis coram, saltem scriptis. Ut hoc sperem, primum est argumentum quod videam ipsum Deum in me excitasse hujus colloquii desiderium, ob idque confido illum ipsum, qui hanc dedit voluntatem, non relicturum inanem et optatis frustratam. Deinde perpendo, animum meum, in quaerendo hoc[a] solatii, interim magis ac magis spernere emolumenta illa et commoditates quas prudentia carnis quaerere solet. Praeterea, legendo et relegendo tuam epistolam[b], considero idem desiderium in corde tuo radices egisse. Itaque his omnibus perpensis certior fio negotium hoc agi potenti manu illius qui dispersiones Israel congregat tempore suae voluntati constituto. Reliquum est, mi frater, ut quam fieri possit pedetentim ac sensim, ut ita dicam, nostrum hoc colloquium aliquo in loco fiat, ne videamur nimis properando invertere illa media quae ad optatum finem inservire possunt. Quod ad me attinet, tibi vere affirmo, teste etiam Divino Spiritu, quod, si a conjuge et socia (quae eo pacto mihi socia est ut sit etiam pars mei ipsius) liber essem, ante triennium jam ad vos advolassem[c], eo inquam tempore quo percepi me absque tua consuetudine vivere non posse. At quia Deus sic disposuit ut maturare gradum non possim, sed bovinum incessum imitando, ut in proverbio apud nos est[d], incedere cogar, ligatus etiam vinculis et loris communi jugo, expectabo Dominum quousque pro ipsius Majestatis arbitrio huic negotio consulatur. Nihilo setius, hisce omnibus impedimentis circumvallatus, anno praeterito decreveram jam me ad iter accingere et te etiam vestigare quamvis in-

---

a) hoc *has been added by me. The original*: veo, que mi intencion en buscar este contento, se desnuda de dia en dia de los interesses que la carne podria buscar.

b) *That letter is wanting.*

c) si estuuiera libre de compañia (la qual de tal manera me es compañia, que es vna parte de mi mismo) mas ha de tres años que vuiesse bolado por alla.

d) al passo de buey (como dizen).

certus de loco ubi ageres. Sed cum aliquot milliaria[a] peregissem coeperunt amici temerariam hanc profectionem et mutabilitatem vocare ac levitatis insimulare, ob idque coactus fui illic quiescere destinatamque differre profectionem. Eodem temporis articulo tuam epistolam accepi modo quodam fere miraculoso, et cum legissem quae scribebas quantumque cuperes meam praesentiam ac Bibliorum impressionem[b] decrevi adhuc hic hiemare, expectans deliberationis tuae certius responsum, quod quamprimum cuperem abs te habere ut ego opportune queam meis hic consulere negotiis ac certi aliquid promittere illis Ecclesiis quae mea opera et functione uti cupiunt. Si tu enim velis huc venire, ego nequaquam solum vertam[c], immo conservare studebo amicos quos hic habeo, ut adjuvent et promoveant nostros conatus. Nam quod attinet ad Bibliorum impressionem, arbitror nos hic habituros paratissima et commodissima omnia, etiam cum loci optione. Tantum erit aliquid difficultatis in correctione. Cui corrigendi muneri si te implicare non vis, deduces tecum Cyprianum qui hoc praestet. Brevius iter erit si Flandrorum navigationem sequaris et illorum classi te conjungas Rupellam[d] usque aut Burdegalam. Et si quid necesse est huc mittere, tute fidere poteris huic mercatori Burdegalensi qui vocatur Petrus de Perreij.[e] Cujus epistolam nuper ad me scriptam tibi mitto ut ex ejus lectione compertam habeas cum meam in scribendo diligentiam, tum ipsius voluntatem ad nostros conatus promovendos. Quodsi fortassis constituas pedestre iter accipere neque audeas tecum ferre pecunias impressioni destinatas, relinquito illas apud fidum aliquem mercatorem Antuerpiensem. Nam hic postea facile inveniemus qui syngraphae debitum persolvant. Et si Jacobus Fichetus[f] tibi certo affirmaverit hunc mercatorem Burdegalensem habere commercium cum Antuerpiensibus, fidito illi, nam, si iste habeat curam persolvendi syngrapham, omnem gratitudinem erga nos exercebit, estque adeo dives ut inopia nequaquam sit retardaturus persolutionem.

Huic etiam mercatori, ut ex ipsius epistola intelliges, provinciam dedi ut tibi daret quattuor coronatos[g] in eum finem ut emas aliquot libros quos mihi utiliores fore arbitrabere. Cupio inter alios habere libros D. Casparis[h] atque Valentini Crotoaldi, item alios qui tractent nostrae religionis doctrinam cum conscientiarum aedificatione, nam Hebraismi et Hellenismi fastidium mihi jam pariunt et prolixorum commentariorum lectio mihi est insipida. Hos libros ad me poteris mittere per hunc Burdegalensem mercatorem qui naulum[i] persolvet.

a) treynta leguas.
b) assi de su deseo de vernos como de la impression de la Biblia. *Accordingly I have written* ac *instead of* ad *which must be a misprint.*
c) yo no haré mudança alguna.
d) *In the Spanish text* la Rochelle.
e) *The Spanish text has* Pierre du Perrey.
f) *The Spanish has by mistake* Fixer, *with* r (Span. *x sounded like French ch*). *In the letter of March.* 25. 1564 *Corro shows his reliance on* Jaques Fichet, *and the endorsement says that the letter is to be delivered to him in case of Reina's absence. Du Perrey sends it April* 4. 1564. Au Sire Jaques Fichet marchant habitant de la cité de Londres. *He had come to England in* 1541, Schickler I 51. *Jaques Fichet antien subscribed with others the letter of the Ecclesia Belgica in London to Calvin March* 18. 1560, Cp. Rf. 46, *letter* 3170. Jaques Fichet *signed together with others the testimonial of the French and Dutch churches of London in favour of Gallasius May* 14. 1563, Hessels III; *the remonstrance against Corro July* 1568 (Hessels *ib. wrongly July* 22. 1569); les articles que l'Egl. Frç. met en avant contre Ant. Corran Nov. 28. 1568; *the letter of the French Consistory about Corro Nov.* 22. 1569. *I think in this last document the name is written* Fischet, *but I do not recollect if by himself. In the protocol, written by Cousin, on the conference held in the Corro affair April* 16. 1567 *it is written* Fischet, *in the subscription of the French articles against Corro Nov.* 28. 1568 *Cousin writes under* Les Anciens: Jaques Fichet, *but in the text of the second confirmation* Jaques Fischet, *where the Latin, Dec.* 1568, *has* Jacobum Fichet seniorem ecclesiae.
g) escudos.
h) *Schwenkfeld. Compare Beza's* Epist. LIX.
i) el flete.

Cuperem etiam ut primis tuis litteris appendicem aliquam adderes ac mihi responderes ei interrogationi quam Lausannae tibi proposui, videlicet: quam cognitionem debeat habere Christianus homo de Christo Jesu, habita ratione trium diversorum temporum hypostaseως sive existentiae ipsius. Ac primum dicas velim quo pacto[a] possimus considerare aut contemplari λόγον illum promissum[b] a Deo in remedium hominis antequam carnem nostram assumeret et in qua hypostasi[c] apparuit Patribus Veteris Testamenti. Item de secundo post incarnationem statu dicas velim quo pacto, cum Christus esset in mundo, simul etiam residebat ad Patris dexteram juxta illud:[d] Et nemo ascendit in caelum nisi qui descendit de caelo, filius hominis qui est in caelo. De tertio denique statu post ipsius glorificationem scire cupio quo pacto Jesus Christus, habitet in cordibus fidelium et quibus similitudinibus hoc possit intelligi. In hunc eundem finem vellem ut ad me mitteres libellos quos Osiander scripsit de justificatione Christiani hominis, quibus ostendit modum quo Christus praesentia sua habitare solet in his qui in ipsum credunt.[e] Pro hac quaestionis elucidatione opto tuam explicationem audire in eum locum Joannis 17 ubi Christus sic ait: Precor ut omnes unum sint sicut tu Pater in me et ego in te ut et ipsi in nobis unum sint ut credat mundus quod tu me miseris.

Desidero abs te intelligere quo in pretio sint apud vos Velsius et Acontius Italus. Nam cum concionator quidam urbis, quae vocatur Sancta fee[f], mentionem de illis faceret, capitis motu innuebat, istos non admodum sibi placere. Cum vero de te quid sentiret interrogarem, plane ostendit valde egregiam de te habere opinionem. Illo vero loquente, intra me dicebam: Si scires donum Dei et quis est qui loquitur tecum &c.[g] Idem concionator mihi dixit, istic male intellectum fuisse[h] libellum Petri Martyris De utraque Christi natura, quo auctor vult impugnare Ubiquitatem. Qua de re cuperem tuam sententiam audire et an existimes necesse esse necne, Christum esse ubique secundum humanam naturam, et an fructum seu utilitatem aliquam assertio haec de praesentia Christi ubique possit afferre homini Christiano. In eundem finem legere vellem libellum a Germanis evulgatum[i] cujus argumentum seu materia est Christum esse ubique.

Praeterea scire vellem quem fructum capere potest conscientia Christiani hominis si disputet an Christus jam in caelis gloriosus creatura dici debeat necne. Nam in Christiana religione, ubi omnia nostra studia collimare debent ad aedificationem, nequaquam debemus obtrudere quaestiones supervacaneas et infrugiferas. Atqui video D. Casparem tam vehementi studio has quaestiones urgere ut existimet actum jam esse de Christiana pietate veroque Dei cultu ni ambabus quod ajunt ulnis hanc doctrinam recipiamus.

Item scire cupio quem modum celebrandae Dominicae cenae habeant Ecclesiae illae circa quas agit Crotoaldus[k] et quam sequantur interpretationem verborum

---

a) En que manera.
b) *This Latin translation shows that the conjecture of Usóz about the Spanish text is not right.*
c) essencia.
d) Jo. 3, 13.
e) Christiana, donde prueua, que essencialmente Christo se comunica a los fieles.
f) Sainte-Foy-la-Grande sur Dordogne, *about 20 kilometres west from Bergerac. At Ste Foy a Protestant synod was held in November* 1561.
g) Jo. 4, 10.
h) que essa gente ha mal entendido. *The book had appeared in* 1561.
i) impresso en Alemaña. *He probably means the work of* Brenz. De majestate domini J. C. ad dextram dei. 1562.
k) las yglesias, donde reside el Señor Crotoaldo.

Christi. Nam in his schedulis^a plus laboris impendit in impugnanda falsitate quam in ostendenda suae opinionis veritate.

Cum tot simul videris hic congestas quaestiones, non dubito quin difficile tibi sit atque arduum, omnibus una epistola satisfacere. Sed ut intelligas meum hac in re animum, scias me hoc pacto voluisse te praemonitum ac praeparatum ad mutuum nostrum colloquium. Deinde ut interea temporis singulis tuis epistolis appendicem aliquam addere hisce de rebus memineris. Proderunt praeterea hae quaestiones ut melius noris quos mihi libros mittendos cupiam, ut eos seligas quos videris esse utiles ad dilucidandas propositas quaestiones. Atque scias hoc apud me decrevisse, nullas alias novitates ad te velle scribere, immo tria aut quattuor exemplaria hujus epistolae ad te mittere constituisse.

Hac ipsa die venit ad me typographus quidam ut conveniremus de pretio excudendorum Bibliorum. Ultra omnes expensas petit iste correctorem typographiae diligentissimum et in quem rejicere possit tuto negotii curam. Deinde conditiones has proponit: Si demus illi chartam, et correctorem nostris expensis alamus, ipse suppeditabit mille et ducenta volumina in folio communi excusa cum versiculorum distinctione, et pro unoquoque exemplari tantum persolvemus quattuor regalia Hispanica cum dimidio. Quodsi ipse chartam suppeditet, vult habere pro unoquoque exemplari sex regalia. Quod autem attinet ad commoditatem inveniendae chartae, hic permagna est, nam prope hunc locum sunt tres aut quattuor officinae illorum qui chartam parant. Lubenti etiam animo typographus vult prelum erigere et aptare eo ipso in loco quem nos selegerimus. Et credo ad hoc perficiendum opus Regina Navarrae nobis permittet aliquod ex suis castellis, ad hoc peragendum commodum.^b Ob idque oportet ut tu responsum mittas tuae deliberationis quam citissime fieri possit, ut ego cum Regina hac de re agam antequam hinc proficiscatur.^c Essetque multo melius si tu huc venires ut ambo simul huic negotio incumberemus. Si quid vero adhuc transfundendum^d superest, hic facile absolvi poterit dum prelum adornatur. Nam hoc compertum habeas velim, duos aut tres menses^e esse necessarios ad paranda omnia quae prelum requirit. Opus est etiam ut ducentos coronatos^f typographo initio demus. De his omnibus precor ut quam citissime queas ad me responsum mittas. Sicque finem faciam salutando omnes eos fratres qui tecum sunt^g, simul ac singulatim.

Theoboni 24. Decembris anno 1563.

[In the Spanish original is added:]

Tuus ex animo.
Antonio d'el Corro.

2.

Lettre envoyée à la majesté du Roy. 1567. D iij foll.:

De la cognoissance de Dieu, puissée de sa saincte Parole.

Dès le commencement que le Seigneur crea les hommes, pour les faire participans de la cognoissance de soymesme, il ordonna trois classes en son Escole: La premiere a esté d'une leçon commune et universelle à toute creature capable de raison, prinse du livre de ce pourpris admirable et machine ronde, où la multitude et diversité des creatures nous servent comme de lettres, lesquelles assemblées nous

---

a) tratadicos.
b) Y para este effecto la Reyna de Nauarra nos prestarà vno de sus castillos que sera mas commodo.
c) antes que se vaya à Francia.
d) algo pot trasladar.
e) mas de dos otros meses. *Usox:* pareze errata, por: dos, o tres meses.
f) escudos.
g) embiando encomiendas à todos essos Señores.

Biblioth. Wiffen. III.

enseignent la puissance, eternité, et divinité de nostre Dieu, tellement que (comme dit le Prophete)[a] les cieux, la terre, le Soleil, la Lune, les Estoilles, la mer, et la reste des creatures comprinses en iceux nous racontent jour et nuict la gloire et excellence de nostre Dieu: et n'y a nation, tant soit elle barbare, qui ne soit capable de la leçon de ceste classe; ce que rend inexcusable[b] un chascun devant la presence de Dieu, lequel justement pourra condamner tous ceux qui vivent en ce theatre universel du monde: d'autant qu'ayans cognu le Seigneur par un tel moyen, ne l'auront point servi et honoré, ainsi qu'il appertient à la grandeur et excellence de telle Majesté.

La seconde classe de son Escole, est singulierement dressée pour ceux qu'il a choisis pour son peuple particulier, afin de se manifester à iceux plus au vif. Nous entendons par ce mot de peuple de Dieu, non seulement les esleus en Jesus Christ son fils, mais aussi les hypocrites et fardez, qui de tout temps ont esté meslez parmy les esleus, voire ont eu la vogue, et la preeminence, pour persecuter les autres... Tels sont en nostre temps les Papes, plusieurs Cardinaux, Archevesques, Evesques, Prestres, et Moines, lesquels entrent bien quelquefois en ceste classe deuxiesme, pour escouter en l'Eglise la parole du Seigneur, ou la lire: mais beaucoup d'eux, en lieu de l'ouir et escouter, pour en faire profit particulier à leur conscience, et pour la communiquer aux autres, en abusent... Et en lieu de cognoistre un vray Jesus Christ, Dieu et homme, ils forgent un Jesus Christ à leur poste, lequel vienne à toute heure entre leurs mains pour leur donner à gaigner...

Au contraire, les esleus en Jesus Christ sont enseignez en toute verité, d'autant que estans sortys de ceste classe deuxiesme, l'Esprit du Seigneur les introduit en une autre troisiesme[c], et leur fait repetition de ce qu'il faut retenir et apprendre en la premiere et seconde leçon. Car les creatures n'estants point regardées des yeux illuminez, et entendement esclairci par l'Esprit de Dieu, ne nous sçauront point enseigner parfaite leçon. Item, si les escritures ne sont point leues avec lunettes de lumiere divine, elles ne nous sçauront jamais conduire à vie eternelle, ains plustost en lieu de nous nourrir de la moelle et substance d'icelles, nous nous contenterons de l'escorce, c'est à dire, de la lettre morte: et en lieu de prendre le glaive trenchant, pour couper la gorge au viel homme, et aux mauvaises affections, qui resident en nous, nous prendrons le foureau qui le couvre, avec lequel quand nous frapperons, ce sera faire grand bruit, et point de playe. Et par ainsi toute nostre vie seroit pleine de tromperie, illusion, et hypocrisie de nousmesmes. Ce que n'avient point aux enfans de Dieu: ains plustost estans spirituels, jugent tous les autres, et les autres ne les peuvent point juger, d'autant qu'ils ont la vraie intelligence de la volonté de Dieu, moyennant les continuelles leçons que le S. Esprit leur enseigne dans leurs coeurs et consciences... enfans de Dieu, lesquels n'ont point esté seulement enseignez en l'escole de la lettre morte: mais ayans passé plus outre, le S. Esprit leur a monstré Jesus Christ leur salut, qui est enfermé et envelopé là dedans...

This reminds us of the 85th Consideration of Valdés. *Corro had certainly read the Hundred and ten considerations of his countryman, published in Italian 1550, and twice in French, 1563 at Lyon, 1565 at Paris. Beza in his letter to Corro 1569 calls them* evanidas speculationes. *Already in 1566 (epist. IV) he called the book* a verbo Dei ad inanas quasdam speculationes, quas falso Spiritum appellant, homines abducentem.

---

a) *Margin*: Pseau. 19.   b) *Margin*: Rom. 1.
c) *Margin*: Troisiesme classe en laquelle sont enseignez les enfans du Royaume.

3—6 *From the* Acta *printed* 1571.

3.

Summa ceu epitome orationis coram habitae
ab Antonio Corrano, divini verbi Ministro,
in Consistorio Londinogallicae Ecclesiae
6. Augusti 1569
et ejusdem Consistorii rogatu scriptis mandata
traditaque 11. die ejusdem mensis.

Carissimi in Christo fratres. Paulus Apostolus nos admonet Ephes. 4. dandam operam esse ne sol supra iram nostram occidat. Unde videre est, fideles, quantumvis regeneratos, frequenter motionibus animi perturbari quae vix possunt simul omnes extingui sedarive. Itaque optandum sit nos in Christianae mortificationis tantum profecisse studio ut irae forte perciti aut humanos nostros impetus frenaremus coerceremusque ne Christianae moderationis limites transiliremus aut certe, errore hic aliquo abducti, ad Apostolicam hanc admonitionem confugeremus. Atqui tanta est animi nostri depravatio ut utriusque fere obliviscamur. Nam quantum ad me attinet, cum me ex eorum numero agnoscam qui his perturbationibus sunt obnoxii, optarem equidem lubenter singulari Dei benignitate tanta munitus instructusque esse patientia ut aut vincere tales affectus aut saltem consopire mihi quamprimum liceret.a Haec eo dico, fratres, quod, cum jam biennium atque etiam paulo plus elapsum sit ex quo inter nos subortae sunt simultatum et irarum causae, non semel optavi, uti nunc quoque facio, tum Pauli tum Doctoris nostri Jesu Christi salutiferis exhortationibus obsequi.

Quamobrem si quis est in hoc consessu qui se a me vel verbo vel facto vel quavis ratione offensum putet, eum ego enixe oro, istud omni oblivione delere, sibique persuadere, id non tam pravo animo quam humana imbecillitate contigisse, adeo ut affirmare ausim, omne prorsus odium omnemque inimicitiarum materiam ac semen ex animo meo Deum expunxisse et obliterasse. Quod ut omnes pro se quisque pariter faciatis, etiam atque etiam precor, sepultis omnibus inter nos ultro citroque hactenus dictis factisque, ut omni sublato offendiculo, propositoque fratribus salutari exemplo, in posterum vitam traducamus cum Christiana caritate et concordia conjunctam, nosque hac ratione unis omnes animis studiisque operi Domini incumbamus diligentissime. Vos ut scripto respondeatis precor.

Vester ex animo

Antonius Corranus.

4.

Responsio Consistorii Londinogallicae Ecclesiae ad scriptum Antonii Corrani.

Care frater. Scimus quam sit necessaria concordia fraterna in Ecclesia et pretiosa coram Deo, sine qua nullum opus nostrum Domino gratum esse potest etiamsi esset sacrificium ex praecepto legis factum. Hoc dicimus ut tuo scripto respondeamus, nobis 11. die hujus mensis exhibito. Multis videri possit ex tuorum verborum contextu, discordiam obortam, quam 28. mensibus durasse vere ais, aeque a nobis ac abs te profectam, atque etiam te frequenter voluisse admonitionem Pauli aliasque salutares Domini nostri sequi, quasi tota culpa penes nos resident. Frater, rogamus te ut verba abs te proposita propius inspicias. Nam hactenus id contra nos pro-

a) *Ms. copy:* lueret.

batum non est et ita rem habere vehementer doloremus ut tam diu sol super iram nostram occidisset ac toties Cœnae divinae communicassemus ad nostri condemnationem. Ceterum quoniam scriptum tuum eo videtur tendere ut videare velle nobis reconciliari, ut haec verba tua ostendunt: Si quis est etc., hoc in loco non possumus dissimulare nec non aperte dicere, nos abs te graviter offensos fuisse libellis tuis diffamatoriis. Neque id tantum dicimus de nobis qui Consistorii nomine censemur, sed de multis etiam aliis qui et citra et ultra mare rem intellexerunt. Interim quoties scandalum accidit si quis proximo offendiculum dederit, quaerendum est remedium et adhibendum prout culpa gravis levisque videatur, ut verbo Dei docemur. Non ignoras qualis fuerit Ecclesiae disciplina et quod in usu Ecclesiae primitivae fuerint haec verba, videlicet paenitentia, confessio, satisfactio, remissio, reconciliatio et similia. Et nobis videtur non esse aliam quaerendam regulam in hoc negotio quam eam quam verbum Dei nobis demonstrat, videlicet ut faciamus alteri quemadmodum nobis ipsis fieri velimus. Hanc autem discordiam adduxisse publicum scandalum, putamus te non dubitare, et si corpus Ecclesiae aut multi tuo scripto offensi fuerunt, satisfaciendum esse contrario scripto. Ergo ut malum e medio tollatur et culpa sarciatur, en tibi formam et progressionem quae nobis videtur necessaria pro ratione et modo scandali oborti, videlicet ut tibi tres articulos proponas, quos tamen subjicimus judicio ejus eorumve ad quos pertinebit secundum ordinem Ecclesiasticae disciplinae. Primum ut tu sententiam D. Episcopi Londinensis, Superintendentis nostri, et Commissariorum suae Majestatis approbes juxta suum tenorem. Secundum ut retractes omnino omnes diffamatorios libellos a te compositos tum in contemptum ordinis hujus Ecclesiae, tum in detrimentum famae Ministrorum et Seniorum et aliorum, quos divulgasti tum Londini tum aliis in locis contra officium Christiani hominis et regulam caritatis, et notanter addes haec verba: quod te paenitet scripsisse, te minus repperisse humanitatis et hospitalitatis in nostra Ecclesia quam reperire potuisses inter Turcas et paganos ceu gentiles et nos exercuisse erga te iniquitatem et tyrannidem majorem quam quanta est illa Inquisitorum Hispanorum. Tertium ut tu nobis fidem des coram Deo, te cum Ecclesia Dei et nobiscum in posterum pacifice acturum neque tumultus aut scandala proximis daturum, quemadmodum nos quoque Deum oramus ut tibi nobisque tantum beneficium largiatur. Postremo dabis operam ut intra paucos dies scripto nobis respondeas supradicta, ut ad Christianam reconciliationem perveniatur. Dominus tecum maneat et per suum Spiritum sanctum dirigat. Amen.

Datum Londini in nostro Consistorio 18. die Augusti anno 1569.

    Totius Ecclesiastici Senatus nomine

                          Jacobus Taphinus.

5.

Responsum Antonii Corrani,
Divini Verbi Concionatoris,
ad scriptum sibi oblatum
a Ministris et Senioribus Ecclesiae Londinogallicae.

Fratres in Christo mihi carissimi,

quo die vobis exposui quam mihi Deus voluntatem injecisset injuriarum obliviscendarum et tuendae reconciliationis, jucundissima vobis fuit mea oratio, Deum ob hunc candorem animi mei collaudantibus. Cumque ejus orationis summam scripto a me petiissetis, pendebam animo dicebamque vereri me ne hinc discordiae renovarentur et scriptorum numerus augeretur quae sepulta esse jam dudum cupiebam. Praesentiebam enim scripta diversis interpretationibus esse obnoxia prout sunt varia lectorum ingenia atque studia. Et tamen, ut vobis morem gererem, in pauca quae dixeram conjeci ac perscripta tradidi. Sed ea video varie explicata fuisse. Unde accidit quod metuebam, ut scripta scriptis cumularentur. Cum vero ita induxeritis animum ut scripto respondeam responsioni vestrae quam mihi duo e vestris Senioribus hujus mensis die 20. tradidere, ab ipsa praefatione vestra auspicabor, ubi postremo scripto meo vobis a me exhibito dicitis affirmare me velle, dissensionem aeque a vobis atque a me ipso profectam esse. Ego sane verus mentis meae interpres profiteor, me in laudanda illa Pauli ad Ephes. 4. admonitione in me solum tum temporis spectasse, ceteris Dei judicio vestraeque conscientiae relictis. Atque ut ordine respondeam tribus mihi propositis capitibus, primum, quo efflagitatis ut sententiam Domini Episcopi Londinensis comprobem, mihi istuc non videtur in arbitrio litigantium positum neque ad eos approbationem pertinere sed observationem duntaxat et obedientiam. In quo hactenus tam me gessi obedienter ac summisse ut nil a me desiderari posse videatur, praesertim cum Domino Episcopo satisfactum sit cujus unius maxime interest. Itaque vos oro ut, obsequio meo ac observatione sententiae contenti, ad reconciliationem, quam cupio esse firmissimam, una mecum incumbatis.

Quod ad secundum caput attinet, tantum praestare sum paratus quantum integra salvaque conscientia licebit. In eo autem postulatis ut retractem aut deleam omnino quos appellatis famosos libellos a me, ut dicitis, editos in contumeliam ordinis vestri Ecclesiastici inque Ministrorum, Seniorum aliorumque ignominiam. Cui postulationi ut respondeam, ingenue fateor affirmoque me nihil magis in votis habuisse quam ut ad sinceram vereque fraternam reconciliationem vobiscum pervenirem, eamque ob rem paratum, si qua in re a me laesi fuistis, candide agnoscere atque eatenus satisfacere quatenus fraterna caritas postulaverit. Cujus rei gratia retractare non recuso, non solum quicquid a me minus modeste aut paulo liberius dictum fuerit in illa mea Apologetica expostulatione, quam duro asperoque vocabulo libellos famosos vocitatis, sed etiam quicquid unquam et usquam a me dictum scriptumve minus honeste ac officiose demonstrabitur. Nam Augustini aliorumque piorum virorum exemplo neque errores meos agnoscere neque eosdem emendare erubescam, quippe qui eam esse Christianorum gloriam sentiam, peccata mutuo inter se ingenue confiteri et se tanquam pro Dei tribunali reos agnoscere. Itaque, fratres, ex animo obsecro ut omnes offensiones oblivioni tradantur et obliviscantur, et quicquid secus admissum est ac factum, quam Christiana caritas postulabat, pro infecto habeatur. Verumtamen sic mihi persuadeo, fratres optimi, vos nunquam induxisse animum ut reconciliationis studio aliud ore proloquar, aliud pectore sentiam. Hac ratione lubenter obliterabo expungamque meis e scriptis quicquid minus recte se habere quisquam ordine me docuerit, ne dicam ea etiam quorum divini Spiritus gratia mihi satis sum conscius. Igitur, ut meum de scriptis meis judicium proferam, illa in duas distribuam partes. Prior ea erit ubi limites Christianae modestiae verbis acerbioribus fortassis excessi, altera vero in querelarum mearum excusatione versatur quarum mihi magnae gravesque causae citra dubium oblatae fuerunt.

Itaque primum omnium circumductum volo vestro admonitu quicquid dictum a me scriptumve fuerit fortassis acerbe in tota illa mea Apologia, unde quispiam ulla ratione offendi potuerit quasi ad contemptionem vestri ordinis Ecclesiastici aut aliquam Ministrorum, Seniorum aliorumve infamiam spectarit, ubivis terrarum quidquam hujusmodi reperiri queat, neque enim is mihi fuit animus. Imprimis autem doleo me tum Turcarum et paganorum, tum Inquisitorum Hispanorum comparatione fuisse usum, quod quidem attinet ad humanitatis hospitalitatisque tenuitatem quam jure querebar a vobis mihi praestitam, ad eamque etiam tyrannidem ac iniquitatem qua me affectum esse vobiscum expostulabam. Eas quidem comparationes quamvis justas ne contumeliae loco ducatis oro, immo etiam omnino obliviscamini.

Quod autem ad alteram partem attinet, excusatione res dignior profecto videtur quam correctione. Atque ut res ipsa fiat dilucidior, sigillatim percurrenda et perstringenda mihi sunt aliqua quam brevissime.

Ante omnia justissimae mihi querelae oblata est occasio cum multi mearum litterarum fasciculi, quas quattuor annorum spatio ad amicos Londinum miseram, resignati fuerint asservatique a vestro Concionatore, nec eis, ad quos mittebantur, ab illo redditi. Porro haec injuria et omnium gentium jus violat et non immerito vel patientissimum quemque accendere ira valet. In quo vacare culpa mihi quidem videor. Et obnixe fratrem oro, apud quem litterae illae adhuc extant, ut eas bona fide mihi restituat, quod rationi plane consentaneum est, ac praesertim illas quae sunt cujusdam mercatoris Burdegalensis de rebus maxime seriis ad me conscriptae.

Deinde jure questus sum quod, cum epistola quadam homini mihi amicissimum ac divini verbi Ministrum egregia eruditione ornatum consulerem super gravibus quibusdam quaestionibus quae controvertuntur hodie inter Ecclesias alioqui Antichristi jugo liberatas, ea non solum patefacta reclusaque fuit, quamvis unius hominis ejusque familiarissimi oculis peculiariter destinata esset, sed etiam in diversa linguarum genera a vestro Concionatore versa, idque vocibus perperam ac maligne aliorsum translatis ac periodis etiam clausulisve detractis, quod ipsum liquido constat ex multis per hoc regnum dissipatis exemplaribus. Unde non mediocriter perturbati sunt plerique boni et simplices viri, utpote insolentes hujus receptae inter eruditos consuetudinis qua solent de omni quaestionum genere inter se tum disputare tum consultare mutuasque sententias exquirere.

Praeterea fuit etiam quod quererer quod, cum haec epistola Domino Episcopo me accusandi gratia tradita est a vestro Ministro, veri alioquin indagatrix, quaedam sententiae subscriptis lineis adnotatae sunt quasi aliquid illae haereseos aut perniciosae doctrinae atque impiae continerent; annotatae sunt autem circiter 24 sententiae. Quod ipsum quantae sinistrae suspicionis et offendiculi afferre potuerit lectoribus, nemo ignorat, praesertim cum earum annotationum nulla redderetur ratio.

Atqui[a] merito cum illo expostulare debeo quod, cum eam ipsam epistolam suspectam haberet, illi tamen curae non fuit quod Jesus Christus praecipit, ut me per litteras admoneret doceretque ne in errore perseverarem quo me prolapsum existimabat, praesertim cum probe sciret me publice litteras sacras profiteri, unde gregi periculum esse posset. Nonne igitur debuit iste e fratrum numero post reclusas litteras, cum ad me scriberet in Gallia tum versantem, me inquam suis litteris ipsis commonefacere offendiculi quo legendis meis fuerat affectus? Debebat, debebat inquam, hoc erga me caritatis officio perfungi potius quam tam diu male de fratre suo suspicari. Adde quod nec tentata prius leniter admonendo docilitate mea aut pertinacia me jam publice traduxerat, contra accuratissimam Jesu Christi praeceptionem, non modo per Angliam, verum etiam primum per Flandriam, deinde etiam

---

a) *Here begin marginal numbers, from 6 to 22, this last at the alinea* Atque ut tandem, *here p.* 88. *Numbers 1—5 are wanting.*

per alias Galliae provincias, tum hujus epistolae nomine, tum aliarum quas e Francia accepisse dictitabat, nec me antea admonito et vero violata caritatis Christianae lege.

Alia fuit justa doloris mei causa quod, cum ex cujusdam Senioris Ecclesiastici denuntiatione Antuerpiam missi[a] ad quaestiones illa epistola comprehensas vobis suspectas respondissem Ecclesiaeque Antuerpianae omnino satisfecissem, quod nec emissarium illum nec eos qui eum miserant latere potest, nihilominus, statim atque Londinum adveni, passim ac praeter modum doctrinae meae sugillabatur puritas. Quod etsi conscientia aequi justique amans non potest aequi bonique consulere, tamen supprimere sum paratus et ita oblivioni mandare quemadmodum ab ipso Deo omnia peccata mea mandari percupio.

Item non injuria conquestus sum quod post meum Londinum adventum quidam ex vobis clam falsos de mea doctrina rumores sparsere, ne verbo quidem quidquam mihi significantes. Et tamen divini verbi efflagitabat ratio ut primum ego ipse separatim semotisque arbitris commonefierem; quod si obfirmato animo et refractario fuissem, supererat admonendae Ecclesiae locus; alias praepostere actum, nemo est qui non videat. Quid dicam quod, cum de me ipso in suo ipsorum coetu audissent doctrinamque meam comprobassent, nullum tamen fecere maledicendi modum.

Nec diffiteor me questum esse quod multis persuadere conati sunt et me in Cenam irrupisse et ea me antea exclusum fuisse. Quod Deo gratia nec factum fuit nec ut fieret ullam cuiquam causam dedi. Constat enim unum ex Senioribus me ad Cenam deduxisse ac loco suo sponte cessisse, quod non fecisset si de sententia Consistorii Cena mihi fuisset interdicta.

Querarne quod uxor mea, cum nomen dare vellet et Catechismo, uti assolet, ad Cenam praeparari, ab iis repulsam est passa, causante scilicet Ministro, nullum e Gallia testimonium ab ipsa proferri. Quae cum modeste respondisset testimonium in promptu esse Ecclesiae suae cujus Minister suus maritus esset, Cena tamen exclusa fuit nec eam participare per eos licuit. Quod ipsum inusitatum ac inauditum est, tum in Ministrorum persona, tum eorum qui ab iis testimonium proferre possunt.

Inter querimonias meas ea vero omnium gravissima et justissima videri debet quod ex quodam Brentii libro collecta sunt pleraque argumenta, eorumque brevia et manu descripta exemplaria multis ostensa, et sparsus rumor eum librum esse a me editum, meis opinionibus consarcinatum et completum. Quae injuria ut inaudita est, ita haud scio an ullo modo sarciri queat et sine gravi querimonia praeterire debeat.

Praeterea vos ego judices appello: postquam a me editi Antuerpiae libelli vicatim ac domesticatim haereseos falso traducti in hac urbe fuere, nonne veritatis, cujus praedicatio mihi commissa est, proditor merito haberer si dissimularem? Enimvero eorum accusatio silentio meo confirmata esset ac vera doctrina abnegata librorum meorum quos et Doctores[b] orthodoxi et Ecclesiae, ac nominatim D. Beza, ut litterae ipsius testantur, non improbarunt.

Illoque vero conqueri[c] possum quod, cum haberem praeclarum Ecclesiae Antuerpiensis testimonium cujus testes sunt ipsum autographum et ejus Ecclesiae Seniores ac Diaconi Londini commorantes, nihilominus fidem quibusdam falso fecerunt, habere quod me ejus nomine accusarent, cujus rei tamen nullum adhuc extitit vestigium.

a) *Cf. in the* Capita *of* Dec. 1568 caput 2.
b) *Ms. copy:* Doctoris.
c) conqueri. *Ms. copy:* non queri.

Quod tantopere expetitis ut ea ipsemet corrigam quae de iniquitate ac tyrannide Hispanorum Inquisitorum cum vestris nunc actionibus a me comparata dixi scripsive, considerate, quaeso, diligentius quis mihi scopus propositus et quis ejus orationis fons ac origo fuerit. Eo loco recitabam me ardentissimis precibus vos in vestro consessu rogasse ut meam epistolam sermone Hispanico descriptam, scandali vestri materiam, mihi exhiberetis ut eam agnoscerem. Quam tantum abfuit ut ulla ratione a vobis impetrare potuerim ut etiam coactus sim[a] pro mea agnoscere alienam alienoque, id est Gallico, sermone conversam a Nicolao olim Gallo, nunc Angelo Victorio, mihi infestissimo, qualem se ostentavit aliquot post diebus cum me domum usque conviciorum et injuriarum tota plaustra effundens prosecutus est. Deinde cum instarem ut liceret saltem meam cum ista aliena conferre et comparare, nec sic quidem quidquam profeci. Postremo illa traductio egregia cum coram lecta fuisset audiente me, supplex efflagitavi ut aut ipsam epistolam meam aut illius translationis exemplar mihi communicaretis ut responderem vobisque satisfacerem, affirmavique ac fidem dedi, nisi vobis a me satisfactum esset, lubenter me vestri Consistorii judicium subiturum. Sed vanae preces et repudiatae a vobis fuere, adhibitis etiam comminationibus a vestro Ministro, fore ut, antequam illa mihi frui liceret, exemplaria in plurimas regiones, ubi maxime opus esset, emitterentur. Itaque in his recitandis has voces usurpavi:[b] Ecclesiam Dei obtestor ut quod aequum est de hac iniquitate statuat ac tyrannide, ad hodiernum usque diem nusquam usurpata nec apud[c] ipsum quidem tribunal Inquisitorum Hispanorum quos isti omnium crudelissimos judicant. Haec ipsa sunt mea verba in art. 22, in quibus fateor quidem collationem hanc esse odiosam et ingratam; si vero quaestio instituenda sit jurene an injuria fecerim, vos quoque judices, omni contentione et discordia sublata extinctaque, non recusabo. Ita enim mihi persuasi ac certo scio, si mihi cum Inquisitoribus illis agendum fuisset, neque illos meae mihi epistolae lectionem aspectumque denegaturos fuisse et certe daturos exemplar ex praescripta juris formula legitime ac diligenter cum prototypo comparatum, ut Dominus Episcopus Londinensis postea facere non est dedignatus.

Si vero querimoniis meis justisque doloribus recitandis, tum his ipsis, tum aliis brevitatis causa praeteritis, digna caritate Christiana fortassis non retinui moderationem, pervicacem idcirco praestare me non decrevi necesse cuiquam offendiculo, sed potius totum illud pervellere qualecumque esse potuit omnemque culpam longissime amoliri. Quam ut oblivioni detis, etiam atque etiam obsecro, vobisque profiteor, haec a me non explicari persequendi aut decertandi studio, sed prorsus ex animo meo delendi.[d] Quod item ut faciatis, vos per nomen Domini nostri Jesu Christi enixissime obtestor. Ille enim fratri condonare nos jubet septuagies septies, et eum etiam, qui nobis injuriam fecerit, reconciliationis causa antevertendum. Oro item ut ne vobis molestum sit quod, dum ex vestra denuntiatione errata agnosco mea, et quae sunt occasiones ipsas dissimulare non potui quibus ad eam scribendam Apologiam impulsus sum.

Atque ut tandem secundum hoc caput finiam, oro vos ne in posterum meas querelas libellorum famosorum nomine infametis, hactenus enim nequaquam compertum neque probatum fuit ignominioso isto nomine vocari posse. Nam si jurisperitis credimus, etiam acerba querimonia aut expostulatio objurgatiove hoc nomine

---

a) *Ms. copy:* sum. *On* Ang. Vict. *see above p.* 34.
b) *In the margin:* Vide Apolog. art. 22.
c) *Ms. copy:* ad.
d) *Ms. copy:* dolendi.

censeri non debet, praesertim cum profiteri vere possum me nunquam scriptum illud evulgasse aut cuiquam ejus exemplar tradidisse nisi forte Domino Episcopo Londinensi, quod necessitate coactus feci, ac D. Bezae cujus sententiam amice ac consilium mihi exposcebam. Nonnullis etiam mihi singulari quadam benevolentia conjunctissimis me praelegisse non diffiteor, ut et consilio me juvarent et causae meae aequitatem perspectam haberent. Quod cur cuivis non liceat non video. Et ut hoc ita esse constet, non ignoratis me Ministro vestro efflagitanti exemplar denegasse.

Postremum illud caput est quo postulatis ut fidem vobis dare velim, me vobiscum cumque Ecclesia Dei pacem ac concordiam conservaturum nec ullam offensionis ansam cuiquam daturum aut tumultus excitaturum. Et me id hactenus praestitisse scio, quae summa est Dei erga me beneficentia, et si quid a me forte cessatum est, profiteor tamen me pro mea virili semper enixum esse ut id, quam maxime possem, praestarem, speroque ac confido in posterum magis magisque daturum operam ut in eadem voluntate ac studio ad extremum usque persistam ac perseverem.

Coronidis loco rogatis ut intra paucos dies scripto responderem. Rogo igitur vicissim ut scriptum hoc meum in bonam partem accipere velitis, utpote quod vestro jussu feci, aliter minime facturus. Ac ut in posterum talium scriptorum omnes occasiones praescindatis oro, illis enim nil aliud quam Christiana caritas labefactari ac incohata conciliatio dissolvi distrahique potest. Itaque profiteor posthac et me nihil omnino de hac causa vobis scripturum et a quovis vestrum scriptum quidquam non accepturum, ut aliorum sit ad quos pertinet judicium. Deum pacis supplex precor, fratres optimi, ut vobis pacem suam impertiat vobisque suas dotes per Spiritum sanctum augeat in suam ipsius gloriam.

Datum Londini 24. die Augusti anno 1569.

6.
Ultima responsio Consistorii.

Care frater, nostra responsio, data 18. Augusti, ut nobis visum est, debebat tibi satisfacere, tum propter suam aequitatem, tum propter submissionem nostram Christianam. Quod autem pertinet ad secundum tuum scriptum, non est nobis propositum, aliud tibi respondere nisi quod nos perseveramus in nostra submissione praedicta, relinquendo omnia judicio Domini Episcopi, nostri Superintendentis, ad evitandas omnes contentiones quae non conveniunt Christianis, et finem imponendo omnibus scriptis, ut optas.

Datum in Consistorio nostro 8. die Septembris anno 1569.

Totius Ecclesiastici Senatus nomine

Nicolaus Fontanus.

7.
Grindal to Cecil.

British Museum, Lansdowne Ms. XI. Fol. 150. Paper. No. 67.

„The document is in a clerk's hand". George J. Warner *of the British Museum who copied it.*
I have made some additions to the punctuation.

A declaration of the begyninge of the controversie betwene Corranus the Spanisshe Preacher, and the Ministers and Seniors of the Frenche churche in London, and of some processes abowte the same.

Anno domini 1563. A pacquett of letters was directed to a frenche merchaunte of London, beinge a member of the frenche churche, and under the direction wer written wordes to thys or like effect: for matters of greate importance touchinge the churche of godde.

In the said Pacquett was founde a letter from Antonius Corranus, the Spanisshe Preacher, then beinge in Fraunce, written to one Cassiodorus, another Spanisshe preacher, not long before remayning here in London, the copie of which letter is sent herwith.

The said Cassiodorus, beinge accused a littell before de peccato Sodomitico, fledde the Realme upon the accusation, no man knew whither.

The said Pacquett directed as above was broughte to the Minister and Seniors of the Frenche churche, who after some consultation, considerynge that the title was for matters of goddes churche, concludid to open the said Pacquett, and also to breake upp the letter directed to Cassiodorus, and fyndinge no publicke matter in it but onlie for the Impression of the Spanisshe bible, they wrote answer to Corranus that Cassiodorus was departed owte of this Realme, and (as they thought) was gone into Germanie: and by channce (as shulde seme rather then of anye purpose) they kepte stille Corranus his said letter in theire custodie.

After the greate trobles in Antwerpe Corranus cam to London and desyred to be admitted into the Frenche churche. The Consistorie called hym before them and burdened hym withe his said letters: which ministered greate occasion of suspicion (as they thought) that the said Corranus did not thincke well in some principall articles of Christian Religion; he answered that his letter was written by the way of questioninge, and not of affirmation; they replied that suche kinde of questioninge was not meette in these tymes for a minister of goddes churche: but in the ende offered that, if he wolde subscribe to true doctrine, and acknowledge that those letters[a]) werr imprudenter scripta, he shulde be receiwed into the churche.

Corranus answered that the letters werr written in goode and lawfull maner and that he did not repent the writtinge of them, and that he wolde (yf neede werr) sett them owte in printe with a defense or Apologie annexed &c. wherupon the Minister and Seniors of the Frenche churche wolde not receive hym.

Corranus thinkinge hym sealf injuried herwith and offended with certeyn speaches uttered by some of the Frenche churche in Lumbarde streete[b] and att tables in London, as he hathe often declared unto me, which I all waies[c] advised hym to contemne, wrote a pamphlet which he called an Apologie, but in dede a sharpe Invective conteyninge many sclaunders against the Ministers and Seniors of the Frenche churche and also sundrie untruthes of myne[d] owne knowledge, which Apologie was communicated unto diverse, and a copie thereof sent to Beza to Geneva.

The copie of the said Apologie is not sent herwithe, partlye by cause it is longe and tediouse, partly bicause the principall poyntes of it are conteyned and answered in Beza his letter sent herewith.[e]

Upon complaynte made by the Ministers and Seniors of the Frenche churche, that they wer by the saide Corranus injustlie diffamed and sclaundred, the matter was hearde twise or thrise att lengthe, and sentence geven againste the said Corranus as appeareth by the copie thereof sent herwith.

a) letters = litterae *evidently means the same letter mentioned before.*
b) Strype, Grindal *p.* 220 (*mrg.* 149) *adds:* „where merchants met before the Exchange was built."
c) Strype *ib.*: „unto the Bishop who always . . ."
d) Strype *ib.*: „of the Bishop's."
e) Strype *ib.*: „answered in a letter of Beza to Corranus; which is published among his epistles."

Att the tyme of hearynge, and before and after sentence, the said Corranus used manie contemptuouse and contumeliouse wordes against the Commissioners, and some towchinge the state[a]: for these, or words of like effecte he then uttered: Apparet vos Anglos non solum civile, sed et ecclesiasticum bellum gerere contra Hispanos, civile capiendo ipsorum naves et pecunias, ecclesiasticum in persona mea.

8—11 *from Geneva mss.*

8.

Apologia Corrani.

Delectis fratribus Consistorii vestrae Ecclesiae
salutem per Jesum Christum unicum humani generis servatorem.

Carissimi in Christo fratres, accepto vestro scripto, quo Tabulam de opere Dei a me sartam et auctam tot modis proscinditis et accusatis, adhibui diligentiam ut vestris objectionibus satisfacerem. Responsum dum paro, intellexi vos iniquo animo ferre meam in respondendo dilationem, adversae meae valetudini et amanuensium penuriae potius adscribendam quam differendi voluntati. Quando igitur tantopere me urgetis et cogitis, tum verbis, tum comminationibus, dicentes, ni responsum ante celebrationem Cenae Dominicae vobis dedero, me fore ejiciendum e vestra communione (ut aliqui ex vestro coetu mihi retulerunt), vestris votis obsequi cogor vestrisque comminationibus parere, cupiens interim ne vera hoc nostro tempore sit Enniana illa sententia a Lactantio alicubi citata: Pellitur e medio lenitas, vi geritur res. Quis enim unquam credidisset Dominicae Cenae celebrationem tam cito conversam fuisse in ferulam et flagellum adversus eos qui ex animi vestri arbitrio non statim scribunt aut respondent. Consulat Dominus suae Ecclesiae. Ceterum quando ita vultis et me in eas angustias redigitis ut intra praescriptos dies vobis respondeam, en vobis mitto impolitum quoddam scriptum vel, ut rectius dicam, indigestam molem mihi soli ipsi paratam. Ex qua postea, veluti ex acervo, majoris momenti argumenta depromere et seligere decreveram ad confirmandum meum responsum quod multo brevius vobis dictare destinaveram. Informem igitur hunc fetum, quem lambendo et relambendo formare sperabam, aequo animo si vultis accipite. Et si hac indigesta materia vestris dubitationibus satisfecerim, quaerite obsecro modum aliquem quo notas infamiae, quas mihi meaeque doctrinae et scriptis inussistis vestris accusationibus, prudenter et Christiane abstergatis. Quod si ita, ut estis homines, vobis non placet, habemus leges aequissimas in hoc regno et Reverendissimos Dominos Commissarios Regiae Majestatis qui jus et aequitatem tribuunt unicuique nostrum. Ad quos, ut ego quidem arbitror, pertinebat provincia examinandi scripta veramque doctrinam a falsa discernendi. Quodsi hae duae rationes ad hoc componendum dissidium vobis minus placent, habetis tertiam et inter utramque mediam, nempe ut seligamus arbitros ex utraque parte viros doctos et pios, sive Anglos sive Flandros sive Gallos sive Italos sive Hispanos aut si mavultis ex omnibus nationibus promiscue quibus omnimoda compromittatur potestas hac de re inter nos judicandi omnemque litem dirimendi. Haec omnia vobis propono ut me agnoscatis et pacis studiosum et fraternae concordiae amantissimum. Obsecro ut mihi scripto respondeatis ut ex hac numerosa et prolixa congerie paginarum et quaternionum possim ea seligere quae meo responso

---

a) Strype *ib.: p.* 217 (*mrg.* 147): „and since, touching his state."

conducere prospexero aut coram judicio et tribunali R^morum D^norum Commissariorum Regiae Majestatis aut coram electis arbitris. Haec enim, quae nunc vobis fere invitus offero, primae lineae tantum sunt quas mihimet ipsi soli paraveram adjuvandae memoriae gratia. Precor Deum opt. max. ut omnes unanimes Christi regno amplificando incumbamus. Datum Londini 8. Decembris anno 1569.

Catalogus locorum communium quos breviter explicat Antonius Corranus in hac Apologia...

Nomina auctorum quorum sententiis stabilitur et confirmatur doctrina quam docet Tabula operum Dei.

Sacra volumina Veteris et Novi Testamenti.

Paraphrasis Chaldaica. Targum Hierosolymitanum. Rabbini Judaei. Versio Graeca LXX interpretum. Irenaeus. Tertullianus. Ambrosius. Arnobius. Clemens Romanus. Origenes. Theodoretus. Chrysostomus. Theophylactus. Hilarius.

Martinus Lutherus. Joannes Calvinus. Musculus Dusanus. Joannes Oecolampadius. Zwinglius. Petrus Artopoeus. Pagninus. Paulus Fagius. Sebastianus Munsterus. Conradus Pelicanus. Philippus Melanthon. Nicolaus Lyranus. Petrus Martyr. Erasmus Roterodamus. Theodorus Beza. Lossius.

P. 17: Si me nunquam[a] audivissent ipsos docentem aut publice concionantem de Christi gloria, de mortis ipsius beneficio, de fide piorum in ejus meritum deque aliis capitibus nostrae religionis, excusari poterant eorum suspiciones aliquo modo, utpote de homine sibi ignoto conceptae et in medium prolatae. Sed cum triennio fere publice hic doceam, non satis mirari possum horum fratrum (ut mihi quidem videtur) praeposteram fraternitatem et caritatem.

P. 56 *sq.*: Melanthon in argu. epist. ad Rom. [Cp. Rf. XV 505—6]: „... Itaque in quaestione de justificatione seponantur aliquantisper disputationes de praedestinatione. Exordiendum est ab Evangelio, quod et arguit omnes et offert omnibus gratiam promissam propter Christum, et quidem gratis offert, modo ut fide accipiant. Intueamur ergo in verbum quod est universale, nec sinamus nos a promissione avelli speculationibus de praedestinatione. Non enim judicandum est de voluntate Dei sine ipsius verbo. Et ut promissiones sunt universales, sic intelligo hoc dictum: Deus vult omnes homines salvos fieri, sicut in promissionibus omnibus offert salutem..." Litem intendant nunc examinatores huic piissimo et doctissimo viro, cujus auctoritatem tanti facio ut, vel mille aliis nescio quibus reclamantibus, huic uni potius fidem praebeam hac in parte.

P. 81 *sq.*: .. aequo animo ferre nequeo quod isti toties repetant et inculcent praedestinationis et reprobationis quaestiones quas illos aut non credere aut non intelligere, ex ipsorum propriis verbis suspicari aliquis posset. Adeo enim pueriliter, frigide et incondite de his rebus garriunt, aut blaterant potius, ut pretio conducti videantur ad hanc fabulam peragendam et venali calamo ista scripta fuisse. Memini me vidisse in Hispaniarum regno mulierculas quasdam lamentatrices quae in exequiis mortuorum ad deploranda funera vel minimo pretio conducuntur; plorant quidem istae, dilacerant capillos, contundunt faciem et pectora, non quidem ex animo id agentes sed tantum ut hac ratione ventri consulant. Tantum enim abest ut hominum mors illas maerore afficiat ut nihil magis in votis habeant. Et dictu mirum: quanto minore dolore afficiuntur, tanto majori vociferatione, clamoribus, suspiriis et lamentationibus replent domos, vicos et compita, ut hac ratione astantibus persuadeant se

---

a) *my copy has* unquam.

maerore confici ob mortuum amicum. Precor Deum opt. max. ut animus illius, qui ista scripsit, longe absit ab hac fictione neque calamo venali id scripserit,
> ut qui conducti plorant in funere, dicunt
> et faciunt prope plura dolentibus ex animo,

ut poetae verbis utar. [Horat. de arte poet. 431—2.]

9.

Responsio Antonii Corrani Hispalensis
ad Animadversiones quorundam in Tabulam divinorum operum.

After the passages printed in Bulletin 1901 *p.* 214. 215 (*ending* Norwichi typis mandare) *from what Corro says here concerning the first edition of his* Tableau de l'œuvre de Dieu, *he continues:*

Quia vero typographus Flandrus erat Gallicique sermonis ignarus, mercator ipse, cujus expensis ista agebantur, prima aliquot exemplaria attulit cuidam concionatori Gallo ut orthographiam corrigeret. Qui lecto meo nomine in calce paginae et certior factus de auctore, idoneam occasionem nactus, ut ipse arbitrabatur, negotium mihi facessendi quod diu multumque desideraverat, relicta orthographiae correctione 25 censuras scripsit in marginibus meae tabellae, vocans doctrinam ibi scriptam absurdam, ineptam, erroneam et αἱρέσεων veneno refertam. Allatis ad me hisce censuris dialogo quodam Gallico Gallicis correctionibus respondere decrevi. Interim dum paro responsum, ecce duo Flandri, Cabellaus[a] nempe et Vandenrinus, in eadem causa accusatores se constituunt in Consistorio nostrae Ecclesiae. Postea vero Londino relicto alio abierunt, nolentes etiam audire Gallicum responsum quod primis illis objectionibus scriptum erat, etiam me saepius illos ad hoc invitante. Post illorum vero discessum duo alii Flandri, eorum amici, Migrodius videlicet et Joannes Henricius medicus, Consistorii nomine mihi Animadversiones ex primis illis Gallicis collectas obtulerunt ut Latino sermone illis satisfacerem, cum antea easdem animadversiones vel ut rectius dicam accusationes obtulissent D. Episcopo Londinensi ut de quibus ab ipsis accusarer certior fieret. Accepto hoc ab illis scripto et adhuc minime lecto dedi eis dialogum meum Gallicum quo omnibus objectionibus pro mea virili satisfacio. Sed quia biduo post idem Migrodius et Joannes dicebant se nolle legere Gallicum responsum sed Latinum, coactus sum aliquid laboris impendere seligendo ex scripturis sacris aliquot sententias quae hanc tabulam confirmant et 36 orthodoxorum doctorum, tum priscorum tum neotericorum, sententias et interpretationes quibus universae phrases hujus tabulae comprobantur et confirmantur ut manifeste appareat has locutiones neque esse novas neque absurdas neque erroneas. Hanc meam lucubratiunculam meis primis schedulis adhuc impolitam et incorrectam dedi legendam nostris fratribus examinatoribus ut ipsorum dubitationibus satisfacerem. Cum vero de scripti prolixitate conquerantur quidam, decrevi breve hoc responsum seligere ex illo numeroso argumentorum et testimoniorum acervo. Quae omnia orthodoxae Ecclesiae judicio submitto....

Praejudicium examinatorum ex loco impressionis: „Hoc scriptum non caret suspicione quia typis excusum Norwichii et non Londini quo loco auctor agit et ubi est major commoditas typographica". Norwichii excusum est quia sic placuit mer-

---

a) Caerle Cabiliau *signed with others the letter of the Norwich Dutch Consistory to the London Dutch Consistory June* 24. 1571. Jan. Cabelyau f. *signed with the Elders and Deacons of Maidstone Dec.* 25. 1572. Hessels III.

catori qui illud suis expensis typis mandandum curavit et suis sumptibus parcere volebat. Londinenses enim typographi minus quam mille et quingenta exemplaria excudere noluissent[a] idque magnis impensis, Norwichensis vero typographus pro coronato centum exemplaria dabat quae satis erant mercatori ut gratificaretur suis amicis. Nec praeterea male suspicari de aliquo scripto licet quia extra urbem in qua auctor agit excusum sit. Alias quidam ex his qui me accusant suspectas redderet suas conciones quas mittebat Basileam excudendas cum Londini ageret ubi magna est typographica commoditas. Et si loci distantia atque circumstantia perpendi debent, magis ille in hac re erit suspectus quam ego. Jam si in animum induxissem meum clandestino scripto falsas aliquas opiniones spargere, nequaquam misissem prima exemplaria Domino Cardinali Chastillione et aliis nobilibus et generosis Gallis[b] qui publice ea omnibus legebant. Multo etiam minus in sermonem Latinum transtulissem ut D. Episcopo Londinensi traderem . . . Videant ergo isti qua conscientia hac de re me accusant cum ista omnia luce clarius illis comperta sint, tum ex meo proprio ore, toto Consistorio audiente, tum ex aliorum bonorum virorum relatione.

Praejudicium ex temporis circumstantia: „Illam ipsam doctrinam quam in hac tabula judicamus esse aut absurdam et novam quod ad phrases attinet aut erroneam quod ad doctrinam, auctor etiam tractavit in aliis quibusdam suis scriptis, maxime autem in illo ad Epist. ad Rom." Si prava dogmata in meis scriptis continerentur, nequaquam Regiae Majestatis Consiliarii publice vendi permitterent, neque D. Archiepiscopus Cantuariensis in vernaculam linguam[c] ea transfundi typisque mandari permisisset, neque quod isti asserunt dici potest citra magnam D. Episcopi Londinensis injuriam qui, antequam mea scripta venalia exponerentur, viris doctis examinanda tradidit. Sed bene res habet quod errores iidem, ut examinatores ajunt, in hac excusa tabella repetantur. Si enim manifestum evaserit, in hac tabula nihil esse reprehensione dignum, nihil etiam aliis meis scriptis impressis neque in dialogo in Epist. ad Rom. nondum typis mandato esse obelisco obnoxium probatum evadit, nam de similibus scriptis simile judicium esse oportet.

Praejudicium ex idiomatis adjuncto: „Quia auctor Gallice scripsit, ex eo non male colligi potest quod voluerit delimare et tanquam compendio comprehensam proponere doctrinam Christianam soli populo et idiotis. Nam si eam operam doctis voluisset dare, conveniebat Latine scribere quae lingua in hoc regno est usitata eruditis, quod tanto magis judicamus illum ita facere potuisse quo se apud quosdam liberaret suspicione falsae doctrinae. Dicimus igitur cum instituerit docere plebem, praeter rem fecisse, tabulam etiam hanc tendere non ad aedificationem sed ad ruinam conscientiarum, quia cum primum principium et fundamentum nostrae salutis positum esse oportebat altum illud et divinum consilium Dei de praedestinatione electorum, de tota hac re verbum nullum praeterquam in fine tabulae sed ad aliud propositum, quomodo etiam verbum nullum de reprobatione impiorum . . ."

Auctor primarius hujus tabellae Gallico sermone eam composuit quia sic illi placuit, ego autem, quando illam correxi et auxi, Gallicum sermonem mutare nolui quia neque id necessarium autumabam neque animus illius amici, in cujus gratiam hoc tantillum laboris suscepi, eo tendebat, utpote qui vernaculo sermone, quo pagella

---

a) *my copy has* voluissent.

b) *Apol.* 86: primum paginae excusae exemplar Domino Cardinali Castillonio, alterum Domino Vidamio Carnutensi, tertium Domino Jumellio generoso Gallo et quibusdam in ipsius hospitio agentibus.

c) *viz. into English. The epistle to the Augsburghians appeared in English in* 1569, cum Privilegio, *the epistle to the King of Spain only in* 1577.

scripta erat, corrigi et amplificari cuperet, in aliud vero idioma transfundi minime, ut in sui musei pariete praecipua religionis capita brevibus comprehensa haberet, cujus paginae assiduo intuitu velut filo Theseio adjutus libros sacros evolvere posset.

... Cuperem enim ut vernacula lingua unicuique populo et nationi brevibus quibusdam positionibus et thesibus totius Christianae religionis summa perspicue ob oculos poneretur et unico intuitu omnia inspicere possent minorique cum negotio memoriae mandare. Usa est hac diligentia Gallicana Ecclesia quae patrio sermone summam quandam sacrorum librorum Bibliis vulgaribus praefixit.

... Qui enim poteram ante triennium divinare aliquos hic suspiciones habituros de me ut Latine scribendo eas praevenirem et a me arcerem? ...

Et si aliquorum conscientiae ex hujus tabellae lectione ruinam sibi parari existimant, id meae intentioni adscribendum minime judico utpote qui omnibus prodesse cupiam sed illorum potius praejudiciis quibus, cum persona fortassis displiceat, illius scripta placere nequeunt, cum veritatem intueri solam oporteat absque ullo προσωποληψίας praejudicio.

... quanto prae istorum morositate laudabilior fuit Joannis Calvini modestia in ferendis aequo animo hujuscemodi omissionibus, etiam in eorum scriptis qui justa volumina de locis communibus et omnibus Christianae religionis dogmatibus scripserunt. Laudat enim vir iste Philippum Melanchthonem eo quod de libero arbitrio parum et modestissime scripserit et difficiles quaestiones de praedestinatione et reprobatione omiserit. Hac de re testatur praefatio ab ipso Calvino scripta et locis communibus Melanchthonis Gallice excusis praefixa (Genevae 1552). Alibi etiam ipse Calvinus hortatur Christi discipulos ut caveant ab inquisitione hujus scientiae de praedestinatione cujus, ut ipse ait, cum stulta atque periculosa atque adeo exitialis est affectatio (Instit.)... Miror etiam quod Apologiam Ecclesiae Anglicanae isti non accusant, in qua tantum abest ut initio posita praedestinationis et reprobationis aeternae doctrina, ut nulla mentio prorsus in toto libro ea de re facta sit. Theodorus Beza veniret etiam hac de re accusandus qui in ea brevi confessione qua religionis Christianae summam comprehendere voluit absque disputatione (vide prooem. confess. Gall.), nullum prorsus articulum praedestinationi neque reprobationi aeternae assignavit... Ad haec in Ecclesia Gallicana his 30 annis excusa sunt plus quam 30 millia exemplaria sacrorum Bibliorum, tum Latino sermone tum Gallico, quibus praefixa est summa totius sacrae scripturae ubi nulla fit mentio de praedestinatione neque reprobatione aeterna. Ut semel finiam, quotusquisque est in Germanicis et Helveticis Ecclesiis qui in sua fidei confessione de praedestinatione et reprobatione aeterna disputet?...

... ingenue fateor me non libenter audire has quaestiones de reprobatione aeterna. Sentio enim de omnibus, quamdiu vixerint, bene esse sperandum, ut optime scripsit auctor Confessionis Helveticarum ecclesiarum, cujus doctrinam in omnibus sequor...

... tum ex sacris scripturis evidentissime comprobo omnes phrases hujus tabulae, tum 36 orthodoxorum doctorum priscorum et recentiorum testimoniis exorno omnes ipsius tabulae articulos...

Quod ajunt me confuse tribuere felicitatem fidei et voluntati obediendi, dissentaneum est veritati. Ego enim soli fidei in solidum tribuo justitiam, at non historicae aut hypocriticae sed verae et vivae fidei quae operatur obedientiam per dilectionem. Conjungo autem causam cum suo effectu, ne rudis plebs arbitretur fidei nomine me intelligere vanas aliquas speculationes et hypocriticas persuasiones de Deo. Hoc pacto doctrinae Pauli et Jacobi de fide et operibus concordant...

10.

Quare a Consistorio Ecclesiae Italicae quae est Londini, Antonio Corrano sit interdicta Cena Dominica.

Cum Antonius Corranus in ea tabella, quam scripsit et edidit *de opere Dei*, se reddidisset suspectum de falsa doctrina, Consistorium Ecclesiae Italicae, cujus erat membrum, nihil intentatum reliquit (quod quidem ipsius esset partium) quo tam infaustum omen averteretur, dum pie et legitime studet de hac suspicione cognoscere. Corranus vero hoc Christianum officium adeo sinistre interpretatus est ut non dubitaret dicere Consistorium agere partes accusatoris et inimici ac propterea se postulare ut omnino sibi non sumeret judicium de doctrina. Quanquam autem Consistorium saepe cum eo egerit perquam benigne et patienter, tantum ut persuaderet, quicquid ejus fecerat, fecisse se fraterno quodam affectu et pro eo quod didicerat sibi incumbere officio, omnimodo cupiens probare suam diligentiam et fidem, qua de tota re porro decreverat cognoscere: ille obstinate semper perstitit in suo proposito et contendit omnino non pertinere ad Consistorium judicium de doctrina. Propter has causas, tum etiam ad vitandas contentiones et tollendam occasionem scandali quam facile hinc arriperent infirmi et nostri adversarii, nos, Consistorium inquam, volentes omnia agere pro nostro jure illo quod speciali quodam privilegio Regia Majestas concedit profugis in hoc regnum peregrinis Ecclesiis, misimus ad Corranum duos Seniores qui eum compellarent de eo quod stipulatus fuerat Consistorio quinto die Septembris „si nos haberemus aliquid adversus illam tabellam et scriberemus, se responsurum et omnem exempturum scrupulum", ut illud suum scriptum adferret, quo, defendendo suam tabellam, nobis satisfaceret, quod si non satisfaceret, nos inituros rationem ut una cum aliis aliquot piis et doctis viris de doctrina in illa tabella proposita exactius cognosceremus. Tandem Corranus ipse nono die Decembris nobis attulit scriptum tabellae suae apologeticum, quod reliquit tanquam fratribus et Consistorio Ecclesiae Christianae Reformatae in hoc regno, cum prius ipsi confirmassemus quod antea Consistorii nomine promiserant duo illi Seniores. Hoc Corrani scriptum fuit postea inventum ita plenum mendacii, maledicentiae, contumeliae et omne genus scommatum adversus Ministrum et Seniores, quae omnia passim permista sunt defensioni illius tabellae, ut, qui Deum sincere revereretur et nomen suum dedit Ecclesiae Reformatae, non possit illud legere sine maxima offensa, cum propter inauditam linguae virulentiam, tum propter doctrinam quae tantum abest ut potuerit adhuc probari, ut reddita sit magis suspecta. De hac re cum alias saepe, tum maxime septimo die Januarii fuit Corranus serio admonitus praesente Ecclesia, quae tunc convocata fuerat propterea quia sequente die celebranda erat Cena Dominica, ad quam decretum erat eum non admittere. Ille tum hanc admonitionem sic admisit ut conaretur sese excusare ac diceret non fuisse sibi consilium dicendi contumeliam, etc., simulans se revocaturum et deleturum ex suo scripto si quid tale in eo inveniretur, pollicitus etiam se omnino satisfacturum de doctrina, ita ut post multas tergiversationes et ambages, libere permitteret trigesimo die Januarii universam cognitionem et doctrinae et contumeliarum toti coetui, qui eo die constabat ex Consistorio, septem aliis fratribus Ecclesiae, duobus Ministris Anglis et duobus Ministris Gallis, qui quattuor Ministri erant convocati consentiente[a] Corrano ab ipso Consistorio, ut essent testes, assessores et consultores in praesenti negotio atque ut una nobiscum et cum aliis fratribus cognoscerent ac judicarent: quibus etiam ille promisit se ob-

a) *The copy*: consentientos.

secuturum et a sententia quae ab eo coetu ferretur non recessurum. Verum postero die, quod praesentibus tot fide dignis testibus sollemniter promiserat, scripto revocat ac ejus rei de qua agitur cognitionem et judicium adimit Ministro et Senioribus, asserens se commisisse negotium quattuor tantum dictis Ministris, quibus etiam praescripsit modum et legem cognoscendi et agendi. In hoc scripto usque adhuc persistit in suo proposito, ut quavis[a] ratione evincat Ministrum et Seniores esse suos inimicos et accusatores, quamvis id aliquando liquido negasset et omnino diversum professus esset; quale et illud est quod, cum seriem rerum a nobis gestarum narrare vellet, alienam omnino a veritate narrationem contexuit, quare etiam statim, praesentibus duobus vocatis Ministris et reliquo universo coetu, fuit convictus mendacii. Propter hanc futilitatem, propter mendacia et inobedientiam conjunctam cum extrema pertinacia et contemptu disciplinae ecclesiasticae, tum etiam propter multas alias controversias et simultates quae ipsi fuerunt tristes et acerbae privatim et publice cum suis fratribus, quibus nunquam voluit reconciliari, cum omnino non possit frangere panem Domini in signum pacis cum iis quos passim clamat et pronuntiat suos inimicos, accusatores et adversarios, quae res in Ecclesia Dei pessimi est exempli, apta nimis ad subvertendam disciplinam ecclesiasticam quae tanquam nervus colligat et continet universum corpus Ecclesiae Domini nostri Jesu Christi, sex ex fratribus Ecclesiae, Magister Duringk, Minister Anglus, Josaer, vir pius et doctus, domesticus Archiepiscopi Cantuariensis, suffectus in locum Magistri Walckeri, Doctoris et Ministri, qui die praecedente adfuerat suo consilio Consistorio, Magister etiam de Feugueray, omnes vocati consentiente Corrano tanquam testes, assessores et consultores, fuerunt auctores, ut tantisper dum suspicio de doctrina et alia illa passim in apologetico nimis petulanter et proterve aspersa in Ministrum et Seniores, non diluerentur, Consistorium arceret Antonium Corranum a Cena Dominica. Quod nos hoc praesente scripto testamur bona conscientia fecisse, quo ille resipiscat, et infirmis adhuc, istis Corrani actionibus nimium offensis, fiat satis. Rogamus autem illum per viscera misericordiae Domini Dei nostri ut hanc coercitionem accipiat in meliorem partem et tanquam castigationem a clemente patre profectam.

Antonius Justinianus Consistorii Ecclesiae Italicae nomine.

11.

Dignissimo et Reverendissimo Domino Episcopo Londinensi reliquisque Verbi Dei fidelibus Doctoribus aut Dominis alioqui in schola Christi doctis, Constitutis in causa doctrinae Corranianae Judicibus S.

Consistorium Ecclesiae Italicae hoc praesente scripto cupit facere testatum, se quicquid superioribus septem aut octo mensibus egit, maxima cum animi mansuetudine et qua fieri potuit minimo cum strepitu, adversus Antonium Corranum Hispanum, ejusdem Ecclesiae membrum, fecisse pro officio optima conscientia et fide, neque unquam voluisse sibi sumere aut agnoscere nomen inimici, adversarii aut partis, quod falso saepe idem Corranus et dicto et scripto illi Consistorio imposuit. Cum autem in illa Tabella, de qua quaeritur an contineat phrases peregrinas aut novas, agatur quoque de justificatione, praecipuo capite religionis Christianae, — quem articulum tractarat antea in suo in epistolam ad Romanos dialogo Hispanico (quem tum etiam faciebat Latinum) eodem fere modo quo hic, id est novo, peregrino

---

a) *The copy:* quamvis.

et perplexo, — aequum erit laudare vigilantiam eorum qui sedulo cavent ne hujusmodi peregrinae novitates invadant in Ecclesiam, tanto magis quod haec Tabella et Consistorii in eam animadversiones, factae jam sunt ab aliquo Corrani discipulo Belgicae et versantur in manibus hominum. Consistorium dictae Ecclesiae obtestatur dignissimum et Reverendissimum Dominum Episcopum Londinensem aliosque Verbi Dei fideles Doctores aut Dominos alioqui doctos in schola Christiana, ut diligenter dispiciant quorsum haec ambitiosa scriptitandi et docendi libido sive intemperies tendat, praesertim illius cui publica auctoritate et lata sententia fuit per totum hoc regnum interdictum munus docendi reliquasque partes Ministerii Ecclesiastici exercendi. Orat autem idem Consistorium Reverendissimum Dominum Episcopum reliquosque Dominos Commissarios ut quam operam et diligentiam impendit praesenti Corrani negotio, ita suo favore et aequitate tueantur ut Ministri et Rectores aliarum Ecclesiarum excitentur hoc exemplo ad similem diligentiam.

Antonius Justinianus, Senior et Lector Ecclesiae Italicae, nomine Consistorii.

12. 13. *from the* Acta *printed* 1571.

12.

Praefatio.
Eximiae pietatis et eruditionis viro,
fratri meo in Christo N et amico multis nominibus observando
s. p. d.

Quidam ex nostris amicis, carissime in Christo frater, e nundinis Francfordiensibus reversus mihi attulit tuas litteras ex quarum lectione percipio te nequaquam hactenus intellexisse causas dissidii inter me et Joannem Cusinum, concionatorem Gallum. Neque arbitreris me conquestum fuisse de humanitatis officiis ab ipso omissis erga me (quamvis Christiano jure id optare potuissem ab Evangelico Pastore, quando talis nominari vult), atqui scias de re majoris momenti ortam fuisse controversiam. Is enim, posthabito Dei timore, plures litterarum mearum fasciculos intercepit, resignavit, vertit, pervertit, et aliquot retinet etiam adhuc apud se. Item libelli cujusdam me fecit auctorem, qui ante 15 annos Brentii nomine excusus fuit. Nunc denique, ut suam malevolentiam evidentioribus argumentis ostendat, eam Tabellam de divinis operibus, quam scripsi, miris modis exagitat et, fortassis non intellectam, condemnat. Cujus rei exitum proximis venturis nundinis ex meis litteris intelliges. Interea haec Acta legito et ex eis cognosces centesimam partem earum rerum de quibus jure conqueri possem si omnia persequi vellem. Mitto etiam ad te exemplar decreti Episcopi Londinensis quo testimonium reddit de mea doctrina et de adversariorum candore. Datum fuit hoc scriptum eo tempore quo Cusinus circumferebat cujusdam meae epistolae Hispanicae depravatas et detruncatas translationes ut mihi apud multos tum Anglos tum peregrinos conflaret[a] invidiam. Credo, cum ista leges, facile agnosces hominis ingenium et ex unguibus dignosces leonem ut posthac caveas et cum Propheta preceris: Defende me ab ore leonis, assere me a cornibus monocerotiis.[b] Vale.

Londini anno MDLXX.

a) *Ms. copy:* constaret.
b) *Psalm* 22, 20, *Castellio's translation*.

13.
F. Q. suo G. R. salutem plurimam.

Satis prolixe ad te scripsi, amantissime frater, postremis meis litteris de dissidio orto in Flandrica Ecclesia ob ceremonias quasdam in baptismi administratione servandas erga susceptores infantum, nunc vero obnixe efflagitas his tuis litteris ut tibi paucis exponam occasiones dissidii inter Joannem Cusinum, Ministrum Londinogallicae Ecclesiae, et Antonium Corranum, concionatorem Hispanum, et quas ob causas hic cessaverit a sua functione, ille vero novas inceperit tragoedias. Tota res ad hunc modum se habet.

Antonius Corranus, cum ministerio fungeretur in Aquitania anno 1560, incidit in aliquot libros in Germania excusos qui quorundam opiniones confutabant, inter alios vero legit Confutationem Joachimi Vadiani, viri uti scis egregiae eruditionis et eximiae pietatis, in libellos Gasparis Schwenckfeldii qui Germanico sermone scripsit. De quo Gaspare, quamvis antagonista, hoc testimonium fert Vadianus in epistola ad Zwiccium et praefixa Antilogiae: Neque id scribo, inquit, velut Gasparem, optimum virum nec parum de pietate postliminio reversa moerentem, invidia sim apud te gravaturus. Fateor enim ex ejus me lucubrationibus non parum profecisse, et ad manum esse etiamnum mihi libellos ejus quos relegere, et quidem magno cum fructu, non piget. Alii mihi memorantur quorum vicem doleo etc. Hos libellos cum legisset Corranus et Dialogum Petri Martyris contra Ubiquistas, ultimas etiam Calvini Institutiones, ubi Osiandri dogmata recensentur, decrevit cuidam amico docto et pio, qui Londini agebat, scribere et, missis pecuniis, ab eo petere ut sibi emeret eos libros quos Calvinus, Vadianus et Petrus Martyr confutabant. Scripsit autem ad amicum Hispanum Hispanice, cujus epistolae exemplar ad te mitto simul cum Latina ut ex ejus lectione scias totius negotii summam et quas quaestiones proposuerit Corranus suo amico et quos libros sibi emendos optaverit, nam hac de re falsissimos et diversissimos rumores spargunt adversarii.

Hanc Corrani epistolam cum multis aliis litterarum fasciculis octo mensium spatio missis accepit aut si mavis intercepit Cusinus (de quibus stratagematis adhuc sub judice lis est) nec eos litterarum fasciculos mittere voluit ei cui dicabantur, jam tum in Germania agenti, immo apud se servavit, reseratis litteris et publice lectis in coetu multorum. Quinquennio vero transacto, cum Corranus Antuerpiam venisset ibique ministerio fungeretur in Gallicana Ecclesia, Cusinus scripsit clancularias litteras ad Consistorium quibus suspectam reddere conabatur doctrinam Corrani ut eum exosum redderet et suspicionibus obnoxium illi Ecclesiae, uti postea fuit omnibus compertum, quamvis, quod conabatur, omnino tunc assequi non potuerit.

Sequenti vero anno cum Corranus, relicta Antuerpia ob inceptum bellum, Londinum venisset, curavit Cusinus Hispanicam illam epistolam transfundi in diversa idiomata et quam plurima exemplaria hinc inde dispergi, ea tamen fidelitate ut translationes tum Latina tum Gallicana et Anglicana multis in locis fuerint depravatae, abscissis etiam in quibusdam exemplaribus plus quam viginti lineis quibus occasio scribendi ostendebatur. Harum litterarum ostensione et publicatione magnum fuit ortum dissidium, quousque opera Episcopi Londinensis fuit compositum, qui, acceptis litteris e Cusini manibus, eas restituit Corrano et satis honorificum testimonium dedit de ejus doctrina. Cujus testimonii exemplar Latinum et Gallicum ad te mitto cum his litteris.

7*

Cum Cusinus videret hujuscemodi factum multis displicuisse, ne videretur omnino frustra sparsisse sinistros illos rumores de Corrano, coepit publice et privatim pravae doctrinae insimulare libros quosdam Gallico sermone a Corrano conscriptos et Antuerpiae excusos. Deinde ut majorem in modum gravaret eundem Corranum, litteras ad diversas regiones scripsit, praesertim vero ad Genevenses concionatores, quibus eundem Corranum multis modis sugillabat et infamabat. Et ne Londini omnino otiosus esset, transscripsit aliquot quaterniones et argumenta ex libello ante 20 annos in Germania excuso cujus titulus est Iudicium Joannis Brentii &c., et abraso auctoris nomine Corrani nomen substituit. Atque ad hunc modum circumferebat haec argumenta inter Anglos concionatores ut adversario conflaret[a] invidiam.

Has injurias, et alias quas in Actis Consistorii leges, cum patienti animo Corranus ferre non posset, scripsit Apologiam quandam Gallico sermone qua et objecta sibi crimina diluebat et, quae adversus eum patrasset Cusinus, narrabat. Ejus exemplar aliquando ad te mittam si quoquo pacto nancisci potero occasionem transscribendi.

Cum hoc scripto compertum esset quam plurimis dissidii exordium et quo pacto Cusinus se gessisset in ejus progressu, coeperunt quidam Generosi Galli, ac praecipue quidam magnae auctoritatis, inflammare animum Episcopi Londinensis contra Corranum eum in modum ut, maledicentiae praetextu in sua Apologia, eum cessare fecerit a concionandi munere, ut praecipua dissidii occasio orta videretur potius ex Corrano quam ex Cusino.

Sed temporis progressu cum nobilis ille Gallus quodammodo mitesceret, melius intellecto negotio, et Episcopum Londinensem rogaret ut finem imponeret controversiae, ex scriptis Consistorii et responsis Corrani manifeste apparuit quis esset primus auctor hujus certaminis.

Haec Consistorii Acta cum epistolio Corrani quidam amicus ad me misit nuper, et ego, diligentia cujusdam correctoris typographici qui Corranum ex animo diligit, aliquot exemplaria typis mandanda curavi in Germania, simul cum his exemplaribus Hispanicae et Latinae versionis, ut pii viri, qui veritatem hujus negotii nosse cupiunt, harum schedularum lectione de initio et progressu hujus controversiae fiant certiores, nam, qualis futurus sit finis, adhuc ignoro. Sed propediem aliquid audies, nam novus Episcopus Londinensis toti huic tragoediae vult finem imponere et utriusque partis querimoniae auditae jam sunt a quibusdam commissariis qui provinciam susceperunt componendi totum dissidium.

De his ad te scribam intra paucos dies, nunc vero vale, Deumque Opt. Max. precor ut te servet incolumem et liberet ab hujuscemodi controversiis.

Londini 1. die Martii anno 1571.

14—16 *from Geneva mss.*

14.

Carissimis in Christo fratribus D. Cousino, D. de la Roche et D. Baptistae, ecclesiae Gallicanae atque Italicae Ministris.

Cupiimus perscribi religionis illos articulos, de quibus apud vos suspecta est Corrani fides, ut, si id nobis necessarium videbitur, sua manu confirmet veritatem. Et vos, si quid praeterea faciendum monebitis, libenter obsequemur desideriis vestris

---

a) *Ms. copy:* constaret.

quatenus ecclesiae Christi sic expedire putaverimus. Rogamus ut coram nobis adsitis duo aut tres vestrum praesentes in aedibus decani Westmonasteriensis die Martis proximo, hora pomeridiana tertia.

N. Cicestrensis.   Gabrielle Goodman.   Tho. Wattes.   Jo. Hammons.   Ed. Deringus.
(Hae litterae allatae sunt [die] Lunae 19. Martii 1571).

15.

Reverendo D. Episcopo Cicestrensi aliisque assessoribus in Christo salutem.

Litteris quas heri ad nos misistis, honorandi Domini, intelligimus vos cupere ut a nobis perscribantur articuli religionis de quibus suspecta sit Antonii Corrani fides. Quo autem nomine aut in quem finem hoc a nobis postuletis ignorantes, operae pretium nobis ac nostris Consistoriis visum est haec duo vobis proponere, primum ut institutum vestrum fusius nobis indicetis, alterum ut dies scribatur quo ad respondendum aut aliquid exhibendum paratiores ad vos accedamus. Valete 20. Martii anno ex stilo calendarii[a] 1571.

16.

Complexio capitum quae de doctrina et moribus Antonii Corrani ponderanda sunt, a ministris ecclesiarum peregrinarum quae sunt Londini, jussu R. D. Episcopi Cicestrensis aliorumque assessorum ad hujus causae informationem sumendam designatorum conscripta.

Primum in collocutione Londini nuper sub fine Augusti habita, praesentibus triginta sex ecclesiarum Galliae Ministris cum quibusdam aliis, Antonius Corranus haereses, errores aliaque pio doctore indigna passim ubique, praecipue in regno Angliae suis tabellis varie ac saepius editis disseminasse convictus fuit, quemadmodum ex sententia sex arbitrorum, omnium consensu selectorum, idem ex certis disputationis capitibus adscriptis, patet. Legantur scripta.

Idem ex litteris Corrani ad Cassiodorum suum consocium scriptis 24. Decembre 1563. Ex his, inquam, apparet jam tunc Corranum parum sincere sensisse, ac multum false dubitasse de primariis Christianae religionis capitibus. Et vero postea fine monitus ab ecclesia Londinogallica ut eas litteras retractaret tanquam imprudenter et non sine offendiculo scriptas, ad hunc diem obstinate restitit. De hac re ex litteris D. Bezae ad Corranum scriptis 11. Martii 1569 documentum petatur.

Idem quam impure sentiat atque etiam scribat Corranus de sacramentis ecclesiae. Dei ac praesertim de mysterio Cenae ex ipsius libello nuper Anglice reddito apparet, cui libello, ut hoc obiter dicamus, non sine fuco insigni affigitur singulis pagellis haec inscriptio: A most christian and godly sermon, cum revera sit epistola plaustris conviciorum et rixarum refertissima. Interpretationen autem Cenae et capernaiticam et spiritualem ex aequo rejicit, ut patet sectionibus 17 et 49. Externa symbola pro re nihili existimare videtur, sect. 23. Subtilitates et phantasmata vocat quaecunque de Dei dextera, ut quae de Christi ubiquitate dicuntur. Idem de Christo pane concluso, aut a nobis absente quattuordecim aut quindecim mille dierum spatiis — Corrani sunt ipsissima verba sect. 24. Quam igitur Christi cognitionem probet Corranus, carnalem an spiritualem, an neutram, aut potius essentialem quandam juxta Osiandri

---

a) *Newyear calendis Januariis.*

delirium, dubitari potest, ad hanc tamen postremam propius accedere videtur, ut haec ipsius verba testantur: Qui panis ego* ipse sum, oportet illum esse in vobis, sect. 22, et sub finem sect. 24. leguntur haec verba: Qui Christum extra cor hominis fidelis quaeret, operam ludet. Quid de baptismo disputaverit ac disseruerit cum aliis doctrinae capitibus, litteris et articulis ab ecclesia Parisiensi missis 3 Junii 1567 colligitur. Negat infantes participes fieri gratiae in baptismo oblatae, ex eo, inquit, quod fidem non habent.

Item tabella quaedam, cui inscribitur titulus Monas theologica, accurate discutiatur, etenim sub obscuris verborum involucris magnum virus delitescere omnino certum est. Non negabit Corranus aut se ejus auctorem aut saltem approbatorem. Item animadversiones Ieronimi Jerliti[b], ad dialogum Hispanicum in epistolam ad Romanos, quem Antonius Corranus scripserat et paraverat prelo, factae, domino Episcopo jubente, expendantur.

Superest ut de moribus Corrani aliquid dicatur. At hic sese offert maxima silva; mensis integer vix sufficeret ad obiter dicendum aut raptim describendum quantum negotii et molestiarum ecclesiis peregrinis Londinensibus abhinc quattuor annis exhibuerit, quot et quam diris criminationibus, quot famosis libellis, quot litteris aculeatis, in omnes, praecipue Ministros, Seniores et Diaconos invectus sit; quam acerbe, inquam, famam omnium praeciderit, vix dici, vix credi posset. Extant documenta, non desunt idonei testes, sed quid multis opus? Ipsa Reverendissimi domini[c], nunc Eboracensis Archiepiscopi sententia, una cum assensu Commissariorum Regiae Majestatis ante duos annos lata in Corranum, fidem facit.

Istud etiam ponderandum quemadmodum tunc pro conviciatore injurioso et maledico, pro ecclesiae turbatore damnatus, nullis piis hortamentis, etsi saepius monitus et rogatus, ad peccati agnitionem et confessionem adduci unquam potuit, ita in eodem amaritudinis felle ad hunc diem (saltem contrarium non constat) manet induratus. Hoc ex litteris Corrani ad illustrissimum D. Comitem Hungtintoniensem 18 Januarii 1571. scriptis apparet. Legatur sententia, legantur litterae.

Praeterea haec nota alienae famae insidiandi, omnes mordendi, bonum nomen quibusvis detrahendi non in Corrano deprehenditur ex quo duntaxat in Angliam venit, verum etiam, si rite expendatur libellus ille de quo supra meminimus, merito dubitare quis potest an destinato consilio Corranus, tanquam spiritus immundus, non inveniens requiem, claustrum et cucullum reliquerit ut reformatiores ecclesias passim exagitet, traducat aut etiam subvertat.

Argumentum libelli sane praeclarum, nimirum ut ecclesiae variis opinionibus distractae ad unitatem fidei et caritatis reducantur. Hoc unice moliri pro se fert Corranus, idque magno pietatis fuco (quo solet omnes adoriri), sed vix stadium ingressus, post praefatiunculam et primam libelli sectionem, mox ad contentiones, ad rixas, ad convicia delabitur, atque adeo ita abripitur suo genio indulgens ut vix se compescat donec sub finem eodem fuco, quo coeperat, libellum absolvat. Judicent omnes ex lectione sitne ita necne. Judicent autem Domini Commissarii an expediat inter Christianos hujusmodi furiosos libellos in luce prodire. Corranus eo libello selectissimis nostrae aetatis spiritus Dei organis laesiones longe turpissimas suaviter appingit; suos quidem naevos habuisse nemo dubitat, sed neotericos omnes doctores, probos aeque ac improbos, nominatim Martinum, Zwinglium, Brentium, Osiandrum,

---

a) *The copy:* ergo.
b) *The copy has* Ferliti, *cf. above p.* 33.
c) *The copy:* Reverendissimo Domine.

Melanchthonem, Calvinum, Petrum, appellare caecos, inscios, sibi deditos, affirmare propriam gloriam cooptasse, se ut idola coli voluisse, discipulos non Christo sed sibi comparasse, quinti evangelii esse auctores, suos commentarios, catechismos, confessiones institutiones obtrusisse pro fidei articulis. Haec et hujusmodi dicteria quae passim leguntur sectionibus 6. 8. 48 et aliis, quis scintilla pietatis praeditus aequo animo feret? Ministri Antuerpienses Corranum serio monuerunt ne excuderentur hujusmodi sed obsequi noluit; hoc ipsorum litteris probatur.

Hinc rabula monachus occasionem nactus, magnum edidit volumen Antuerpiae quo miris sannis ecclesias reformatas, sinceros Christi Ministros, puriorem denique evangelii doctrinam petulantissime perstringit. A quo et ipse Corranus Archipraedicantis Calvinelli nota insignitur.

Insuper testimonia Ministrorum ecclesiarum Genevensis, Parisiensis, Aurelianensis, Cadornensis, Antuerpiensis aliorumque locorum de moribus Corrani ad ecclesiam Londinogallicam abhinc tribus aut quattuor annis missa; idem litterae R. D. nunc Eboracensis Archiepiscopi; idem litterae D. Cardinalis Castilionei in confirmationem superiorum legantur et expendantur.

Quoniam autem ex superioribus testimoniis quaedam non nisi Gallico sermone habentur, si Domini Informatores jusserint Latine verti, ad aliquot dies exhibebuntur.

Tandem nos peregrinarum ecclesiarum Londinensium Ministri, ne ex stomacho minus Christiano agere quicquam intemperantius videamur in hoc negotio, obnixe precamur D. Episcopum Cicestrensem aliosque designatos Informatores, ut haec singula maturo primum examine considerent, cum ad nostras ecclesias in futurum conservandas in concordia et tranquillitate, tum etiam ad rixosos cum homine refractorio et versipelli progressus vitandos, ac etiam ne ipsi Corrano ullum a nobis absque merito adferatur praejudicium.

Data Veneris 23. Martii anno ex stilo calendarii 1571.

17.

The original in the Hottinger *collection vl.* XXII *in the city-library at Zurich. A copy in the* Simler *collection there.*

Amico meo carissimo
D. Rudolpho Gualthero.

Carissime Gualthere. Mitto ad te aliquot folia illius articuli de praedestinatione cum censuris magni illius Aristarchi quem nosti. Exemplar unum dabis D. Henrico Bullingero[a] simul cum meo libello typis tradendo et tabella argumentum epistolae ad Romanos continente[b]. Alterum exemplar trades patri[c] tuo mihi multis nominibus amantissimo. Reliqua vero distribues pro tuo arbitrio ubicumque videris ejus lectione meam innocentiam ostendi posse et meorum adversariorum malignitatem. Curabis, mi frater, omni adhibita diligentia et tui parentis favore, ut libellus meus Tiguri excudatur, et pauca quaedam exemplaria, quae hic excusa sunt, supprimentur, nam

---

a) *In the letter to Bullinger Corro says:* Specimen hujus malignitatis perspicies in folio quodam hic Latino et Anglico sermone excuso cum censuris cujusdam Aristarchi.
b) *The* Dialogus *explaining Paul's epistle to the Romans*, London 1574, *which Corro wished to be reprinted in Zurich or Basle. See the letter to Bullinger.*
c) patrio *in the original, according to the copy sent to me.* Menendex 489 *has* patri. *And certainly Corro means him, Zwingli's son-in-law.*

innumeris scatent erratis. Quod si videris rem esse perdifficilem, obsecro te ut libellum simul cum tabula mittas Basileam ad Petrum Pernam. Scribes autem epistolium cuidam nobili Italo qui vocatur Franciscus Beti[a], qui quamvis mihi sit facie ignotus, existimo tamen eum lubenti animo, quae est ejus humanitas, accepturum librum et typographo traditurum. Tu interea de toto negotio brevi epistolio me facies certiorem, ut ad Petrum Pernam scribere tempestive queam: optarem enim proximis nundinis libellum in lucem emitti. Cum voles ad me scribere, includito tuas litteras cum iis quas pater tuus mittere solet D. Episcopo Londinensi, et ex ejus manu ego eas accipiam, ne mei adversarii, uti saepius fecerunt, eas intercipiant. Vale. Londini.

Tui amantissimus J. Antonius Corranus.

In the original without date, the Simler copy adds: Nonis Julii 1574, *the date of the letter to Bullinger, and no doubt both letters have been written about the same time.*

18.

From Cohelet 1579, Epistola Dedicatoria A 4*f.*:

.. egregium, mea quidem sententia, reformationis genus esset renascentia: qua homines suae Christianae professionis memores, dissidiis et litibus supersederent, atque in memoriam revocantes Servatoris nostri dogmata, intelligerent (ut pie quidam[b] annotavit) Christum, caelestem doctorem, eum populum in terris instituisse qui totus e coelo penderet et, omnibus hujus mundi praesidiis diffisus, alio quodam modo dives esset, alio sapiens, alio nobilis, alio potens, alio felix, quippe contemptu rerum omnium, quas vulgus admiratur, felicitatem consequeretur; qui nesciret spurcam libidinem, utpote sponte sua castratus, Angelorum vitam in carne meditans; qui nesciret divortium, quippe nihil non malorum vel ferens vel emendans; qui nesciret jusjurandum, ut qui nec diffideret cuiquam nec falleret quemquam; nesciret pecuniae studium, ut cujus thesaurus in caelis esset repositus; non titillaretur inani gloria, ut qui ad unius Christi gloriam referret omnia; nesciret ambitionem, utpote qui quo major esset, hoc magis propter Christum se submitteret omnibus; qui nesciret ne lacessitus quidem vel irasci, nedum ulcisci, quippe qui et de male merentibus bene mereri studeret; qui ea morum esset innocentia ut vel ab Ethnicis comprobaretur; qui ad infantulorum puritatem et simplicitatem veluti renatus esset; qui volucrum ritu in diem viveret; apud quem summa esset concordia nec alia prorsus quam membrorum corporis inter sese; in quo mutua caritas omnia faceret communia, ut sive quid esset boni, succurreretur cui deesset, sive mali quippiam, aut tolleretur aut leniretur officio; qui doctore spiritu sancto sic saperet, qui ad exemplum Christi sic viveret, ut sal, ut lux esset orbis, ut civitas esset in edito sita omnibusque undique conspicua; qui quicquid posset, id omnibus juvandis posset; cui vita haec vilis esset, mors optanda immortalitatis desiderio; qui nec tyrannidem timeret nec mortem, nec ipsum adeo Satanam, unius Christi fretus praesidio; qui modis denique omnibus sic ageret ut ad extremum illum atque optatissimum diem semper esset accinctus ac paratus, ad capessendam videlicet verae atque aeternae felicitatis possessionem.

a) *vix.* Betti.
b) *This* quidam *is Erasmus. From his* Ratio seu methodus compendio perveniendi ad veram theologiam *(p.* 41 *f. in the edition* Basileae MDXX, *which is now at my disposal) is taken almost word for word the whole passage beginning with* Christum caelestem doctorem, *and ending with* accinctus ac paratus.

19.

From British Museum, Cottonian Mss. Galba, C.VI pt. 2, fol. 340.
(Museum number 349.)

Muỹ Magnifico S^{or}

Viendo que el Sor Culpepers y va por essas partes no quise deaar passar esta occasion da saludar a V. m. con esta cartita: y suplicarle que ofreciendose oportunidad se acuerde de mi negocio, reduziendo en memoria al yllustrissimo señor Conde su promessa en la promocion de los obispos que agora se haze. Suplicole tambien que si aquella carta que los meses passados escriuieron en mi fauor les doctores de esta universidad no es perdida; q̃ la quiera guardar entre sus papeles: por q̃ el Sor Doctor Mathew holgaria que no se perdiesse por algun buen officio que con ella se podria hazer en mi favor. En lo demas estoy tan confiado de la buena voluntad q̃ v. m. me tiene que no dudo de importunarlo con mis cartas y nuevos ruegos. Pero ofreciendose occasion en q̃ v. m. quiera emplear me; sere muy aparẽsado para servirle El S^{or} sea con v. m. y le guarde. De Auxford a 22 de Nov. 1579.

Su muy afficionado
amigo para servirle
Antonio
del Corro.

Addressed, not by Corro himself:
Monsr
Arthurus Ateius
Secretaire de monseigneur
le conte de leysester
Londres.

Another contemporary hand has written inside the letter: To the Worshippefull my very good friende Mr Arthure Atey secretaire to the right honorable the Earl of Leycester at ye Courte.
Before Antonio *a flourish.*

20.

De sacrae scripturae auctoritate. 1588.

Lectori Christianae pietatis studioso s. p.

Ea est sempiterni Numinis erga humanum genus philanthropia ut nos omnes salvos fieri velit et ad veritatis tramitem multifariam atque multipliciter nos alloquens adhortetur. Ex hoc Divinae benignitatis fonte diversae rationes cognoscendi Deum, aetatumque omnium, naturalis et scriptae legis atque evangelicae philosophiae oriuntur. Hae enim sunt scholae tres diversis temporibus apertae quas Divino spiritu ducente ac docente possumus identidem frequentare. Namque superior et inferior caelorum regio schola est qua homines vel ipso tantum spectaculo illius discordis concordiae rerum atque effectuum ab ipsa editorum sapientiam Dei virtutemque sempiternam docentur. Praelectiones autem hujus scholae nunquam intermittuntur, immo assiduae sunt, nam dies suam partem docet, nox rursus etiam suam. Neque opus est longo itinere ut perveniatur ad scholam hanc, namque ipsa omnes homines ubique continet. Neque varias linguas discere opus est in quibus haec sapientia contineatur, namque caelorum sermo cunctis est notus et vox etiam sine sono ullo auditur. Ipsi praeceptores caelum, dies, nox, aether et ceteri suas sententias perferunt in omnes hominum regiones, hoc est suis motibus et efficientiis omnes, qui instrui velint, instruunt. Porro inter hos praecones et praelectores unus maxime conspicuus est sol qui lumine efficientiisque suis omnia lustrat et pervadit, idque celerrime. Quodsi quispiam caecus sit qui solem sibi visum neget, at non negare potest ejusdem caloris sensum qui ad infimas usque terrae partes et maris penetrat. De hac visibili schola atque rerum creatarum libro ad hunc modum olim cecinit Regius vates[a]: „Caeli enarrant, inquit, Dei gloriam, et opus ejus manuum ostendit aether. Cujus rei cognitionem parit dierum noctiumque vicissitudo, quasi fundens orationem, idque it aut nullus sermo, nulla lingua sit, ubi non audiatur eorum vox; quorum regula ad omnes terras, quorum oratio ad ultimum pertingat orbem. In illis quidem tabernaculum posuit solis qui quasi sponsus prodit ex suo lecto geniali, exultans ut athleta ad decurrendum curriculum. Atque ab ultimis caeli carceribus profectus, ad alterum pergit extremum, nec quicquam est quod ejus lateat ardorem." Verum enimvero quanquam magna, clara et manifesta sit doctrina quae ex hac naturae contemplatione Deum cognoscere docet, adeo ut teste Apostolo[b] „quod Dei cognosci potest, id apud omnes manifestum sit, utpote cum Deus eis patefecerit, etenim quae ejus sunt inaspectabilia, cujusmodi est ejus sempiterna potentia atque Divinitas, ea ex mundi opificio, dum considerantur per opera, perspiciuntur, adeo ut (quotquot rationis sunt participes) inexcusabiles reddantur", nihilominus altera schola scriptae legis ab ipso Deo aperta atque publicata est, in qua singulari Numinis beneficio longe melius ac plenius animos hominum non modo erudit, verum etiam docet, instruit, illustrat et afficit. Namque hac schola non tantum naturales, sed supernaturales etiam et morales disciplinas continet. Scripturae enim sanctae si recte cognoscantur atque intelligantur, Domini timorem in hominum animis efficiunt qui initium sapientiae, disciplina sapientiae et corona sapientiae est. Continet hoc sacrum verbum aequitatis ac juris fundamenta omnia et complectitur omnia quae scitu utilia sunt, elegantissima oratione pertractata. De hac secunda schola rursus cecinit Divinus vates[c]: „Jehovae, inquit, lex integra animum recreat, Jehovae fidum oraculum ex infante reddit sapientem. Jehovae mandata recta mentem exhilarant, Jehovae pura disciplina illustrat oculos. Jehovae castus metus perpetuo manet, Jehovae sententiae verae simul et aequae sunt, favorum dulciores nectare". Quid quod integer psalmus centesimus decimus nonus ordine alphabetico conscriptas laudes indicibiles secundae hujus scholae Divinarum scripturarum congerit ut nos ad earum studium trahat? Certe vel unicum Apostoli testimonium satis superque esset ad alliciendos hominum animos ad magnificentissime sentiendum de sacrarum scripturarum excellentia, ita ut ad earum assiduam lectionem jugemque meditationem incitaremur. Sic enim suum Timotheum alloquitur Paulus[d]: „Tu vero, inquit, in eis persevera quae didicisti et per quae fidens factus es, cum scias a quo didiceris et a puero sacras litteras noveris quae te possunt erudire ad salutem per fidem Jesu Christo habendam. Omne scriptum divinitus inspiratum est et utile ad doctrinam, ad reprehensionem, ad correctionem, ad justitiae disciplinam, ut compositus sit Divinus homo, ad omne recte factum comparatus."

---

a) *In the margin:* Psal. 19. ver. 1. *Castellio's translation, also in the following words of the same psalm, and in those of Rom. and 2 Tim.*

b) *Rom.* 1, 19 *f.*

c) *In the margin:* Psal. 19. ver. 7. *Castellio has throughout* Jovae.

d) 2 *Tim.* 3, 14 *f.*

Equidem si nostri saeculi homines praestantissimas has Divinorum librorum utilitates animo attento perpenderent, relictis humanorum scriptorum lacunis ipsos caelestis veritatis fontes adirent suamque sitim aquis limpidissimis sedarent. Verum, proh dolor! ea est nostri saeculi morum corruptela atque victoriae potius quam veritatis studium ut plures sint qui rixando, altercando, disputando tempus terere malint quam pie atque modeste Theologiam religiosam rixis posthabitis profiteri. Quid quod non desunt athei qui suis cavillis atque calumniis, uti olim fecit Julianus imperator, apostata dictus, sacrorum librorum auctoritatem elevare conantur? Genus certe hominum non tam commiseratione, si malitia, non inscitia peccant, quam insectatione dignum. Verum quia tantisper, dum spirant, bene de illis sperare non desinimus, tractatulum hunc de sacrarum litterarum auctoritate tanquam praesens pestifero morbo quo laborant remedium praebere voluimus. Faxit Deus ut eos fructus ex hujus scripti lectione percipiant quos opusculi auctor Christiano zelo excitus discupit. Ceterum ut de ultimo propositae partitionis membro seu tertia schola aliquid breviter dicamus, cum lex litteris exarata peccatum et concupiscentiam peccati evellere non possit neque littera sine spiritu salutem afferre queat, reliquum est Evangelium atque Divini spiritus schola in qua credentibus et obedientibus Spiritus Christi donatur. In quem Christum, aeternum Dei verbum, Prophetae omnes intendebant, cujus spiritus^a mundum arguit de peccato, de justitia atque judicio. De peccato quidem quia in Christum non credunt, de justitia vero quia in caelis jam regnantem superstitioso cultu eum demereri mundus vult, de judicio denique quia plus Satanicae tyrannidi quam Christi victoriae tribuere videtur. Cujus tamen spiritus virtute et efficientia superantur etiam occulta et latentia veteris hominis vitia atque purgantur. Ut tandem concludam: cum satis superque compertum sit Ethnicos in prima schola rerum creatarum et Israelitas in secunda sacrarum litterarum absque Divini spiritus unctione parum aut nihil profecisse, quin potius coram Divino tribunali sese inexcusabiles reddidisse, invocandus est clementissimus Jehova ut per aeternum verbum suum Christum se nobis patefaciat perque suum sanctum Spiritum se nobis communicare nostrasque mentes suum domicilium efficere dignetur ut eo pacto rerum creatarum spectaculum nobis sit tanquam Divinae potentiae atque providentiae speculum, et sacrarum scripturarum volumina tanquam Divinae erga humanum genus benevolentiae testimonia atque oracula veneremur et exosculemur. Vale pie lector.

a) *Jo.* 16, 8 *f.*

LIST OF CORRO'S WRITINGS, AND TITLE-COPIES, TOGETHER WITH A REGISTER OF DOCUMENTS CONCERNING HIM.

Here, as well as in the preceding Life, some abbreviated titles refer to the following works:
Bulletin historique et littéraire *of the* Société de l'histoire du protestantisme français. Paris.
Some separate copies of my article on Corro in the set of 1901 *have been paged* 1—16, *corresponding to pages* 201—216 *of the volume.*
Clark. Register of the University of Oxford. Vol. II edited by Andrew Clark, Oxford. Part I *and* II 1887, Part III 1888.
Hessels. Ecclesiae Londino-Batavae Archivum. Edidit Hessels. Cantabrigiae T. II 1889, III 1897.
Menendez Pelayo. Historia de los heterodoxos españoles. Madrid T. II 1880.
Schickler. Les églises du refuge en Angleterre par le Baron F. de Schickler. T. I—III. Paris 1892.
Sepp. Christian Sepp's *works published at* Leiden: Geschiedkundige nasporingen. I 1872, II 1873, III 1875. — Die Evangeliedienaren, 1879. — Polemische en irenische theologie, 1881. Tweede druk 1882. *This one corresponds page for page with the first edition, at least in the article on Corro which I have compared. The second has some corrections in the text of the documents.* — Bibliographische mededeelingen, 1883. — Kerkhistorische studien, 1885. — Verboden lectuur, 1889. — Uit het predikantenleven van vroegere tijden, 1890.
Strype. *I quote the pages of the old editions, found in the margin of the* Oxford *reprints which I use.* The Lives *of* Parker *and* Grindal 1821, *of* Whitgift 1822, *the* Annals of the church of England during Elizabeth's reign, vol. 1—4, 1824.
Correspondence of Parker. Ed. by Bruce and Thomason Perowne, Cambridge 1853.
The remains of Grindal. Ed. by Nicholson. Cambridge 1843.
Wood's Athenae Oxonienses. History *and* Fasti. Two vols. Second edition, London 1721.

1558 *in lent. Corro is mentioned as a fugitive.* Documentos inéditos para la historia de España. T. 5. 1844. p. 531.
1559 *April* 19. *Corro to Calvin, Lausanne. Latin.* Corpus Reformatorum, vol. XLVI. 1878. N°. 3182.
— *May* 26. *Calvin to La Gaucherie.* Cp. Rf. XLVI.
1561 *October* 27. *Corro to Calvin, Bordeaux. Latin.* Cp. Rf. XLVI. N° 3266.
1561 *December* 26. *Beaumont to Renée.* Denkwürdigkeiten der Häuser Este & Lothringen. Heraus. von v. Münch. Stuttgart 1840.
1562 *January. Grené to Calvin.* Cp. Rf. XLVII 229 f. *On the date see* Bulletin 1901 *p.* 202 f.

1562 *Corro at Toulouse.* France protestante ² II. 1879. *col.* 226 *f.* Sepp, Mededeel. 82 *noted that* Bellerive *should be read for* Bellerue.

Antoine de Corro *in the list of persons to be arrested at Toulouse.* France protest *l. c. col.* 147. n° 63. *On the persecution at Toulouse cf.* Histoire ecclesiastique, livre X *and* Bulletin XI 258 f.

— *April* 26. *Corro and others of S. Isidro burned in effigy at Seville.* *Official* Relacion *in* Schäfer's Beiträge zur Geschichte des spanischen Protestantismus und der Inquisition im sechzehnten Jahrhundert. Gütersloh 1902. Bd. 1, *p.* 454.

1563 *July* 23. *Merlin to Calvin.* Cp. Rf. XLVIII.

— *Dec.* 24. *Corro to Reina, Teobon. Spanish. With Latin translation in the* Acta 1571.

Spanish in Reformistas Españoles. XVIII. Madrid 1862. *p.* 59 *f.*

Spanish some extracts in Menendez Pelayo, Heterodoxos II. *p.* 485—6.

Latinized a few passages in Beza's letter to Corro 1569.

French from the ms in the Bibliothèque publique de Genève, *printed by* Aguiléra *in the* Revue théologique. Quatrième vol. Huitième et neuvième années. Montauban 1883 *p.* 329 *f. Part of the Spanish original has been left out in this translation, see* Bulletin 1901, *p.* 203 *f.*

Les questions posées par Corranus. *From the same French ms by* Schickler I 169. 170.

Quaestiones propositae Cassiodoro *(Not from the Latin of* 1571). *In* Theses 1576, *printed by* Sepp, Polem. *p.* 57. 58.

Latin the whole letter from the Acta 1571 *above here p.* 78 *f.*

English by Wiffen. *Ms bound together with* Ref. Esp. XVIII. *In my possession.*

1564 *March* 25. *Corro to Reina,* cerca de Bergerac. *The greater part in French, dictated by Corro, who wrote at the end some lines in Spanish. Endorsed by a third hand in French: to Fichet for Cassiodore or his parents. From the original,* Hessels III *p.* 32—4.

— *April* 4. *Du Perrey to Fichet, Bordeaux. French. With a* paquet *from Corro for Reina.* Hessels III *p.* 34.

— *Cousin to Corro. Mentioned in Corro's report* 1568 *on the facts which led to Grindal's testimonial for him, and in Corro's letter* 1569 *August* 24, *also in Grindal's letter to Cecil.* 1569 *Sept.* 20.

1566 *May* 28. *The French ministers of Antwerp to Renée.* v. Münch *l. c.* Bulletin XXX 451 *f.* Sepp, Predikantenleven 26 *f.*

— *August* 13. *The Consistory of the French church at Antwerp to Corro. French.* Hessels III *p.* 44.

— *Aug.* 18. *Corro to du Jon. Missing.*

— *Sept. The Antwerp French Consistory to Renée. Missing. Both mentioned in the letter of* 18. *Sept.*

— — 18. *The same Consistory to Corro. French.* Hessels III *p.* 44—5.

— *Oct.* 12. Tesmoignage de la classe de Montargis et Chastillon pour Corro. *Missing.*

Part of it in the letter of the London French Consistory May 17. 1567.

— — 20. *Corro to Renée. From the* mss. de Bethune, Bibliothèque Nationale, Paris, *ed. by* v. Münch *l. c. p.* 130—1. (Retour *means recovery from illness.*)

Reprinted *in the* Bulletin 1881 T. XXX *p.* 456—7. *From the* Bulletin *in* Sepp's Predikantenleven *p.* 29—31. P. 29, 13 *a. i. write* ont, *p.* 31, 4. d'Octobre 1566, 5 *at the end add* Bellerive. *On the year see* Bulletin 1901 *p.* 205—6.

1567 *foll.* Corro's two Antwerp publications.

Corro 1569 *Aug.* 24: a me editi Antuerpiae libelli. *PQ* 1571 *March* 1: libros quosdam Gallico sermone a Corrano conscriptos et Antuerpiae excusos.

Epistle to the Augsburg Confessionists.

1567 *Jan.* Epistre | et amiable | remonstrance | D'vn Ministre de l'Euangile de nostre | Redempteur Iesvs Christ, en- | uoyée aux Pasteurs de l'Eglise Flamen- | gue d'Anuers, lesquelz se nomment de | la Confession d'Augsbourg, les exhor- | tant à concorde & amitié auec les | autres Ministres de l'Euangile. | 1. Cor. 1. & 3. |

Ie vous prie, Freres, par le nom de nostre Seigneur | Iesus Christ, que vous disiez tous vne mesme chose, | & qui'l n'y ayt point de partialitez entre vous, ains | que soyez bien vnis en mesme sens & mesme aduis. | Car comme ainsi soit, qu'il y ait entre vous enuie, | & noises, & partialitez, n'estes vous pas charnelz, | & ne cheminez vous pas selon l'hōme? Car quand | l'vn dit, Ie suis de Paul: & l'autre, Ie suis d'Apollos, | n'estes vous pas charnelz? Mais l'œuure d'vn chas. | cun sera manifestée, car le iour la declarera, d'autāt | qu'elle seva manifestée par le feu, & le feu esprou- | uera quelle sera lœuure d'vn chacun. |

Icy pourra veoir le Chrestien Lecteur | quelle est la vraye participation du | corps de Christ, & quel est l'v- | sage legitime de la S. Cene. | M. D. LXVII.

Small oct. 40 leaves unnumbered, including title, A — E.

E iij: Anuers ce. 2. de Ianuier de 1567. ||| Antoine Corran, dit Belle riue.

On the verso an epilogue. On the following last five leaves extracts from the Holy Scripture.

STUTTGART *Royal.* BRITISH MUSEUM. BODLEIAN. OXFORD *Wadham,* Wiffen's *copy (from an auction at Antwerp* 1859). *A ms copy made for* Usox, *in Madrid National.*

Rahlenbeck, Bulletin du bibliophile belge, t. XV 1859, *p.* 371: M. Frédéric Muller a été modeste, suivant nous, en le cotant à neuf florins des Pays-Bas. Bibliotheek van Pamfletten, enz., n° 71.

Among Wiffen's *tracings is found a facsimile reprint of the title.*

1567 Eenen Brief eñ vriendelycke bewysinghe, Van eenē Dienaer des Evangeliums ons verlossers Jesu Christi, gesonden aen den Herders der Duytscher gemeynten binnē Antwerpen, die hun noemen vande Confessie van Ausborch: hun vermanende tot eendrachticheyt eñ vrientschap te hondē metten anderen Dienaren des Evangeliums. Waer in den Christelycken Leser sal moghen sien, welcke de warachtighe mededeelachtich3 des lichaems Christi, eñ welck het wettich gabruyck des H. Avontmaels is. Nu eerst in Nederlansch overgeset. 1. Cor. 1. eñ 3. Ik bid u, Broeders &c. 1567. 46 *leaves* = 92 *pages*. *On the last but one:* In dese Stadt van Antwerpen, den 2. Januarij, 1567. By uwen seer jonstighen Broeder eñ ootmoedigen Medegheselle in dwerck Gods Antonius Corranus, ghenoemt Belle rive.

HAGUE Royal. Its chief librarian, Mr. Campbell, *made for me in* 1871 *the above title-copy with the other remarks.* Wiffen *had got his notices on this edition from the same library, and also* Sepp, Naspor. III *p.* 111*f. and* van Lennep, De hervorming in Spanje, Haarlem 1901, *p.* 396, *used the Hague copy.* Sepp *calls it a* duodecimo. *He mentions p.* 110 *that another copy was sold in* 1875 *by the bookseller Frederik Muller to a Belgian* liefhebber.

Prohibited in the Antwerp Index 1570, Appendix.

1569 „*An epistle or godlie admonition, of a learned Minister of the Gospel of our Sauiour Christ, Sent to the Pastoures of the Flemish Church in Antwerp, (who name themselues of the Confession of Auspurge,) exhorting them to concord with the other Ministers of the Gospell. Translated out of French by* Geffray Fenton.... *Printed at London, by Henry Bynneman, Anno.* 1569. Cum Privilegio. sm. 8 vo. At the end is the following imprint: Imprinted at London, by Henry Bynneman, dwelling in Knyghtryder streete, at the signe of the Marmayd. Anno Domini. 1569.

A copy in the British Museum (press-mark 1351, a. 28). Another copy in the Cambridge University Library with the date 1570 on the title-page." Hessels II 990.

Sir Geoffrey Fenton *had published in* 1567 Tragicall Discourses, *which work is one of the sources used by the old English dramatists.*

1570 An epistle | or godlie admoniti- | on, of a learned Minister of the | Gospel of our Sauiour Christ, | *Sent to the Pastoures of* | *the Flemish Church in* Antwerp, | *(who name themselues of the* | *Confession of* Auspurge,) | *exhorting them to concord with* | *the other Ministers of* | *the Gospell.* | Translated out of French by | Geffray Fenton | Here may the christian Reader lerne | to know what is the true participatiō | of the body of Christ, & what is | the lauful vse of the holy Supper. | Printed at Lon- | don, by Henry Bynneman | Anno. 1570. | Cvm Privilegio. | *Title in borders. Colophon: [Printer's device a mermaid etc.]* Imprinted at London, | by Henry Bynneman, dwelling in | Knyghtryder streete, at the | signe of the Marmayd. | Anno Domini. 1569. | Cvm Privilegio. |

What is here in Italics, is there black-letter, the rest Roman. The book mostly black-letter. Fenton's dedication to John Byron Esquire *is dated* 10th *of December* 1569. *At folio* 48 *the work is signed:* In the towne of Antwerp ij of Janua. 1567 *by* Anthonie de Corro. *Fol.* 48*f.:* To the Churche of Antwerpe, *and* 1 *leaf of imprint.* [VIII] *(title included)* + 56 *leares* 8°.

CAMBRIDGE Univ.

Probably the edition of 1569, *with a different title.*

Addition from Wiffen's papers concerning a copy in „CAMBRIDGE, Trinity E 15. 79"*:* After Fenton's Dedication, a prayer of the author for concord of doctrine, and a prayer to Jesus Christ for peace by Fenton, Corro's Epistle folio 1—48 with the running title: a most Christian and godly sermon, and an Epistle to the church of Antwerp, explaining the reason of the publication, last leaf Imprint.

Menendez Pelayo II 770: An epistle to the pastoures of the Flemish Church in Antwerp of the Confession of Ausburgh. (Heidelberg, 1570; en 8°. Universidad de Cambridge.) *But* Heidelberg *is a mistake.*

Wood Ath. I 252 *registering this edition of* 1570: „originally written in Latin, but the copy of it I have not yet seen." *Certainly the French was the original.*

Wiffen has written with pencil on a scrip: Antonii Corrani dicti Belleriue Epistola ad Fratres Augustanæ Confessionis data Antwerpiæ 21 Januarii 1567. *Without any further remark. I do not think that he had seen the treatise in Latin or knew whether it existed at present. The* 21 *is strange, the right date is* 2, *Bor's mistake* 22 *has been repeated by others.*

Letter to the king of Spain.

1567 Lettre | envoyée a la | maiesté dv roy | des Espaignes. &c. | Nostre Sire. | Par laquelle vn sien treshumble subiect | lui rend raison de son departement du | Royaume d'Espaigne, & presente à sa Ma. | la confession des principaux poinctz de | nostre Religion Chrestienne: luy mon- | strant les griefues persecutions, qu'endu- | rent ses subiets du Pais bas pour main- | tenir ladite Religion, & le moyen | duquel sa Ma. pourroit vser | pour y remedier. |

Soyez subiets à tout ordre humain pour l'amour | de Dieu: soit au Roy, comme au superieur: soit | aux gouuerneurs, comme à ceux qui sont enuoyez | de par luy, à la vengeance des malfaiteurs, & à la | louange de ceux qui font bien. Car telle est la vo- | lonté de Dieu, qu'en faisant bien, vous fermiez la | bouche à l'ignorance des hommes fols: comme li- | bres & non point cōme ayans la liberté pour cou- | uerture de malice, ains comme seruiteurs de Dieu: | portez honneur à tous: aimez fraternité: | craignez Dieu: honorez le Roy. | 1. Pier. 2. | M. D. LXVII.

On the next leaf the verses 12—19 *of* 1. Pier. 4. *and the verses* 14—18 *to* pechez *of* 1. Pier. 3.

Colophon: Escripte en vostre ville d'Anuers le. 15. | de Mars l'An 1567. par vostre tres- | humble & loyal Vasau, & tresaf- | fectionné à faire seruice à | vostre Royale Ma.^{te} | Antoine du Corran. |

Sm. Oct., unnumbered; including title, A--M[IV].

STUTTGART Royal. *BRITISH MUS. BODLEIAN. CAMBRIDGE* Christ Church.

In the National library at Madrid a ms copy which was made for Usox.

1902 Carta de Antonio del Corro al Rey Felipe II fielmente traducida del original francés y publicada ahora por primera vez en español.

Begun in the Revista Cristiana, Madrid *and* Barcelona, 31 de Enero de 1902, *and ended there* 31 de Diciembre.

The translation has lately been made in Spain.

In the preceding number of that periodical, January 15., *a short sketch of Corro's life, written by me.*

Both letters together.

1577 ¶ A Supplication exhibi- | ted to the moste Mightie | Prince Philip king of Spain &c. | Wherin is contained the summe of our Chri- | stian Religion, for the profession whereof | the Protestants in the lowe Countries of Flaunders, &c. | doe suffer persecution, wyth the meanes | to acquiet and appease the | troubles in those | partes. | There is annexed an | Epistle written to the Ministers of Antwerpe, | which are called of the Confession of Au- | spurge, concerning the Supper | of our Sauiour Jesus | Christ. | Written in French and | Latine, by Anthonie Corranus of Siuill, | professor of Diuinitie. | Imprinted at London by | Francis Coldocke, and Henrie | Bynneman. | Anno. 1577. | Sm. oct.

The title, the preface to the Christian reader and the inscription of the dedication as well as the marginal notes and the word Finis *on the last page are in Roman type, the text Gothic. Title leaf, one leaf preface, then* 284 *numbered pages. The annexed* Epistle *is numbered separately,* 55 *folios, with three unnumbered leaves before them, two of these containing a prayer, one the following title framed by an ornament:* An epi- | stle or Godlye | Admoniton *[sic]*, | sente to the Pa- | stors of the Flemish | Church in Antwerp, | who name thē- selues | of the cōfession of Au- | spurgh: exhorting them | to concord with the o- | ther Ministers of the Gospell. | *This title has Roman, Italic and Gothic types. The text Gothic with Roman heads and inscriptions and subscriptions.*

BRITISH MUS.

Licensed on August 4. 1577 *to* master Coldock a booke intituled a Confession of faithe with a supplicacon wherein in shewed to the kinge of Spayne with howe manie and howe greate Calamities the people of Fflaunders are troubled and opressed. *See* A Transcript of the Registers of the Company of Stationers of London; 1554—1640. Edited by Edward Arber. Vol. II. London 1875, *p.* 317.

The book of 1577 *says in the address to the reader:* The author was determined to prefixe before these treatises an Apology wherein he declareth and defendeth certain places specially challenged in thē, which his defence, for certain respects, he hath reserved to be imprinted with the Latine Copie (which by God's grace shall shortly come forth) and in the mean time refereth this as it is to the iudgement of the learned and impartial reader.

Wood Ath. I 252: Supplication to the King of Spain; wherein is shewed the Sum of Religion, for the Profession whereof the Protestants do suffer Persecution in the Low Countries. Lond. 1577. oct. *[The differences from the title copied by me, seem to be only inaccuracies of Wood].* 'twas written in Latin and French; but who put it into English, I know not, unless the Author.

In the preface of the Articuli fidei *appended to the* Dialogus theologicus 1574 *Corro says fol.* 96: ante octo annos cum Antuerpiae docerem Gallico sermone, scripsi meae fidei confessionem eadem lingua, quae etiam propediem Deo favente prodibit in lucem Latino et Anglicano sermone.

The Confession alluded to is contained in the letter to the king printed in French, and the French text of the whole letter is naturally the original. The English translation of the Confession did not appear prope diem, *but three years later, in the whole letter, together with the English translation of the former letter. On the English title-page of both is said:* Written in French and Latin, *in the preface to the reader the hope is expressed that the Latin copy shall shortly come forth. On the Latin copy Wiffen:* it is not known that it was ever printed, Hessels l. c. p. 990: no trace of such an edition has yet be found.

I cannot but believe that the Latin never has been printed, nor the defence which in 1577 he intended to prefix.

Extracts.

From the letter to the Augsburghians: Dutch *in the works on church-reformation in the Netherlands by* Bor, Uytenbogaert, Brandt, Uyttenhoven, Sepp Naspor. III 112*f.* — *French:* Porthaise, *cf.* Sepp *l. c.* 146*f. French abridgment of* Brandt's *work.* — *Spanish from French some lines* Menendez Pel. II 484. — *English. Translation of* Brandt's *work. And here above p.* 21*f.*

From the letter to the king:

English. Wiffen *in the* Preface *to* Constantino's Confession of a sinner, *transl. by* Betts. *My extracts here p.* 3*f., with the use of those by* Wiffen *just mentioned, and p.* 26*f.*

1567 *April. Notices by Cousin from conversations with Corro in London April* 11.—13. *French.* Hessels III *p.* 45. 46. *Most of what he deciphered from Cousin's scribble remains unintelligible.* Angelus „perhaps Michael Angelus Florentinus", Hessels, *who refers to* II 272. 301; *but I think it is* Angelus Victorius, infestissimus *to* Corro, *see above p.* 88. *On* Phares, *see above p.* 7, *on* Baltasar *p.* 30.

— — 16. *Advices of Cousin and Elders of the London French* (Simon, Botteler, Chastelain, Charles Durant, Carprat, Fischet, Chaudron, Cappel, Marebout, Chellos, Ponchel) *concerning a remonstrance to be made to Corro. French. Draft by Cousin.* Hessels III *p.* 47. 48.

[—] *On the same day Corro to the London French Consistory. Alleged in the* Capita *of* 1568 *under* Litt. D. *Missing.*

— May, 7. *The London French Consistory to the Reformed Church at Paris. French. Copy made by Cousin.* Hessels III *p.* 48. 49.

— *Cousin to Saules. Mentioned in the letter of* June 16. *Missing.*
— *Answer of Saules. See* Capita [M.]. *Missing.*

1567 „circa May or June", *I think May. The London French Consistory's questions to the Reformed Church of Antwerp. French. Copy by Cousin.* Hessels III *p.* 51.
— June 3. *The Paris Church to the London French. See* Capita *and letter of* March 23. 71. *Missing.*
— *The Antwerp answer.* Capita. F. *Missing.*
— — 5. *Bishop Grindal's testimonial for Corro. Latin. Printed by Corro in* 1568 *on a separate sheet with a French translation. Such a printed copy is in the GENEVA library among the Corro papers.*
Both texts reprinted in the Acta Consistorii 1571.
From these Acta *reprinted in Latin with an English translation in the* Grindal Remains *p.* 313—4. *The correction* ista *proposed by the editor and translator is confirmed by the old printed copy in the Geneva library.*
Reprinted by Schickler III 73 *f. from the* feuille volante *among the Geneva papers.* (*He notes:* Bibl. de Genève. Lettres et pièces diverses, n° 2; *the exact reference he gives* I 170, *where, however, read* portef.). *P.* 74, *line* 6 *correct* est *instead of* estre, 11 soubhaitans *instead of* soubhaitons, 13 chascun, nous *instead of* chascun. Nous. *I take these corrections from the copy made for me at Geneva; they agree with the* Acta *and correspond with the Latin.*
— — 16. *The council of the London French Church to François de S*^{t.} *Pol* (*on him see* Schickler I 293). *French. Copy by Cousin.* Hessels III *p.* 50.
— July 18. *Episcopus Londin. ad Cusinum and*
— — 19. *Cusini responsio.* Hessels II n° 82. 83.
— *Sept.* 1.—7. *The National Synod at Vertueil on Corro.* Aymon *p.* 78. *where* Antoine de la Rodit Bellariva *means* Corro, *see* Bulletin 1901 *p.* 207. *Quick has the same article, likewise writing* Anthony de la Rodit Bellariva; *not, however, in the* Roll of Vagrants, *as* Aymon, *but in the* General Avertisements *given unto the Churches* of France *p.* 76.
1567 *An apology of Corro. Mentioned in the next paper of* Dec. 8 *and* 9. *Missing.*
— *Dec.* 8 *and* 9. *Conference of Cousin and four other ministers of the London French Church. Protocol by Cousin. French.* Hessels III *p.* 52—55.
1568 *Jan.* 16. *Corro to Archbishop* Parker. *Latin. Printed in* Corresp. of Parker 339 *f. from the* Parker Mss. C. C. Coll. Camb. CXIV. art. 334. *p.* 935. Rahlenbeck, Bibliophile Belge t. XV. 1859 *p.* 371 *says that the letter is at Oxford in the library of Queen's College, but the librarian of that college informed me Dec.* 18. 1879 *that the letter is not found there in the library nor registered in the minute catalogue.* Rahlenbeck *gives the date* 16 janvier 1568, *while* Strype, Parker 271, *only mentions this year. As* Strype *places it in* 1568 *according to the English style, it would have been written in* 1569 *new style, and so in the* Parker Corresp. *is printed* 16. Jan. 1568—9. *But it must have been written in* 1568 *new style.*
— *Corro's report on the facts which led to the Bishop's testimonial of June* 5. 1567 *was in* 1568 *presented in ms. to several persons and July* 21. *to one of the French ministers. French. Printed in* Bulletin 1901 *p.* 208 *f.*
— *July.* 1. *Du Croissant to Cousin. Latin.* Hessels III *p.* 57.
— — 15. *Letter of Corro to the Bishop of London, containing articles against* Cousin *and adherents. French. Printed from the copy in* Geneva *by* Schickler III 74 *f.*
I note the different readings (excluding orthographical variants) of my copy of the same Geneva paper, and I add some redintegrations. The begin-

ning: [Copie] d'une lettre. *L. Dufour, my copyist:* Le mot a été coupé, mais je pense qu'il faut le rétablir ainsi. *(The Geneva ms. has indeed* 1567 *as the year of the death of Perez, but it is a mistake for* 1566; *see* Bulletin 1901 *p.* 204*f.)* P. 74, *line* 3 *a. i., the Geneva paper has* ces, *but it means* ses. 75, 2 leurs *instead of* les. 13 vousissent. 15 inventarizer. 18 Madame [de Ferrare pour avoir des] deniers. 19 tirer. *Last line* craignoient. 76 *first line* il eust. 14 Synodes [ou Consistoires gener]aulx. *Dufour.* 15 [peu]. *Dufour.* 16 leurs. 20*f. the words* pour comble &c. *to* prescheurs *and* sergens et boutefeux *are underlined. Likewise soon the words* absence contre toute loy divine et humaine. 10—9 *a. i.* contre ma personne. *The* ma *(which Sch. has not) is surprising as Corro speaks of himself in the third person.* 8 *a. i.* sachans. 6 *a. i.* la formalité. — *Sch. says p.* 77 *on the underlined words which he prints in italics:* paroissent l'avoir été par les accusateurs pour en faire ressortir la violence.

1568 *end of July. Remonstrance of the French Ministers, Elders and Deacons to the Bishop. French.* Schickler III 85*f. without year.* Hessels III *p.* 81—82 *(he misplaced it* 22 July 1569).

— *July ? Cousin to somebody at Geneva. See Beza's* Epist. LIX. *Missing.*

— — *? Beza to Cousin. See the same* Epist. LIX. *Missing.*

— *August ? Corro to Beza, complaining of Beza's letter to Cousin. See the same* Epist. LIX *p.* 271, secunda ed. *p.* 248—9. *It was probably in this letter that Corro spoke of the many testimonials favorable to him, and of Nerac, of* Merlin, *of* Calvin's *and* Beza's *choleric temper, points mentioned by* Beza *p.* 282*f.* sec. ed. *p.* 258*f. Missing.*

— *Aug.* 31. *Corro to the London French Consistory. Latin. From Cousin's transcript* Hessels III *p.* 58. 59.

— *Sept.* 2. *The London French Consistory to the Bishop. Latin.* Hessels III *p.* 60.

— *Sept.* 3. *Corro to Beza. French. Printed from a copy of the Geneva ms., in* Bulletin 1901 *p.* 209—214. *According to a later notice sent to me, it is written by a contemporary copyist whose last words are:* de Londres ce 3 jor de septembre 1568. *Only the subscription* tuus &c. *is by another hand, certainly Corro's.*

— *An Apology of Corro.* Grindal *mentions it to Cecil in March* 1569 *and says that it was long and that Beza answered the principal points. It must be the* codicillus *of at least* 79 *articles which was appended to the* Capita *of the end of* 1568. *Missing.* Strype, Appd. to Grindal, *at the very end, under the* „Manuscripts used or mentioned in Archbishop Grindal's History: Apology of Anth. Corranus, a Spanish Preacher, against the Ministers of the French Church, London." *Most likely* Strype *registers it without having seen it, only because it is mentioned in the letter of Grindal to Cecil, printed here above p.* 89*f., used by* Strype, Grindal 149 *where he notes at the margin:* „Corranus's Apology"; *cf.* 126.

— *Nov.* 28. *Articles of the London French Church against Corro. French. Cousin's handwriting.* Hessels III *p.* 62—72.

— — 29. *Grindal to Cousin.* Hessels III *p.* 72—75.

— *[Dec.] The Articles of Nov.* 28 *in Latin:* Capita. *From the copy in Geneva* Schickler III *p.* 77*f.*

From the London copy together with the French Hessels III *p.* 62—72.

The copy which was made for me from the Geneva ms. of the Capita, *and* Schickler's *publication from the same ms. differ in many places, and* Hessel's *Latin text from the London ms. differs in many places from the Geneva ms. The French original (with the subscribed names of ministers, elders, deacons) in Cousin's handwriting is important for the meaning. I have made the desirable comparative notices. Here only some remarks for the reconstruction of the list of the missing* appendix. *Where* Schickler 80, 6 a. i. *has* B, *my copy has* F, Hessels' *Latin* C. *the French gives* E, *and this is evidently the right.* Schickler 81, 21 *after* judicabit H, *my copy* B, Hessels *in the Latin* K, *in the French* Lz. *Also in the document itself referred to,* Hessels *read:* l'enuelope des lettres. Lettre Lz. *This endorsement as well as the French* Articles *are both in Cousin's handwriting. Certainly Cousin's figure meant in both places* K, *which has been misread in different ways.* Hessels *Latin* C, *French* E *as in the Geneva Latin* Schickler 82, 6 *and in my copy, and this is evidently the right.*

Cousin wrote on that cover the other (probably the first) notice: L'enveloppe d'un paquet d'Ant. Corran, *and on the letter itself:* Lettres d'Antoine Corran.

The papers of the missing Appendix *must have been the following:*

A. *The Bishop's testimonial of June* 5. 67 *with Corro's translation and introduction.*

B. *Corrani* codicillus. 79 *articles or more. Certainly the* Apologia, *as Corro had called it, of which the Bishop said that it was long, see above p.* 90.

C. *Episcopi Londinensis epistola ad consistorium ecclesiae Gallicanae Londinensis. Compare the Bishop's letter to Cousin July* 18. 67.

D. *Corrani epistola ad consistorium Apr.* 16. [67.]

E. *Corrani epistola ad consistorium Aug.* 31. 68.

F. *Ministri ecclesiae Gallicanae Antuerpiensis epistola ad Londinensem.*

G. *Corro's letter to Reina of Dec.* 24. 63.

H. *Ecclesiae Gallicanae Londinensis epistola ad synodum in Germania inferiore.*

I. *Ecclesiae Parisiensis epistola ad Gallicanam Londinensem [June* 3. 67]. *See above p.* 31.

K. *The cover of a letter of Corro to Reina.*

L. *Commonefactiones Corrano factae.*

[M.] *Sauli epistola. Cf. above* 1567, *May.*

[N.] *Bexae testimonium. Certainly the letter of which Bexa speaks in the beginning of his letter to Corro March* 11. 69.

Besides, the Capita *refer to several* sections *of Corro's Epistle to the Augsburg Confessionists. Moreover they propose to the Bishop to ask the cardinal of Chastillon and certain ministers of churches of France for their opinion on Corro's letter to Reina which created all these controversies. Also in other respects they wish that some ministers be interrogated.*

1568 *probably. Corro's answer to the* Capita *which the Bishop had given him* exceptis probationibus *i. e. without the appended documents. See the notice at the end of the* Capita.

1569 *probably. The French Church's reply. See ibid. Both these papers are missing.*

1568 *end or* 69 *beginning. Certificate of the Lord mayor on the strangers in London.*

The misdate 1607 *in* Strype's Supplement *to his* Annals vol. IV Oxf. 1824 *p.* 571*f. is explained by Mr.* George Warner *of the British Museum, whom I consulted, in a letter to me of* Febr. 9. 1880:

„On looking at the folio ed. of 1731, vol. IV. I find that in the margin at the top of p. 403 (the last recto page before the supplement) is rightly enough „Anno 1607". On the first recto page of the supplement is „Anno 1568", but on the second recto page is „Anno 1607", evidently repeated by a printer's blunder from p. 403. The Oxford editors, not observing this, have made the error worse by placing 1607 in the margin halfway down the page opposite the line which happened to be at the top of the page in the folio. There can be no doubt that 1607 is a mistake, for the whole list certainly refers to 1568. It is in fact an abstract of the «Great book»[a], but not from the copy in Lansd. Ms. 202, as I infer from the fact that some names are there given in full for which Strype leaves blanks. Where he quotes the actual words, however, they are precisely the same as in that copy. I see that a French Cardinal is mentioned in that part of the list which appears to belong to 1607 in exactly the same terms as in Lansd. Ms. 202. Would this be possible if the date 1607 was right?"

Strype *p. 3 under* 1607: „Westminster: the French Cardinal, living in Hans Hunter's house, hath to the number of forty servants". *Under* 1568 *there was mentioned* „Laur. Bourghinomus [*i. e.* Bourgignon], minister of the gospel, of the household of cardinal Castilion." *This is the cardinal de Chastillon who arrived in England in* 1568 *in September and died there in* 1571.

On the official lists of foreigners in 1567 *and* 68 *cf. also* Southerden Burn, Refugees *p. 6 f.* Schickler I 147 f.

1569 *March* 11. *Beza ad Episcopum Londinensem.* Epist. LVIII. *It is dated there* 8. Martii; *I, however, think it written on the* 11th *as the two other letters.*

— — — *Beza ad Cognatum.* Epist. LVII. *This is dated* 8. March, *but in the original, from which it is printed by* Hessels II *p.* 308—310, *it is dated March* 11.

— — — *Beza ad Corranum.* Epist. LIX. *This is not dated, but according to the document of March* 23. 1571 *it was dated March* 11.

Corro is not named in the first edition of Beza's Epistolae, Genevae 1573, *in the letters to Cousin and to the Bishop; and the letter to Corro has only the address* N, *but p.* 281 *there is printed by inadvertence:* tu, tu, Corrane. *In this passage the name is cancelled in the second edition, Geneva* 1575, *but the letter is addressed* Antonio Corrano, *and the name appears also in the other two letters, and consequently in the reprint contained in the third volume of Beza's* Tractatienes theologicae, *Geneva* 1582, *and in the so called* editio tertia, ab ipso auctore recognita, *of the Epistles,* Hanoviae 1597.

Part of Beza's letter to Corro, Hessels III 73—75. *The editor wrote to me on this fragment:* N° 125 *is written by an amanuensis (an ordinary scribe of the period), as is clear from the letter following* N° 125, *which is likewise written by an amanuensis, and signed by Beza.*

The fragment begins with istos contemplatores *which occurs in the ed.* 1573 *p.* 277 *below and* 1575 *p.* 254 *below. Differences of both ed. from the fragment (I only note the place of the first ed.):* 277 *2 a. i.* N: Cassiodoro | 278 *1 &c.: without* &c | *2* vel: Antoni uel | *3* N: Cassiodoro | *7* &: *without* & | *18* Tantum dico: Tantum tandem dico | *22* eiaculatus: iaculatus | *7 a. i.* vulgo: *without* vulgo | 279 *2* αὐτολέξει: αὐτολεξεὶ | *4* sunt ea: sunt, Corrane, ea | *5* tueris?: tutaris. | *6* N: Cognato | *15* superiore: superiori | *9 a. i.* enuntiatio: [enunciatio]. *So Hessels* | *8 a. i.* ista: istae | 280

---

a) *mentioned in the inscription of the document,* Strype *p.* 1.

7 N: Cognatus | *13 a. i.* tu: tu Antoni | *7 a. i.* agnoscerent: suspicerent | *5 a. i.* non dubito quin de multis: fortassis aliquid etiam | 280 *end* — 281 *1* Certe quod tam scurriliter fratribus illudis excusare non potes: *Wanting* | 281 *6* indi: in Deum. *Mistake of a copyist* | *10* commento *is the last word of the fragment. The* secunda editio, ab ipso auctore recognita 1575 *has some additional changementy while the first ed. coincides with the fragment. Second ed.* 255 *7 a. i.* N: Cognatus | 256 *15* angustiora non dici, de iis: de angustioribus non dici | *16—17* genus de specie,: speciem de indiuiduis: speciem de genere, indiuidua de specie | 257 *1. 2.* quod.. coeperis: te .. coepisse (*ed. 1:* cepisse) | *11* peroeciae: parochiae | *5 a. i.* Caspar: Gaspar.

From this letter to Corro it appears that Beza had received the following writings of Corro:
 Copy of Corro's Spanish letter to Reina dated Dec. 24. 63.
 A printed copy of Corro's Lettre au Roy. *In that letter occurs* C VIII *the passage:* Dieu estoit cette parole là, Beza's Epist. 1573 *p.* 278.
 A printed copy of Grindal's testimonial June 5. 67. Beza *p.* 274.
 Copy of Corro's letter to the Bishop July 15. 68. *There the comparison with the Spanish Inquisitors*, Beza 282.
 Corro to Beza Sept. 3. 68.
 Copy of Corro's apologetic codicillus *(see above p.* 117*). The passage* Beza 278*f.:* Si Minister non aliam linguam didicit quam sui pagi, ut vulgo dicunt *is alleged in the* Capita *of the end of* 1568, Confirm. 4, *from* article 51 *of that* codicillus. *Perhaps from the same what* Beza p. 255 *refers from* cujusdam scripti conclusione.
 In the same time Beza wrote to Grindal: Accepi his diebus ab Ant. Corrano literas minimum septenas, *and to Cousin:* Accepi hac hyeme septem quaedam scripta Ant. Corrani, eaque copiosissima. *To the same:* omnia ad rev. Dominum Londinensem misi, *and to this one:* Volui ea ipsa ad te mittere. *There are, however, still at* Geneva Grindal's testimonial *of* June 67, *a copy of* Corro's letter *of* July 15. 68 *to the Bishop and* Corro's letter to Beza Sept. 3. 68.
 Large Dutch analysis of Beza's letter to Corro by Sepp Naspor. III 170*f.*

1569 (1568) *March* 17. Sententia commissariorum contra Corranum. Schickler III 84*f. from the Geneva copy. Missing in the papers of the London Dutch.*

[1569] *Corro's dialogue on the epistle to the Romans, in Spanish and Latin. Written before the publication of his* Tableau de l'œuvre de Dieu.
 The Animadversiones *of autumn* 1569 *mention* § 2 *a work of Corro on the epistle to the Romans. In his* Apologia ad Italos *p.* 86 *and in the* Epitome *of it (see here below p.* 124*) he says that this dialogue on the epistle to the Romans is not yet printed, and in that Apology p.* 99 *he calls it his Spanish dialogue. It is mentioned also in* Giustiniano's *letter Febr.* 1570, *here above p.* 97: in epistolam ad Romanos dialogo Hispanico (quem tum etiam faciebat Latinum). *The Spanish as well as the Latin of that time are both missing. The Spanish has never been printed, the Latin, certainly after revision, was printed in* 1574.
 The letter of the London foreigners' churches March 23. 1571 *refers to* Animadversiones Jeronimi Jerliti *(cf. above p.* 32*f.)* ad dialogum Hispanicum in epistolam ad Romanos quem Ant. Corranus scripserat et parauerat prelo *(see above p.* 102). *Missing.*

a) In Luna's *edition of* Dialogos, 1619, *in* Dial. 6: no sabe leer sino en el libro de su aldea. Dr. R. Heiligbrodt *sent me parallels from* Caro y Cejudo, Refranes, 1792, *p.* 258, *and* Sbarbi, Florilegio, 1873, *p.* 184.

1569 f.   *Table of the work of God.*

1569 *July* 15. Tableau de l'œuure de Dieu 1569. *Gothic. At the bottom:* A. C. (*meaning* Antonius Corranus) 15/7 (*meaning* July 15.). *CAMBRIDGE University.*

It was printed at Norwich, *as is stated by Corro himself in his* Apologia ad Italos *and in its* Epitome, Bulletin 1901, *p.* 215, *and here above p.* 93. 94, *and likewise by his opponents in the letter accompanying the* Theses *and* Antitheses 1576.

Wiffen: „*From a* catalogue of C. J. Stewart, 11 King William St. West Strand: Tableau de l'Oeuure de Dieu 1569 . . . A. C. 15/7 . . . *evidently from the press of* Anth. de Solempne (*who introduced printing into* Norwich), *being in the same Dutch type as* «De CL Psalmen David, &c». *It is a broadside in double columns within a border, measuring to the outside* $14^{3}/_{4} \times 11^{1}/_{4}$ *inches, and consists of twenty-two heads or articles, unnumbered.*" *In fact there are only twenty articles; they are unnumbered, but the ms. Latin translation, made in autumn* 1569 *by Hieronymus, numbers them* 1—20. *The misstatement is to be explained in this way:* Stewart *who had got also an edition with* 24 *numbered articles (see here p.* 122*), observed that* n° 23 *and* 24 *were added after the* 4th *partition which ended the first edition. He concluded therefore that the first edition had 22 articles. But both art.* 14 *and* 16 *of the later edition are not found in the first.*

The edition of 1569 *has been reprinted in* 1897 *by* Hessels III *p.* 75—80.

— *Latin by the Italian minister Hieronymus,* additis animadversionibus a Ministro et Senioribus Ecclesiae Italicae. *Geneva ms. I have a copy of it. Cf. above p.* 44 *and below p.* 124. *Twenty numbered articles and* Partitio *and* Divisio 2. 3. 4.

— *Latin by Corro himself* — ut Dom. Episcopo Londin. traderem, *see* Apol. ad It. 86 *and* Epit. *above p.* 94.

The BRITISH MUS. has Lansdowne Ms. XCVI, n° 47. f. 108 6 *in handwriting:* Divinorvm opervm tabvla. *At the end* Auctore Antonio Corrano Hispallensj. *One folio patent. I have seen it. Also* Sepp *mentions it* Naspor. III 154. Hessels *p.* 991: *the headings over the columns* Articuli *or* Articles *are here omitted.* Wiffen: „*Not quite complete as compared with the French printed copy.*" *He means the second French, dedicated to* Mad. de Staffort, *which he had registered just before.* „*This ms. is probably the Latin translation which Grindal caused to be made by Jerome Ferlito the Italian minister.*"

1570 Wiffen: „Tableau de l'Œuure de Dieu. *Colophon:* A la tres noble Dame Madame de Staffort pour estrennes de ceste nouvelle Année 1570.   Antoyne du Corro.

A broad sheet printed in two columns, within a border.
BRITISH MUS., Lansdowne Ms XI 66. *I have seen it.*

Rahlenbeck, in the Bulletin du bibliophile belge, *t.* XV. 1859, *p.* 372 (*describing, no doubt, the same copy, although he quotes* Lansdowne, v. XII): Ce sont deux feuilles collées ensemble et formant un placard avec encadrement long de 65 centimètres et large de 30. Le texte est partagé en deux colonnes; la première porte en tête: Articles de l'Ancien Testament, la seconde: Articles du Nouveau Testament.

Hessels II p. 991: Arranged exactly like the foregoing Latin edition [of 1570], but everything in French. Instead of the dedication to queen Elizabeth, we read: „A la tresnoble Dame" *etc., see above.*

This French edition of 1570 *has been reprinted from the Brit. Mus. copy by* Sepp 1875, Naspor. III 155—165.

Differences between the first and the second edition of the Tableau de l'œuvre de Dieu, *as reprinted by* Hessels *and* Sepp. *I pass over the insignificant or unimportant variants.*

All the marginal references of the second to the holy scripture are wanting in the first which in the text refers thrice to Gen. 3 *and once respectively to* 1. Tim. 4. Ephes. 1, *twice to* Rom. 8. Matth. 25 (*the second time misprinted* 15). *In the first the* articles *are not numbered. Before art.* 1 *is added in the second ed.* Articles de l'Ancien Testament.

6 sans Dieu. *Second:* et ce toutefois sans la faveur de Dieu. *At the end is added:* mais le péché qui est œuvre de Sathan.

11 *at the end after the words that the serpent shall only bruise his heel, the second ed. adds:* Item l'éternel communiqua à l'homme régénéré la force et vertu de son S. Esprit, afin qu'il obtînt victoire contre l'ennemi.

12 s'ils croient et veulent obeir. *Second:* pourvu qu'ils croient et obéissent. *In the first* partition *to* Dextre *is added:* c'est à dire amitié de Dieu, *to* Senestre: c'est à dire inimitié de Dieu.

13 les enfans de Dieu. *Addition:* fortifié[s] par le saint Esprit.

14 *is addition.*

Addition before 16: Articles du Nouveau Testament.

16 *is addition.*

17 sa parolle eternelle faicte chair. *Second:* par. et. qui fut sainte chair. *At the end the words:* obtenu par son moyen, *are added.*

18 *Inscription:* sacrement et exemple aulx hommes. *Second:* Mystère ou sacrament aux hommes, pour engendrer foi en eux. *Also in the text of the art. instead of* sacrement, 1. Tim. 4: mystère ou sacrament. *In beginning of the article instead of* sa peruerse apprehension: son infidélité et perv. appr.

19 aiant destruit le peche. *Second:* et détruire le péché.

20 le peche du monde. *Scnd:* les péchés du monde, s'offrant pour redemption et satisfaction d'iceux. de sa perdition et malheur. *Scnd:* qui est cause de sa perd. et malh.

Third division. n'y veulent croire n'obeir. *Scnd:* n'y croient et obéissent.

21 et Roy eternel. *Scnd:* (qui avoit déjà accompli l'office de Rédempteur), le constituant Roy éternel.

After celeste, *the words* dextre et Paradis *are cancelled in the scnd.*

After chef *the scnd adds:* et avocat éternel.

22 visiblement *is added,* Soufflement *cancelled. Ended thus:* gouuernant (*scd adds:* et soulageant) leurs consciences, il les enseignat (*scd adds* et confirmât) en toute verité, et par le droit chemin (*scd:* en t. verité, par la prédication de sa parole et administration du Saint Baptême et de la Sainte Cène, qui sont comme sceaux de notre régénération. Et que par tels moyens) les menat a la vie eternelle, a la-

quelle ils estoient predestinez et esleuz (sed: étoient élus) des le commencement, Ephes. 1. *(sed has* Eph. 1. *in the margin with other references).*
23 *and* 24 *are addition of the send.*

1570 Diuinorum operum Tabula.

At the end of the second column:

Serenissimæ Elizabethæ, Angliæ, Franciæ, Hiberniæ Reginæ: non tam Regii fastigij | amplitudine, quam praestantissinis moribus insigni, literarum, multarumq3 lingua- | rum scientia, & alijs elegantissimis animi corporisq3 dotibus ad miraculum vsq3 orna- | tissimae, Antonius Corranus Hispallensis, in signum memoriamq3 grati animi, ob ho- | spitalitatem in hoc Regno acceptam, quum in Angliam, propter Euangelicæ veritatis | professionem extorris appulisset, humanissimeq3 esset exceptus: offert hanc | Tabulam, pro xeniolo huius noui Anni. 1570. |

Broadside within borders on two conglutinated sheets in two columns under the headings: Articuli veteris Testamenti *and* Articuli noui Testamenti.

CAMBRIDGE University.

Wiffen: „Sold 1862 at Putticks to C. J. Stewart who writes in his catalogue: The Latin is a similar broadside, but executed on two separate sheets of paper, as is obvious from the watermarks: it is also within a border, measuring $21^5/_8 \times 13^5/_8$. It has two additional heads, or twenty four in all, and numbered, with the scriptural authorities or texts in the margins, which the French [*of* 1569] has not, and at the end the Dedication to Elizabeth... These Tables [*French and Latin*] are folded in two, and placed loose, but secured between pieces of vellum to preserve them from friction, in a morocco case, which may be placed as a book on the shelves of a library. The price is £ 21."

Wood, Ath. I 252: Tabulae divinorum operum de humani generis creatione — Printed 1574 &c. &c. oct. Hessels *p.* 991 *remarks on* 1574: There is no trace of this edition.

1584 Tabvla divi- | norvm ope- | rvm, | in qva | De Hvmani Generis | creatione ac restauratione ex sa- | cris voluminibus aphoris- | mi continentur: | Antonij Corrani Hispal. operâ | collecti. | Beati pacifici, quoniam filij | Dei vocabuntur. | Matth. 5. | *[Ornament]* | Excvsvm Londini, | Anno 1584. | *Octavo.*

After this title-leaf the dedication on A. ij.:

Serenissimae Elizabethae, *and so on just as in* 1570, *but ending* exceptus: hanc divinorum operum Tabulam offerebat.

A. ij. *verso quotation from* Joan. 3.

A. iii: Divinorvm opervm Tabvla. 1 Creatio mundi ...

[*B VII*] Finis Tabvlae. *Verso and B VIII* Gratiarum actio pro beneficio creationis & restaurationis humanæ naturæ per Christum.

Therein: victimam piacularem eum esse voluit; ut humana natura servaretur, atque diffidentiae peccatum (omnium criminum et scelerum fundamentum) e mortalium animis tolleretur.

. . hoc obnixe petimus, ut indies magis ac magis nos tibi devincias, consubstantiali tuo sermone (qui Christus est) edoceas, sempiterno tuo spiritu, afflatu, atque energetico impulsu ad fidem obedientem, atque obedientiam fidelem indesinenter excitare nostram secordiam digneris ...

B VIII verso: Finis.

BERN City. I have got a ms copy, made by my wife, page for page, line for line, literally.

I could not compare this edition with the former Latin one, but I found no essential difference from the second French which was contemporaneous to the first Latin.

„Tabulæ Diuinorum operum, in qua de humani generi *[sic]* creatione & restauratione ex sacris voluminibus aphorismi continentur. Londini. 1588. V. in 8."

From Collectio in vnvm corpvs, omnivm librorvm... qui in nundinis Francofurtensibus ab anno 1564. vsque ad nundinas Autumnales anni 1592... venales extiterunt: desumpta ex omnibus Catalogis VVillerianis... Francofvrti. Ex officina Typographica Nicolai Bassæi. M. D. XCII. *First part (Hebreæ, Greek, Latin), p.* 14. *The author's name is to be repeated from the foregoing article (below here p.* 130 Romans 1588): Antonii Corrani. *The notice* 1588. V. *means (cf. also my remark* Sp. Rf. II *p.* 241) *Willer's vernal catalogue of* 1588 *(a copy in Mainz city library) where fol.* A. 3 *is registered:* 1584. Tabula diuinorum operum, in qua de humani generis creatione & restauratione ex sacris voluminibus aphorismi continentur. Antonij Corrani Hispal. operâ collecti, excusum Londini, oct. Dr. M. Spirgatis (*author of the plentiful articles on* Leipziger Messkataloge *and on* Englische Litteratur auf der Frankfurter Messe *in* Dziatzko's Sammlung bibliothekswissenschaftlicher Arbeiten, Leipzig 1901. 1902) *informed me that the catalogues* of the Augsburg firm Hans Görg Portenbach *and* Tobias Lutz, *have in the list of that vernal fair fol.* A 2ᵃ *the title:* Tabula Diuinorum operum in qua de humani generis creatione ac restauratione ex sacris voluminibus aphorismi continentur: Antonii Corrani opera collecti. Londini in 8°. 1584.

Draudius, Bibliotheca classica 1611 *p.* 155 *gives the same as the* Collectio Bassæi, *only* generis *and without* V.

Corro in the preface to the Articuli fidei *appended to the* Dialogus theologicus 1574 *fol.* 96: Londini scripsi tabulas de divinis operibus quae excusae sunt quatuor linguis Latina, Gallica, Germanica et Anglicana. Germanica *means Dutch. In the English translation* 1575: I wrote at London certayne tables concerning God's works, which were printed in four languages Latin French Dutch and English. Strype. Parker 271: This learned man wrote also certain Tables concerning the Works of God, which appeared abroad in Four Languages, Latin, French, Dutch, and English. abroad *means: published.*

Joris Wijbo Sylvanus *on Corro's* Table *which soon after the publication was read to him from a Dutch translation.* Sepp, Naspor. III 166*f, according to a later letter of* Sylvanus, *printed in the* Bijdragen tot de Oudheidk. en Gesch. van Zeeuwsch Vlaanderen, door Janken en Van Dale II 317*f. A Dutch translation of the* Tableau *and of the* Animadversiones Consistorii Ital. *circulated in* Febr. 1570, *see* Giustiniano's *letter to the bishop, above p.* 98.

Wood, Ath. I 252: „Translated also into English, under the Title of Tables of God's Works, &."

1569 *Censures of a French minister at Norwich on Corro's* Tableau de l'œuvre de Dieu. *Cf. above p.* 93. *Missing.*

1569 *Corro answered in French* prolixo satis dialogo, *as he says in the* Apologia ad Italos *Dec.* 1569 *p.* 88. *It was before the* Animadversiones *of autumn* 1569 *were given to him, see extract from the* Epitome *of Dec.* 1569 *above p.* 93. *This French dialogue was probably on the whole the same as the Spanish dialogue on the epistle to the Romans, cf. above p.* 119. *Missing.*

— *Aug.* 6. Epitome orationis habitae ab A. Corrano in Consistorio Londinogallicae ecclesiae.

— — 18. Responsio Consistorii ad scriptum Corrani.

— — 24. Responsum Corrani.

— *Sept.* 8. Ultima Responsio Consistorii.

These four pieces are printed in the Acta 1571, *reprinted above p.* 83*f.*

— *[Sept.]* Cecil to Grindal. *Missing.*

— *Sept.* 20. Grindal's answer to Cecil. *English. Used by* Strype, Grindal 147—8, *without noting the provenience. From* Lansdowne Ms. 11 n° 65 *printed in the* Grindal Remains *p.* 309*f.*

— *[probably not later than Oct.]. The same to the same. The report promised in the letter of* Sept. 20. *Printed above here p.* 89*f. from* Lansdowne ms. *Used by* Strype, Grindal 147—9 (*also* Annals I 237). *He does not say where he has seen it.*

Rahlenbeck, Bulletin du bibliophile belge, t. XV. 1859, *p.* 372 *translated in French a passage on the* Apology *from* „Musée brit., Burghley's Papers, II". (*Instead of* II *read* 11?)

— *Nov.* 7. Episcopus Cusino. Hessels II n° 97, *p.* 328—9.

— — 12. Cusinus Episcopo. Hessels II n° 98, *p.* 331.

— — 22. The London French consistory to the Bishop. *French. Copy.* Hessels III *p.* 95—98.

— *[autumn].* Tabula de opere Dei translata de Gallico quam proxime fieri potunt et tanquam ad verbum, nuper primo scripta et edita ab Antonio Corano, nunc autem examinata, additis in eam brevibus animadversionibus a Ministro et senioribus Ecclesiae Italicae Londinensis. *Ms copy among the Corro papers at Geneva; I have got a copy of the Geneva copy. Translator and author was the Italian minister* Hieronymus, *see* Grindal's *letter Sept.* 20. 69 *and the letter of* the foreign churches at London 1576, Sepp, Polem. *p.* 26:

Almost entirely repeated in the following Apologia.

— *Dec.* 8. Apologia ad Italos, *as we may call it. Ms. in* Geneva, „58 feuillets petit fol." *I have got it copied.*

A passage from it with French translation in Bulletin 1901 *p.* 215—6.

Some more extracts above here p. 91*f.*

— — Responsio Corrani ad Animadversiones quorundam in Tabulum divinorum operum. *Ms. in Geneva; copy in my possession.*

Magni responsi epitome, *as it is called in that letter of the three foreign churches,* Sepp *l. c., viz. an abridgment of the* Apologia *of Dec.* 8.

An extract from it with French translation in Bulletin 1901, *p.* 214—5. *More extracts above here p.* 93*f.*

Another Epitome *by* Lanius, *see* Sepp. ib. *Missing.*

1570 *[Febr.]* Quare Corrano interdicta Cena in Ecclesia Italica. *Signed* Justinianus Consistorii nomine. *Geneva ms. Printed above p.* 96*f.*

1570 [*Febr.*] *Italica Ecclesia ad Episcopum.* Signed Justinianus nomine Consistorii *Geneva ms. Printed above p.* 97 f.

[— *spring*] Ecclesiae Italicae responsio ad prolixam Apologiam Corrani. *Geneva ms.; I have a copy.*

[— *about Febr.?*] Monas theologica. *Printed* Hessels III *p.* 99—101 *with the date* [1570?] *which he derived from the letter of* de Changy *of Febr.* 18. 1571. *Hessels wrote to me of this* Monas: it is a manuscript, written by an ordinary scribe of the time. *The ministers of the foreign churches of London speak of the* Monas *in their letter* of March 23. 1571, *above here p.* 102, *and again in* 1576, Sepp, Polem. *p.* 26. *It is evident that in the* Theses *of* 1576 *the numbers* 4—7. 9. 10. 54 *are taken from the* Monas; *there are, however, some differences from* Hessels' *edition.*

— *about Febr. ?* Corro to Longastre. *See* de Changy's *letter. Missing.*

— *spring.* Coran Antonius *among the* Auctores primae Classis *p.* 58 *of the* Appendix *to the Tridentine* Index prohibitorum, Antverpiae 1570. *The king's mandatum to compose such an* Appendix *was given in September* 1569 (*p.* 53); *his* Edictum (*printed separately, the title giving* 1570) *on the observation of* Index *and* Appendix *is dated February* 15. 1569 *which means* 1570 *new style; the* Privilege (*joined to the edict) for the printer* Chr. Plantin *has the date Febr.* 16. 1569. *The duke of Alba's letter April* 28. 1570 (Sepp, Verboden lectuur 159 f.) *shows that* Index *and* Appendix *had been published already.*

In the Index Sandoval y Rojas, Palermo *reprint* 1628, Prohib. *p.* 8 Antonius Corranus *in the* Prima classis auctorum damnatorum, quorum opera edita, et edenda prohibentur.

— [*summer*]. *Corro's* Praefatio *to the* Acta Consistorii. *Printed with the* Acta 1571, *reprinted above p.* 98.

— *Aug.* 16. *The Cardinal de Chastillon to the Ministers and Elders of the Dutch and Walloon Churches at London.* Schin XVj^e D'aoust. *French.* Recepta le 17^e. Hessels III *p.* 108 (*who takes* XVj^e *for* 15th).

— *Aug.* Corro to Villiers. *See* Franciotto's *letter of Jan.* 71. *Missing.*

— *Record on the institution of a colloquy between Corro and his opponents on Corro's* Tableau;

— *Aug.* 30. *the submission of Corro and the others to the decision to be given by a commission of French Ministers;*

— *Sept.* 4. *the decision;*

— — 5. *the* extrait de la dispute *and the sentence, both read to Corro;*

— — *Corro's refuse to subscribe. All this in French in Cousin's hand.* Hessels III *p.* 108—114.

The extensive report in Latin on the dispute, ib. p. 114—123.

— *Dec.* 31. Cousin to Beze. *Missing.*

1571 *Jan.* 8. *The Ministers and Elders of the three foreign Churches resolve to give a declaration of the Corro affair to their people. French. Cousin's hand.* Hessels III *p.* 114.

— — 18. *Corro to Henry, third Earl of Huntingdon. Latin. Printed* „*from what seemed to be a transcript*". Hessels III *p.* 130—133.

— [—] *Cousin's short notice on this letter.* Hessels III *p.* 114.

— [—] Annotationes in literas Corrani ad comitem Hungtintonianum. *Handwriting of Cousin.* Hessels III *p.* 133—136.

1571 *Jan. 27. Captain Franchiotto* to the *Earl of Huntingdon. French.* Hessels III *p.* 137—8.

— *Febr.* 14. *Beza's answer to Cousin's letter of Dec.* 31. 1570. Hessels II *p.* 371—2.

— 18. *De Changy [minister] to [the minister Jean] Baptiste [Aurelius] at London. French.* Hessels III *p.* 139. *He sends a copy of the letter which Corro wrote about a year ago to Mr. de Longastre to whom he sent the* tableau *which has the inscription* Monas theologica, *of which de Changy had sent before* (par cy devant) *a copy to Cousin.*

— *March* 1. PQ suo GR. *In* Acta 1571. *Reprinted above p.* 99 *f.*

— — Acta consistorii | ecclesiæ Londinogalli- | cæ, cvm responso Anto- | nii Corrani. | Ex qvorvm lectione facile | qvivis intelligere poterit sta- | tum controuersiæ inter Ioannem Cusinum, eiusdem | Ecclesiæ Ministrum, & Antonium Corra- | num, Hispanorum peregrinorum | Concionatorem. | Pavlina admonitio. | Si Spiritu agimini, non estis sub lege. Sunt autem manifesta carnis | opera, videlicet, adulterium, stuprum, impuritas, falacitas, deastro- | rum cultus, veneficium, inimicitiæ, lis, æmulationes, iracundiæ, con- | tentiones, seditiones, sectæ, inuidiæ, ebrietates, comessationes, & his | similia, quæ qui faciunt (hoc vobis prædico, quemadmodum iam | prædixi) ij diuinum regnum non obtinebunt. At Spiritus fructus | est charitas, alacritas, pax, clementia, benignitas, bonitas, fides, le- | nitas, continentia. Contra talia non est lex. Qui sunt autem Christi, | ij carnem vnà cum libidinibus & cupiditatibus crucifixerunt. Si | Spiritu viuimus, etiam Spiritu gradiamur, ne simus gloriosi, inui- | cem prouocantes, inuicem inuidentes. Fratres, si quis aliquo de- | licto anticipatus fuerit, uos eum, qui spirituales estis, reficite cum | animi comitate, aspicientes vos ipsos, ne vos quoque tentemini. | Alij aliorum onera ferte, atque ita Christi lege perfungimini. | Nam si quis sibi videtur esse aliquid, cùm nihil sit, ipse | se animo fallit. Exploret autem suum quisque | opus, ita demùm in seipso tantùm quod glo- | rietur habebit, non in altero. Nam | suum quisque feret onus. | Galat. 5. & 6. | Anno M.D.LXXI. |

Text beginning on the back of the title-leaf. Then A 2, A 3, A 4, B, B 2, B 3. *[B 4] verso blank. Second series* A *to* A 5 *and [A 6]. No paging. Total 14 leaves.*

MADRID National from Usóz. My title-copy follows the tracing among Wiffen's *papers. A ms. copy of the whole pamphlet has been made for me at Madrid (the copyist has, however, made some mistakes, as the comparison with the tracing shows).*

The translation of the Bible-verses on the title is Castellio's; only 5, 22 alacritas *is new, while Cast. and Vulg. have* gaudium. 5, 21 homicidia *has been left out.*

Contents:
- [1.] Præfatio. *A letter of Corro to a friend.* Londini 1570. *Fol. A verso.*
- [2.] Summa.. orationis.. habitæ ab Ant. Corrano in Consistorio Londinogall. Ecclesiæ 6. Aug. 1569. A 2.
- [3.] Responsio Consistorii. Lond. 18. Aug. 1569. A 2 *verso.* A 3 *recto.*
- [4.] Responsum Corrani. Lond. 24. Aug. 1569. A 3 *verso to* B 3 *recto.*
- [5.] Ultima responsio Consistorii. 8. Sept. 1509. B 3 *recto.*
- [6] *Testimonium episcopi Londin. pro Corrano.* 5. Junii 1567. B 3 *verso.*
- [7.] *The same judgment in French.* B 4 *recto.*
- [8.] F. Q. suo G. R. Lond. 1. Mart. 1571. A *to* A 2 *recto.*

The writer says: the papers contained in this pamphlet typis mandanda curavi in Germania.

- [9.] Corrani Epistola ad Cassiodorum, missa ex Aquitania A. 1563. A 2 *verso to* A 4 *verso.*
- [10.] *The Spanish original of the same letter dated* Teobon 24. Dez. 1563. A 4 *verso to* A 6 *verso.*

Hessels *p.* 991 *f.*: „This work is mentioned in the List of Corranus' works drawn up by Benj. B. Wiffen found in Bliss' copy of Wood's Athenae Oxonienses, preserved in the Bodleian Library. Wiffen refers in the margin of his List to „L. de U. R." which I do not know how to explain [*it means* Luis de Usóz i Rio], and to Grindal's Remains, where the work is mentioned on p. 313. Nicholson, the Editor of the Remains (Parker Society, 1843), informs us on p. XX that Mr. C. J. Stewart, bookseller, London, possessed a copy of this work, and it is, indeed, mentioned on p. 128 (No. 2401) of the latter's Catalogue of 1845, part 1, of which a copy is preserved in the Bodleian Library." *Among Wiffen's papers I found adjoined to the title-tracing of these* Acta *some printed lines from an antiquarian's catalogue containing n°* 2401 Corrani (Acta Consistorii &c.). Price 2 l. 2 s.

In the margin is written: comprar este, *and by the same hand underneath the tracing:* 4 hojas impresas, en este tamaño: o sea 28 pajinas. *It is clear: Wiffen bought n°* 2401 *by order of Usóz, and Usóz sent him the tracing. It follows that the Madrid copy is the only one that has hitherto appeared.*

The numbers 1—5. 8. 10. *are reprinted above p.* 98 *f.*

Some passages from the Acta *in* Menendez Pelayo II 486—7.

1571 *March* 19. Episcopus Cicestrensis ministris Ecclesiae Gallicanae atque Italicae.

— — 20. *Responsum ministrorum.*

— — 23. Ministri Ecclesiarum peregrinarum quae sunt Londini de doctrina et moribus Corrani. *Geneva mss. of these three papers, printed above p.* 100 *f.*

The Bishop had asked only the French and the Italian. Had the Dutch volunteered to ally themselves to the brethren?

1571 *April* 2.—11. *the National Synod at La Rochelle on Corro.* Aymon *p.* 99. Quick *p.* 91.

— — 6. *Cousin to Bexe.* Hessels II *n°* 107. *The passage relating to Corro remains doubtful, as the draft, a facsimile of which accompanies this volume, cannot be read completely.*

— *July* 3. Scriptum allatum ad aedes Ioannis Cousin Die Martis 3° Juli 1571. „*These two lines are in the handwriting of Cousin. Corran himself has merely signed the document which is not in his handwriting.*" Hessels III *p.* 144—6.

1571 [*July*]. *Corro lecturer in the Temples. He had not yet joined a* coetus *when he wrote the declaration received on July* 3. *by* Cousin. *In the dedication, signed May* 31. 1574, *of his dialogue on the epistle to the Romans Corro says that he was called by the Templars* integrum triennium *before. The Bishop must have given his consent after having approved of Corro's declaration which thereupon was certainly sent without delay to Cousin who received it on July* 3.

1572 *Letter of the ministers in England to the National Synod at Nimes. Mentioned in the protocol of the Synod. Missing.*

— *May* 6.—8. *National Synod at Nimes on Corro.* Aymon *p.* 122. 124. Quick *p.* 111. 113. *That* Lozain, Cozain, Cozin *in* Aymon's *and* Quick's *texts of the Synods of* 1571 *and* 1572 *mean* Corranus, *has been observed by* Bernus, Bulletin 1901 *p.* 326 *f. In* 1571 Aymon *has* doctrine *where* Quick *has* Table. *Mr.* N. Weiss *in answer to my questions on the readings of the mss. of the* Bibliothèque du Protestantisme français, *containing protocols of the national synods, says that in* 1571 *ms. n° 23 writes* Coran *and* la table du dit Coran, *and another ms. twice* Coranus *and in an injured place the initial* t *of* table, *and that in* 1572 n° 23 *has* Coran *and to send to England* les livres de Coran *where* Aymon *writes* le livre de Cozin *and* Quick Cozin's Book.

— [*May*]. *The answer to the ministers in England which Saules was asked by the Synod to write. Missing.*

1574 foll. **Commentary on Paul's epistle to the Romans.**
Cf. p. 119. 124.

1574 Dialogvs theologicvs. | Qvo epistola | divi Pavli apostoli ad | Romanos explanatvr. | Ex prælectionibus Antonij | Corrani Hispalensis, sacræ theolo- | giæ professoris, collectus, | & concinnatus. | *[Ornament.]* | Psal. 122. | ⁋ Jehoua, libera animam meam à labijs falsitatis, | à lingua doli. Quid dabit tibi, aut quid ad- | det tibi lingua doli? sagitta robusti viri acutæ | cum carbonibus iuniperorum. | ⁋ Londini Pridie calendas | Iunij, excudebat prælum Thomæ | Purfœtij ad Lucretiæ | symbolum. | ⁋ Cum Priuilegio. 1574. |

On the back of the title it is noted that there are added articuli orthodoxae fidei *and a* tabella *giving a summary of Paul's epistle. The title-leaf is part of a layer of four leaves. On the second leaf begins Corro's epistle* Generosis viris vtrivsque Templi, *which is continued on the second likewise fourfold layer and ends, dated* pridie Cal. Junij. 1574, *on the second leaf of the third layer. This one is signed* A. *On* A 3 *and* [4] Argvmentvm generale in omnes Epistolas Apostolicas, *on the two following leaves* Argvmentvm Epistolæ Pauli Apostoli ad Romanos, ex libris Athanasij Episcopi Alexandrini.

After these 14 *unnumbered leaves (which must have been printed last of all) commences the* Dialogvs *on* B. 1; Finis *fol.* 95. *The numeration of the leaves begins only with* N. 1, *which is numbered* 89. Articuli fidei orthodoxæ *fol.* 96—107. *The last leaf which would be* 108 *has on the verso* Purfoet's *device,* Lucretia killing herself, *and* Excusum Londini apud | Thomam Purfœtum. Anno | M. D. LXXIIII.

The recto of this leaf is blank in Merck's copy, but has Errata *in the Bodleian copy.* B *till* O *are octavo,* P *comprises the last four leaves. Besides a folding table in folio:* Breuis dispositio illius Epistolæ.

MERCK's copy is the remarkable one on which Sepp, Mededeel. 65 f. *and* Studiën 221 f. *BODLEIAN. According to* Hessels p. 992 *also in CAMBRIDGE University and in Trinity College there.*

On July 7. 1574. Corro sent a copy to Henry Bullinger *and wrote:* optarem ut alius aliquis typographus dialogum hunc typis exprimeret, et exemplaria ad summum trecenta, quae hic depravatissime excusa sunt, supprimerentur. *And further on:* si quid est quod tibi minus arrideat in hoc libello, pro tuo arbitrio et insigni prudentia corrigas, et correctum typis tradi jubeas. Quod si feceris, majorem in modum me meumque obsequium tibi perpetuo devincies. *Bullinger fell dangerously ill shortly after receiving this letter and died the next year; so it is not surprising that Corro's wish was not fulfilled.*

Excerpts in Latin, mostly from the dedication, by Sepp, Mededeel. 66—73.

1575 A theo- | logical dia- | logve. | Wherin the Epistle of S. Paul the | Apostle to the Romanes is | expounded. | Gathered and set together | out of the Readings of Anto- | nie Corranus of Siuille, pro- | fessor of Diuinitie. | Psalm 122. | Lorde deliuer my soule from false lippes | and a deceiptfull tung. What shall he | giue thee, or what shal he put vnto thee | thou deceiptfull tung? The sharpe ar- | rowes of a strong man, with the coles | of Juniper. | Imprinted at London | by Thomas Purfoote, dwelling | in Paules Churchyarde at the | signe of the Lucrece. | An. 1575. | *Title in a frame.*

Fol. 139ᵇ *to* 154ᵇ: The articles of the Catholike fayth which Anthonie Coranus Spaniarde Student of Diuinitie professeth, and alwayes hath professed: Nowe set out in Print for their sakes which have not bene present at his Readings.

After the title dedication to the Earl of Leicester, Latin and English. Epistle to the Templars, May 31. 74. *Two arguments. Title-leaf, 26 leaves epistles and arguments. The work* 155 *numbered leaves, small octavo. Gothic and Latin. In the title Roman, Italic, Gothic.*

BRITISH MUS. BODLEIAN. CAMBRIDGE Univ.

Menendez Pelayo II 489: Exposition of the Epistle to the Romans. Heydelbergae, 1575. (En. 8°; Biblioteca de Cambridge.) *I cannot verify this strange notice, after which follows immediately as a new item:* A Theological dialogue ... London, by Th. Purfoot, 1575. (Bodleiana.)

Wood, Ath. I 252 *after the* Dialogus theologicus, Lond. 1574: „Printed in English there, 1579. oct." 1579 *is probably a misprint for* 1575.

Strype, Parker 271, *telling that Corro sent to the Archbishop two French books he had published (the two Antwerp publications, cf. above p.* 36, *says:* One of these books was a confession of his faith: which he afterward set forth in Latin and English. Strype *means the* Articuli fidei *appended to the* Dialogus theologicus *and this English translation of them.*

Biblioth. Wiffen. III.

1581 Epistola beati | Pavli apostoli ad | Romanos, e Graeco in La- | tinum μεταφραςικῶς versa, & in Dialogi | formam redacta, vt instar Christia- | næ Catecheseως iuuentuti | esse possit. | Per Ant. Corranum Hispalensem, | Theologiæ Professorem. | *Device: anchor surrounded by an olive wreath and the words:* Anchora spei. | Londini, | Excudebat Thomas Vautrollerius | Typographus. | 1581. |

From Wiffen's tracing.

Hessels *p.* 993: „Collation $a^8 b^4$, 12 leaves, preliminary matter; $ABCD^8 E^6$, 38 leaves, together 50 leaves, 8°.

.. dedicated: «Ornatissimis Viris, D. Vicecancellario, D. Præsidibus Collegiorum, atque Præfectis Aularum Academiæ Oxoniensis», which dedication is dated: «Oxonio. Calendis. Aprilis anno à Christo nato 1581. Vestræ academiæ inseruire paratissimus: Antonius Corranus.» After this follows an Epistle of Corranus «iuventuti Oxoniensis Academiæ.»

Copy in Bodleian library (pressmark: Z. 568. Th.); in York Cath[1] library, and (slightly imperfect) in Trinity College Library, Cambridge (pressmark VI[d]. 2. 9)."

Wiffen *notes:* „Sm. 8 vo. YORK minster. USOZ i Rio." *A correspondent of Wiffen remarks of the copy at York Minster:* At the end of the Epistle to the students: Autoris Symbolum τὰ παθήματα μαθήματα. The Dialogue occupies 73 pages. *No doubt from Usoz's copy,* Menendez Pelayo II 489: 73 páginas. *This number would correspond to the 38 leaves, if the last three pages are blank.*

1587 Dialogvs | in epistolam | d. Pavli ad | Romanos, | Antonio Corrano Hisp. | Hisp. [*twice* Hisp.] in academia Oxonien- | si Professore, Theologo, | autore. | *A device: a nude Fortuna erect on an overturned wheel; different from the representation in Reina's S. John and S. Mathew from the same press, and without the words there, see above vol.* II *p.* 301. | Francofvrti, | Ex Officina Typographica | Nicolai Bassæi. | $\overline{C\mid\mathfrak{I}.\mid\mathfrak{I}}$.LXXXVII. |

A 2 *and* 3 Argvmentvm generale in omnes epistolas Apostolicas. A 4 — [6] Argvmentvm epistolae Pavli apostoli, ad Romanos, ex libris Athanasij Episcopi Alexandrini. [A 7] *and* [8] *blank.* P. 1—199 Dialogvs. *P.* 199 *again* Francofvrti, Ex Officina Typographica Nicolai Bassæi. $\overline{C\mid\mathfrak{I}.\mid\mathfrak{I}.\text{LXXXVII}}$. Octavo.

FRANKFORT a. M., City. BASLE, Public. LEIDEN, Univ. BODLEIAN.

The Frankfort copy served for my description. Wiffen noted in the margin of his title-tracing: Title Argument ded. to the reader 14 leaves. The work paged 1 to 199.

„Antonii Corrani Dialogus in Epistolam D. Pauli ad Romanos. Francof. apud Nicol. Bassæum. 1588. V. in 8." *From the* Collectio *in vnvm corpus by the same Nic. Bassæus* 1592 (*see above here p.* 123), *p.* 13. *This edition is the only one catalogued in the* Collectio, *and in* Draudius, Bibliotheca classica 1611 *p.* 145 *(without* V).

1588 V. *means* Willer's *vernal catalogue of* 1588, *where fol.* A 3: 1887. Dialogus in epistolam D. Pauli ad Romanos, Antonio Corrano Hisp. Hisp. in Academia Oxonienis Professore, Theologo Authore. Francofurti apud Nicolaum Bassæum, oct.

Wiffen: Perhaps there is a mistake in the date and that this is the same edition as 1587.

That the University-library of Leiden possesses an edition of MDLXXXVIII, *as is said by* Menendez Pelayo II 489, *is an error. In the Leiden library there is only one edition of this* Dialogus, *that of* 1587, *as the librarian informed me in* 1901.

Extracts in Latin from the Leiden copy of 1587 *in* Sepp's Naspor. III 184 f.

The edition of 1587 *is not simply a reprint of the edition of* 1574. *I found many small differences: omissions, transpositions, changes, additions, not affecting the sense, as far as I observed during a rapid perusal. It is notable that* V 12 f. *while corresponding to* τοῦ ἑνὸς ἀνθρώπου Ἰησοῦ Χριστοῦ 1574 *is said:* sic etiam homo Christus, 1587 *has:* sic etiam consubstantialis ille atque coaeternalis Dei λόγος, seu verbum Dei, factus homo Christus. *But also* 1574: VII 24: nisi adsit ipse Christus coeternalis Dei sermo qui suo spiritu nos armet *and* X 3: Fidei autem subiectum quod fides intuetur, coeternalis & coessentialis Dei filius est, factus caro. *(I have not the corresponding passages of* 1587.*) —* VI 8 Tantis (1574 adeo, 1587 nempe) praeteritorum peccatorum illecebris deliniti sumus ac (1574 *at*) inescati, 1587 *adds:* ut malimus falsa dogmata comminisci quam vitiositati nostrae bellum indicere.

1613 A Dialogue vpon the whole epistl[e] of Saint Paule to the Romans.

Licensed, April 13. 1613, *by the London Stationers to* William Jaggard (*Arber* 3, 519). *Probably Corro's work. Reprint of the translation of* 1575 *or a new one?*

1618 *From* Sepp, Studiën 226 f.:

justificatio fidei, Christianae, Antiquae, Catholicae et Orthodoxae. Op Dutz, proevesteen en oprechte wechtschale, van het goede olde, algemene Christlicke gelove: van Godt geschapen tot salicheit. Tegens het quade nye historische Montgelove, doer ouruwige Menschen erdichtet. By Vrage ende Antwort doer einen vornemen Godtsaligen man, voer 38 jaer in groot Britannien int Papyr gestelt. Ende nu onder de dicke Duisternisse van verscheiden strydige Secten ende opinien, wth leve der eentfoldige Warheit, weder ant Licht uthgegeven. Doer einen Olden mede Patriot, ende Leeffhebber van de goede Rust ende Vrede, van de Kercke ende gemene beste, vant hoch gesegende algemeene verenichde Vaderlandt. *Follow passages from* Jeremiae 6 *and* 1 Joan 4. Gedruckt tot Groningen. By David Lip van Augspurch. Boeckdrucker, in 't jaer onses Heeren, 1618.

Small 4 to. *After the editor's dedication,* epistola beati Pauli Apostoli ad Romanos, in dialogi formam, perspicuitatis ergo, redacta, ut instar Christianae Catecheseως juventuti esse possit. Interloquutores: discipulus, praeceptor. *With the letter* juventuti Oxoniensis Academiae.

According to Sepp *p.* 222 *a copy of the book is in HAGUE Royal: another in the library of the Remonstrant church at AMSTERDAM which was already denoted in its printed Catalogue* 1866.

The editor was Doede van Answeer, fidei reformatae apud Groninganos antistes gravissimus, *as a ms. notice in a copy (at present in Merck's possession) of Corros* Dialogus *of* 1574 *says. See* Sepp Mededeel. 73, Studien 221. Answeer *says, the book was* 38 *years ago* int Papyr gestelt. *The* 38th *year ended* April 1. 1619, *counting from the date of Corro's dedication of* 1581. *In that edition Corro said, as from the edition of* 1618 *is repeated by* Sepp, Studiën 228 *(I add the years in brackets):* ego etiam ante annos octo in gratiam meorum auditorum, qui in Novo

Templo Londinensi hujus epistolae explanationem a me audiverunt, paraphrasticum Dialogum conscripsi [1573] ac Latino sermone [1574] et Anglicano [1575] in lucem emisi. Sepp *gives p.* 229 *some passages from Corro's epistle to the youth of Oxford.*

Uytenbogaert, Kerkel. hist. 1646, *p.* 159: *That Corro had other opinions on predestination than Calvin and Beza, was clear* uyt seecker Corrani boeck dat ick voor veele jaren hebbe gesien over Corinth. 9. 10. ende 11. Capittelen des Briefs Pauli aen de Romeynen, hoewel ick de passagien daer uyt niet verhalen en kan, om dat ick dat boeck nu niet weet te bekomen. *The text is corrupt;* Corinth. *(without first or second) is out of place here. The author must mean Corro's exposition of Rom.* 9. 10. *and* 11.

Sepp, Nasp. III 190: Aan welk geschrift van Corranus Uyttenbogaert denkt, sprekende „van een boeck Corrani dat ick voor vele jaren hebbe gesien over Cor. 9 en 10 en de 11ᵉ Capit. des Briefs Pauli aan de Romeinen", kan ik niet bepalen.

Sepp has written en de *instead of* ende (= en, *and*), *but* Capittelen *is plural.*

[1574] Corro to Henric Bullinger July 7. 74: Specimen hujus malignitatis perspicies in folio quodam hic Latino et Anglicano sermone excuso cum censuris cujusdam Aristarchi. *This specimen is missing.*

1574 July 7. Corranus Henrico Bullinger. Londino nonis Julii 1574. In The Zurich letters (second series) ... translated ... and edited for the Parker society by ... Hastings Robinson ... Cambridge ... M. DCCC. XLV. Latin part: Epistolæ Tigurinæ, *p.* 156. *English translation in the* English part *p.* 254—5.

[1574 July 7.] Corranus Rodolfo Gualthero ... Londini. *Part of it, from the* papeles de Usóz, *in* Menendez Pel. II 489.

The whole above here p. 103*f. Copied by Mr.* H. Escher.

1575 Jan. 25. *Will. Barlow to Josia Simler.* Zurich letters (second series), Latin part *p.* 160. *In the* English part *p.* 261*f.* translation of Hastings Robinson; *I have retouched it above p.* 62*f. according to the original.*

— March 4. *Grindal to Parker.* Remains of Grindal 353*f.*

— — 17. *Parker to Grindal.* Correspondence of Parker 476. *Both these English letters are used by* Strype, Grindal 186*f.*, Parker 482.

[*About new year* **1576.**] *Corro to Cambridge University, applying for DD.*

[**1576**] *The Chancellor's answer. Both these letters are mentioned in Corro's letters of March* 20. *Both missing.*

1576 *beginning of March.* (*This date is given* Ath. I). *The Earl of Leicester to Oxford University in favour of Corro. Extract by* Clark I 153.

— March 20. *Corro to the Vice-chancellor of Oxford, supplicating for the degree of DD.* Latin. *Printed in* Sepp's Polem. *p.* 5—8. — *P.* 7 *first edition:* Itaque aut vix fiat Cantabrigiensibus statutis aut in re tantilla dispensanda R. Mᵗᵉᵐ interpellem: cuperem ... *Sec*ᵈ *ed.:* Itaque ut fiat ex Cantabrigiensibus statutis, in re tantilla autem dispensandis, R. Mᵗᵉᵐ interpellarem: cuperem ... *I think there must at least be written* interpellarem? Cuperem ... *P.* 8: moribus insimulari ... deserti judicii. *Sec*ᵈ: nominibus insimulare ... deserto judicio.

— April 2. *Registered at Oxford the letter of Leicester, and:* Supplicat Antonius Corranus ad incipiendum in theologia. Concessa, modo purget se haereticarum opinionum. Clark I 153.

— — *Corro's thanks in reply. Mentioned in the letter of Apr.* 10. *Missing.*

1576 *April* 10. *An unnamed Oxford man from Oxford to Villiers. Latin. Printed in* Sepp, Polem. *p.* 11. 12.

— — 20. *Registered at Oxford that Villiers supplicates* ad incipiendum in theologia.

— *May* 1. Humfrey to Villiers. *Latin. Printed in* Sepp, Polem. *p.* 15. 16; *on the date see p.* 1.

— — 6. *An unnamed Oxford man from New College to Villiers. Latin. Ibid. p.* 16. 17.

— *about May.* Letter *of the Ministers of the three foreign Churches in London to the Archbishop of Canterbury and the Bishop of London against Corro. Latin.* Ibid. *p.* 22—27. *With* Theses *from his writings and sayings, and the* Antitheses *of the ministers. Latin. Ibid. p.* 30—60. Copy of this letter to the archbishop and the bishop, and of the Theses and Antitheses was sent by the ministers to Oxford University with a Latin Letter which is printed *ibid.* 28—30. *All these papers are printed without any date.* — *P.* 29 *the second ed. has some corrections, line* 1: Episcopis (*first ed.* Epistolis) *and no comma after* ejus; *and on the same page:* etsi non obscure nos. *P.* 30 *in the title of the* Theses *write* Ministri *and* provocati.

— *June* 7. Jo. Reynolds of Crp. Ch. College to Humfrey against Corro. *The* contents *given by* Wood, *see above p.* 67 *f.*

— — 13. The Oxford convocation's debate and decree on Corro. *Latin. Printed by* Clark I 153—4.

— [—]. Corro to the Vice-chancellor of Oxford against Villiers. *Mentioned in the next item. Missing.*

— *July* 4. The defence of Villiers before Convocation is allowed to stand instead of responding in the Comitia [*which were held on July* 9]. Clark I 154.

— — 6. Petrus Lozilerius Villerius, D. D., was dispens. pro habitu gradui suo competente ad quem per statuta tenetur inter quindenum comparandum. Clark I 154. *The person admitted to the degree should take oath to provide himself with D. D. robes of his own within* 15 *days. Ibid.* 143.

— *Dec.* 15. Villerius was allowed to defer his lectiones. Clark I 154.

[**1577**?]. Corro was examined by royal commissioners and held some public lectures. *Mentioned in the item of July* 7. 1578.

1578 *March* 7. Bogaert to the London Dutch. Hessels III *p.* 501.

— *July* 7. In consequence of letters from each of the three London foreign churches against Corro and of Corro's wish to purge himself, a committee was appointed. Clark I 155.

— — 10. Corro's declarations in the convocation. *Ibid.*

1579 *May* 2. Stated that Corro was lector catechismi in three Halls. *Ibid.* 156. *On the functions of the lectors ibid.* 155 f.

1579 *foll.*   **Commentary on Cohelet.**

In the Stationers' register, May 16. 1579 (*Arber* 2, 353): Ihon Wolf. Lycenced vnto him under th[e h]andes of the bishop of London and the wardens. A booke in Latin intituled. Cohelet. seu conico Salomonis de summo hominis bono paraphrasi explanata. ex prelectionibus Anthoni Corani Hispalensis. cum noua uersione marginibus addita. eodem. Corani interprete. Londini 25 Martij 1575. The which booke is graunted to him condycionally that he shall haue it printed by Ihon Marlwood. *There is no trace of an earlier edition than that of 1579.*

1579 Sapientissimi | regis Salomonis | concio | De summo hominis bono, quam Hebræi | Cohelet, Græci & Latini Eccle- | siasten vocant, | In Latinam linguam ab Antonio Corra- | no Hispalensi versa, & ex eiusdem præ- | lectionibus Paraphrasi il- | lustrata. | Accesserunt & notæ quædam in singula capita; quibus to- | tius concionis œconomia, ac singularum ferè sen- | tentiarum Dialectica connexio; simul cum | Rhetorica elocutione | ostenditur. | [*Ornament*.] | Londini, | Per Iohannem VVolfium, expensis ipsius Authoris. | 1579. |

On the back of the title-leaf verses and sentences.

A 2: Honoratissimo viro d. Thomae Bromleio Summo Angliae Cancellario, Domino mihi multis nominibus obseruando. *This* Epistola Dedicatoria *ends* [A 7], *dated* Oxonio; ex Ecclesia Christi. Idibus Julij 1579 ... Ant. Corranus. *On the reverse of* [A 7] *Corrections of the press.* [A 8]: Antonivs Corranvs Hispalensis Candido Lectori, *an* Epistola *ending* [B 8] *verso:* Londino anno Domini 1574. P. [33]—273 *Latin translation and paraphrase of Salomon's sermon.* P. 274 (*in some copies misprinted* 742)—382 (*misprinted* 381; *in all copies?*) Annotationes *on the first page of the last leaf:* Argumentum cohelet, id est concionatoris. per A. C. [*Ant. Corranum*], *three Saphic stanzas, on the last page* [384]: Solomon alloquitur Lectorem *in hexameters.*

Octavo. [384] *pages, title included, numbers beginning p.* 34.

Besides a folding table, printed on only one side, with the title:

Delineatio totius concionis, seu mauis disputationis, de summo | hominis bono à Salomone instituta. | Per Ant. Corranum Hispalensem. |

BODLEIAN. CAMBRIDGE Univ. LAMBETH, see Maitland's Index 35. *YORK Cathedral, Hessels p.* 993. *MEMMINGEN. STUTTGART Royal. MERCK. ZURICH City. MADRID National from Usóz. PARIS National,* Menendez Pel. II 490.

Merck's copy has p. 274, *Stuttg. and Memm.* 742. *In these three copies and in the Zurich one* 381 *instead of* 382. *The folding table is wanting in Stuttg.; I noticed the existence in other copies; in Merck's it is found between sheets* A *and* B, *some few words of it are damaged.*

(*Only some weeks before the date of the dedication,* on May 20. 1579, Jo. Serranus *dated* Nemausi *the preface to his commentary in* Ecclesiasten *which appeared Geneva* 1580. *A copy in Zurich City libr.* Anglice cura Jo. Stockwood, Lond. 1585, *according to* Rosenmüller *in the work referred to below p.* 135).

Menendez Pelayo II 490 *gives the distichs of the title-back* (male praesens *instead of* praesens male), *some few words of the dedication* (idem *instead of* ibidem; est *is addition*), *the first five hexameters of the last leaf* (divorum *instead of* diuinus).

Sepp, Mededeel., *reprinted p.* 76. 77 *some passages from the dedication, p.* 77. 78 *a larger extract from the* epistola ad lectorem, *p.* 80. 81 *the back of the title-leaf and the verses of the last leaf.*

In Willer's *vernal catalogue for* 1581 *folio* A 4ᵃ (*notice sent me by Dr. Spirgatis*):

Sapientiss. Regis Salomonis concio de summo hominis bono, quam Hebraei Cohelet, Graeci & Latini Ecclesiasten vocant, in Latinam linguam ab Antonio Corrano Hispalensi versa, & ex eiusdem praelectionibus paraphrasi illustrata. 8°. Londini, 1581.

In the Collectio in unum corpus 1592 (*cf. above here p.* 123), *part* 1, *p.* 24:

Corrani Hispalensis translatio Concionis Sapientissimi regis Salomonis de summo hominis bono, in latinam linguam. Londini per Ioann. VVolfium 1581. V. in 8.

In Vnivs secvli... ab Anno Dom. 1500 ad 1602... Elenchus consummatissimus librorvm... Avctore Ioanne Clessio... Francofvrti... MDC. II. *p.* 51 *the notice quite as in the* Collectio, *only* Ioannem Wolffium, *and without* V. *The same in* Draudius, Bibliotheca classica 1611 *p.* 139, *only* Wolphium (*also without* V).

Wood, Ath. I 252: Lond. 1579 and 81 in oct. The version of which into Latin was done by Corranus also.

1585 Wood, Ath. I 252:

„Sermons on Ecclesiastes — Abridged by Thomas Pitt-Oxon. 1585. oct. which is called by some Pitt's Paraphrase on Ecclesiastes."

Wiffen: Symon Patrick (Bishop of Ely) adapted Corranus's work in his Paraphrase upon the books of Ecclesiastes and the song of Solomon 1685. 1700 &c.

1586 Solomons Sermon: | of mans chief | felicitie: called | in Hebrew Koheleth, | in Greeke and Latin | Ecclesiastes. | With a learned, godly, and familiar pa- | raphrase vppon the same: gathe- | red out of the Lectures of A. | C. & now englished for | the benefit of the | vnlearned. | *[Ornament with the words on the four sides:]* Viue | pius | moriere | pius. | Imprinted at Oxford by Joseph Barnes | Printer to the Vniuersitie. | 1586. | 8 *leaves, title included*) + *p.* 1—219. Sm. oct. *Translated by* T. P. *who dedicated it to* Lady Marie Dudley, Oxford March 8. 1586.

OXFORD, *Wadham, Wiffen's copy. The copy of Usóz at present in* MADRID *National* (Menendez Pelayo *registers this edition* II 771).

In Portenbach & Lutz *auctumnal catalogue of* 1588 (*Many city libr.*) *Folio* Aij: 1588. Sapientissimi Regis Salomonis Concio de summo hominis bono, quam Hebræi Cohelet, Græci & Latini Ecclesiasten vocant. In Latinam linguam ab Antonio Corrano Hispalensi versa, &c. cum quibusdam, ad singula capita, Notis. Londini, per Ioann. VVolfium. in 8°.

Nowhere else is an edition of 1588 *mentioned. On the same page is registered* Beza's *Ecclesiastes of* 1588. (*A copy of it in* ZURICH *City*). *Beza does not name Corro therein, and it may be that he had not read his book. Perhaps the appearance of Beza's book has occasioned the printing of a new title-leaf for some copies of Corro's* Ecclesiastes.

Follows a preface to the Christian reader by Th. Pie B. *On* Thomas Pie *cf.* Clark III 133.

1591 *An edition of this year I found mentioned only in the following passage of* Rosenmülleri Scholia in Vetus testamentum. Partis nonae vol. II. Lps. 1830. *p.* 28 *in the* Elenchus Interpretum: Anton. Corrani Ecclesiastes, paraphrasi et notis illustratus, Lond. 1579. 1591 in octon.; iterum cum analysi, studio Abr. Sculteti, Frcof. 1618 et Heidelberg 1619 in octon.

(1596 Nov. 11 *licensed to* Richard Feilde: Ecclesiastes in Englishe verse. Arber III 73).

Metaphrasis Libri Salomonis qui inscribitur Ecclesiastes. *Licensed, on August* 1. 1603, *to* Master Man, in Latin as in English. Provided that he gett sufficient Aucthority for yt before he publish or print yt. Arber 3, 243.

1618 Wood, Ath. I 252: The said Notes [*of Corro on* Ecclesiastes] were adorn'd with a learned Analysis by Abrah. Scultet. Printed at Francf. 1618. oct.

1619 Ecclesiastes | regis Sa- | lomonis: | Sive, | De Summo hominis bono | concio verè regia, | Antonii Corrani | Hispalensis Hispani, | Theologi orthodoxi, | Interpretatione latinâ, | Paraphrasi perspicuâ, | Analysi eruditâ, | Exposita, & nunc primùm in Germania edita, | studio | Abrahami Sculteti. | *[Ornament.]* Heidelbergæ, | Impensis Jonæ Rosæ, librarij Francofurtensis, | Typis Johannis Lancelloti, Academiae Typogr. | CIƆIƆCXIX *Octavo.* 16 *leaves and p.* 1 — 326 *and a folding sheet. Two pages preface by* Scultetus. Wiffen: „Title 1 leaf. Sacrarvm literarvm studiosis s. Heidelbergâ 1610 A. Scultetus 1 lf. Corro's ded. Bromleio 1579 11 pgs. Corranus ad Lectorem Londini 1574 17 pgs. 1 folding sheet Delineatio totius Concionis &c. The work 218 pgs. Annotationes 218 to 324. Latin verses of Corro 2 pgs. = 358 p. & Sheet."

CAMBRIDGE Univ. (*In the BODLEIAN according to Menendez Pelayo* II 490.

Hessels *p.* 994: Benjamin B. Wiffen, in his List referred to above [*here* p. 127], says that Symon Patrick (Bishop of Ely) largely adopted Corrano's work in his Paraphrase upon the Books of Ecclesiastes and the Song of Solomon 1685 and 1700.

1579 *Nov.* 22. *Corro to Arthur Atye. An autograph notice of Usóz among his papers in the* Biblioteca Nacional *of* Madrid *says:* Este año de 1579, por lo menos et 22 de Septiembre, Corro estaba en Oxford. Porque con esa fecha escribió desde alli una carta á Mr. Attey pidiendole se interesase á su favor con Lord Leicester, en la promocion de Obispos que debia por entonces verificarse (Vease la carta N° ..). *Menendez Pelayo, when sending me in* 1901 *a copy of this notice, stated that after* N° *the cipher is wanting and that a copy of the letter could not be found in the* Bibliot. Nac. *He had formerly used it when preparing his vol.* II *where p.* 489 *he speaks of Leicester's* promesa *which is not mentioned in that notice of Usóz. I then got the letter copied by Hessels; it is printed above here p.* 105. *The date is* Nov. 22., *not* Sept. 22. *as* Usóz *wrote, nor* Apr. 23. *as Menendez Pel. printed* II 489. *Hessels informed me that the addressee signed* Atye *in a letter of June* 12. 1585. *Two letters of* Arthur Atye *in the* Cecil Mss. Part VI. 1895, *to Sir Robert Cecil* 1595 — 6 March 6., *to William Downhall* 1596 Oct. 5.

1582 *May* 7. *The Chancellor to Oxford University on Corro.*

— — 14. *The Vice-chancellor's reply. Both* Clark I 157.

1583 *January* 2. *Corro to John Hotman. Oxford. Latin. In* Hotomanorum epistolae. 1700. *Instead of* Altey *write* Attey.

Part of it in Menendez Pel. II 491.

1584 *Aug.* 26. *Castol to Beza. French.* Schickler III 138. *Instead of* est en credit *read* sont en cr.

1585 *Travers on Corro.* Hooker's works, Oxford 1841, vol. I, *p.* 48. II, *p.* 662.

1586 *Oct.* 1. Christ Church. Matriculated Anthony Corrano, Hispalensis, LL. D. filius, aged 59. Clark II 154 *with the adnotation:* Fil. Anthoni Corrani Doctoris Utriusque Juris. (Ath. I 578.)

— — — *[on the same day]:* Ch. Ch. matric. John Thorie, Lond., M. D. f., aged 18. Clark *ibid. with the adnot.:* Fil. Johannis Thorii Doctoris in Medicina Bellavi (i. e. of Bailleul, Flanders). (Ath. I 624.) — Clark III 138: (Ch. Ch.) Thorius, John; suppl. B. A. Apr. 15. 1586.

Spanish grammar.

1586 „Reglas gramaticales para aprender la lengua Espannola y Francesa, confiriendo la una con la otra, segun el orden de las partes de la oration Latinas. Octavo."
Printed by Joseph Barnes at Oxford. There had not been any printing at Oxford for 66 years, as it seems, when in 1585 the Chancellor, the Earl of Leicester, presented a new printing press to the University. Four publications were issued by it as early as 1585.
I take all this from Ames, Typographical Antiquities, London 1749, *p.* 452.
Underhill: Spanish literature in the England of the Tudors, New York 1899, *registers this book p.* 195 *and* 393 *(he writes* francesca), *naming* Corro *as its author and stating that* an English translation appeared in London in 1590.

1590 The Spanish *[these first two words in a border]* | Grammer: | With certeine Rules teaching both the | Spanish and French tongues. | By which they that haue some knowledge in the French | tongue, may the easier attaine to the Spanish, and like- | wise they that haue the Spanish, with more facilitie | learne the French: and they that are acquain- | ted with neither of them, learne either or | both. Made in Spanish, by M. An- | thonie de Corro. | With a Dictionarie adioyned vnto it, of all the Spanish | wordes cited in this Booke: and other more wordes | most necessarie for all such as desire the know- | ledge of the same tongue. | By John Thorius, Graduate in Oxenford. | Imprinted at London by John Wolfe. | 1590. | *Quarto.*

Dedication by John Thorius *to* John Whitgift, Epistle *and* Table 2 *leaves. The Grammar paged* 1—119. *The Spanish* Dictionarie 7 *leaves. This grammar was, according to the Epistle to the reader, written in Spanish and a little of the end in French, and translated and altered by* John Thorius, *who also added the Dictionary.*

BRITISH MUS. BODLEIAN.

Stationers' license April 7. 1590 *to* John Wolf *for* The Spanishe Gramer with certen rules teaching the Spanish and Frenche tonges, with a dictionarye adioyned vnto yt with Spanishe words. (*Arber* II 544.)

1587 *July* 12. *in an album:*

τα παθηματα μαθηματα.

Non si male nunc, et olim sic erit. Doctiss. Viro Joh. Caes. Rhen. etc. amoris ac benevolentiae Symbolum scripsi Oxon. 12 Jul. 1587.

Anton. Corrano Hispalensis.

Published in de Navorscher 1857. bl. 25. *Therefrom copied for me by* M. F van Lennep, *who says that* Joh. Caes. Rhen. *is* Johan de Keyser *from* Rhenen. *Part of it in* Sepp's Naspor. III 97. *Cf. above p.* 75 *and* 130.

1588 De sacræ scri- | ptvræ avcto-ritate. | Opvscvlvm tem- | poribvs his nostris | vtilissimum. | Qvemadmodvm intel- | ligi potest ex præcipuis capitibus rerum, | quæ in ipso continentur. | Ea autem notata sequenti inuenies pagellâ. | Per R. P. Dominicum Lopez | Societatis Iesu. | *Ornament.* | Hispali. | Apud Lazarum Ferrerium. | 1588. | Cum Priuilegio superiorum. |

A 2—4 Lectori Christianæ pietatis studioso. A 4 *blank.* A 5—D 2 *p.* 1—80. De avctoritate sacræ scriptvræ. ABC 12°, D 6°, *again* D *two leaves.*

MUNICH Royal. B—r.

Corro's preface Lectori *has been reprinted* above *p.* 105 *f.*

1590 *June* 13. Corro T. John Hotman. *Latin. Oxford. In* Hotomanorum epistolae. 1700. *Part of it in* Menendez II 491. *The greater part of the letter in* Sepp's Naspor. III 182—3.

About the *Tableau de l'ocuvre de Dieu*.

My learned friend, Professor Aug. Bernus at Lausanne, who kindly directed to me a *Lettre ouverte* in the *Bulletin du Protestantisme français*, June 1901, has received my thanks in an answer which, owing to untoward circumstances, has remained hitherto unpublished. Revised and more detailed, it now may stand in this befitting place, to be submitted to Dr. Bernus's fine judgment. I am, however, treating here only the *Tableau de l'ocuvre de Dieu*, having referred above p. 10 and 128 to other valuable remarks of that *Lettre*.

Bernus supposes that Corro used a *Tableau* of Beza.

From what Corro in December 1569 in both his Apologies (see the passages in the *Bulletin* April 1901 p. 214f.) states on the Tableau which he remodelled, we learn the following. It was anonymous. It consisted of positions and partitions. Instead of positions Corro in his own Tableau says articles, and in both French editions partition is used by him only in the first instance, the three following ones being called divisions; in the Latin of 1584 *partitio; Altera partitio; Tertia partitio*, in the beginning called also *diuisio; Quarta Distributio*, in the beginning called *vltima diuisio*. He made changes in many periods and added twelve articles (*duodecim* he says in the larger apology p. 85). His Tableau has 20 articles (unnumbered), therefore the former one had only eight. They occupied one page. They were written in French and had the title *Tableau de l'ocuvre de Dieu*. When this collective use of *oeurre* in the title of Corro's Tableau was found fault with by his French judges in September 1570, he answered *se in hoc authorem imitatum*, viz. the author of the former publication (Hessels III p. 114). This had been printed (*excusa*) in France in 1556. When he remodelled it at Antwerp, he had only a manuscript copy; we do not know whether he ever saw a printed one.

It is clear from these notices that the original *Tableau*, revised by Corro, was neither the *Summa totius Christianismi* nor the *Brevis explicatio praecedentis tabulae*, which *tabula* is that *Summa*, both printed in Beza's *Tractationes theologicae* 1570, and was neither a French original of either of these tracts nor a French translation of either of them. In fact the *Summa* or *Tabula* only occupies one foliopage, but it consists merely of headings. It begins:

Deus cujus viae impervestigabiles.

Propositum ejus aeternum et immatabile, omnes causas ordine quoque antegrediens, quo in semet ipso decrevit ab aeterno, certos homines ad suam ipsius gloriam

eligere in Christo   *rejicere, sua ipsorum culpa*
servandos   *damnandos.*

Creatio hominis in recto statu, sed mutabili.

This *decrevit* is the only verbum finitum in the whole table which does not contain any period (we must abstract, of course, from the quotation from the epistle to the Romans at the end of the table). The *Brevis explicatio* on 35 folio-pages contains 43 so called Aphorisms, short and long ones, with the biblical proofs, exhibited in full tenor. In Corro's Table there is not a single passage which might seem to derive from a passage of this treatise of Beza.

Summa and *Explicatio* are repeated in *Vol. primum Tractationum Theologicarum. Ed. secunda ab ipso Auctore recognita. Genevae* 1582. The *Summa* has on the whole remained the same. Instead of *Reiicere sua ipsorum culpa damnandos* is said *Reiicere, & propter suam ipsorum voluntariam culpam aeternis poenis addicere*, and to *Fides* another place has been assigned. Each post is artificially framed and they are connected by lines, which had not been done in 1570. The German translation of *Summa* and *Explicatio* by Heppe in his book on Beza 1861 p. 321f. evidently follows the edition of 1582. — The stem of the Sum has seven heads, but there is no numeration at all in either of these editions of the Sum. Those seven are: (to say it here shortly) inscrutability, predestination, creation, perversion, judgment, justice, glory.

The *Tabula*, called *Summa*, and its *Explicatio* had first appeared in a separate edition. Beza sent to Calvin with a highly interesting letter on July 29. 1555 a ms. tabula which principally treated of predestination; if it pleased Calvin it should be printed with an appendix which Beza would send. This appendix was certainly the *explicatio*. The work appeared, according to Gessner (as alleged by Bernus in his *Lettre* and in his *Bèze* à Lausanne, 1900, p. 66) with the title: *Summa totius Christianismi, sive descriptio et distributio causarum salutis Electorum et exitii Reproborum, ex sacris literis collecta et explicata*. Bernus thinks that this publication served to explain and develop a placard in-folio, the *Tabula proprement dite qui a peut-être d'abord paru seule*. But, as we just stated, Beza did not wish the first edition of the Sum to appear without the Appendix. And the title of 1555 comprises both the Summa and the explication. Except the words *et explicata* the title is verbally the same as that of the *Summa* in the Tractationes. That *Summa collecta et explicata* was printed *in minima forma*, as Gessner says. It must have been a rather thick little volume, if the *Explicatio* was not much shorter than in the *Tractationes*. The *Tabula* was probably printed on a small folding-leaf. As year of the publication Bernus gives 1555 from Gessner, in *Bèze à Lausanne*, but in the *Lettre* 1555 or 56, I do not understand why. (At Geneva the new year began with Christmas.)

Bernus has not seen this first edition nor a separate placard, nor the translation, mentioned by du Verdier, as quoted by Bernus: *Briefve exposition de la Table*. 1560, *in*-16. Nor have I succeeded in finding these publications of 1555 and 1560.[a]

At all events neither the Latin of 1555 nor the French of 1560 is the *Tableau* of 1556.

But one can scarcely doubt that its author was moved by the recent Geneva publication to compose with the use of parts of it a French *Tableau* less laconic than

---

a) Of course I did not ask in Bernus's neighbourhood, at Lausanne, Geneva, Bern, nor in Paris whence our learned and obliging friend N. Weiss would have pointed to the place. I got negative answers, respecting both publications, from Zurich City and Basle University, from the University libraries at Halle, Heidelberg, Marburg, Munich, the City libraries Frankfort o. M. and Hamburg, the Ducal at Gotha, the Royal at Berlin, the Hof- und Staatsbibl. at Munich, and from the British Mus. May others try elsewhere.

the *Summa* and not as verbose as its *Explicatio*. In so far I am therefore in agreement with Bernus, that I think it improbable that Corro's *Tableau* was altogether independent of Beza's direct or indirect influence in regard to the method. However, we nowhere find Corro's adversaries mentioning Beza's Table, nor are we entitled to distrust Corro's statement (Bulletin 1901 p. 215) that he never knew who was the author of the Table of 1556. When he said so at the end of 1569, Beza's *Tractationes* had not yet appeared; their dedication is dated *III Cal. Martias* 1570. But most likely Corro guessed that the method which pleased him in the *Tableau* of 1556 (Bulletin 1901 p. 214f.) was somehow Beza's whose opinions were probably followed there. The *Tabula* of 1555 had appeared anonymously, but Beza's authorship was soon discovered, and raised in the Bernese territory a lasting anger (Bernus, Bèze à Lausanne p. 66f.), facts of which Corro, during his studies at Lausanne in 1557 and 58, could not have been unaware, even if he had not seen that *Tabula*. When in 1569 in London he defended the doctrine of his own *Tabula*, he avoided to name Beza in connection with the Tableau of 1556; he, however, stated that its method pleased him.

On the treatise *De sacrae scripturae auctoritate 1588*.

Sand, Bibliotheca Anti-trinitariorum. 1684. *P.* 67: Idem Gallice sub hoc titulo: Livre de L'Authoritè de la Saincte Ecriture, traducit [*write* traduict] par Nicolas Bernaud gentilhomme Daulphinois, avec L'advertissement de Messieurs les Theologiens de Basle, sur quelques endroits dudit escrit. 1592. *I do not know whether the translation comprises the preface of* 1588.

In form of a letter to his amicus Nicolaus Bernaudus, medicus ac philosophus eximius, *Fausto Sozzino published in* 1595 Defensio disputationis suae de loco septimi capitis epistolae ad Romanos, sub nomine Dysidæi ab se editæ. Sand 74.

Willer's *vernal fair catalogue of* 1589 (*Mainz City library*) fol. B 4 [*misprinted* B 2]: 1588. De sacrę scripturę auctoritate per R. P. Dominicum Lopoz [*sic*] Societatis Iesu. Hispali apud Lazarum Ferreriū. 12. — *From* Basse's Collectio 1592 *p.* 129 *the* Elenchus *of* Cless 1602 *p.* 104 *has exactly copied:* R. P. Dominicus Lopoz [*sic*] Soc. Iesu. De sacrae scripturae authoritate. Hispali apud Lazarum Ferrerium 1589 in 12°. (*Communication of Dr. M. Spirgatis*); *the date* 1589 *refers, according to Basse's method, to the appearence in Willer's catalogue.*

Catalogvs clarorvm Hispaniae scriptorvm.. Opera ac studio, Valerii Andreæ Taxandri. Maguntiæ 1607. [*Preface:* Valerivs Andreas S. D.]. *P.* 44: Dominicvs Lopoz [*sic*] Hispalensis De S. Scripturæ auctoritate, 1589. 12. Sed aduertat Lector esse confictum & librum & nomen apud Allobrogas (*i. e. at Geneva*) ab hæreticis, quibus mentiri religio non est.

Draudius, Bibliotheca classica 1611 *p.* 370 *among the* Libri theologici Pontificiorum: R. P. Dominicus Lopoz [*sic*], De sacræ scripturæ authorite, Hispali apud Lazarum Ferrerium, 1589 in 12. *The* Index *has correctly* Lopez.

Copies of the two Latin editions of 1611 *and of the separate one of* 1656 (*also the folio-ed. of the same year, not the ed. of* 1588) *are in Guicciardini's collection in the National Library at Florence. My information on those three consists in what I obtained, partly copied, partly related, from my dear old friend Professor Comba there.*

De Auctoritate S. Scripturae Opusculum his temporibus nostris utilissimum. Quemadmodum intelligi potest ex praecipuis rerum, q̄ in ipso tractantur, capitibus. Ea verò proximè seqq pagellis notata sunt. In praefatione ad lectorem ratio huius Editionis exponitur. *A bird with the circumscription* Caput Inter Nubila Condit. Steinfurti excudit Theoph. Caesar. Anno MDC. XI. *According to the Guicciardini* Catalogo 323 : 8°. *The* Praefatio Apologetica *of 20 pages is subscribed:* Steinfurti X. Julii, Anno 1611. Conr. Vorstius D. *On him, an Arminian theologer, see the article in* Real-Encyklopädie für protestant. Theologie. 2. Aufl. Bd. 16. 1885 *and the dissertation of* Mellby, Lpz. 1901. *Vorst says in his preface that, when* (exemplaribus antiquis jam plane deficientibus) *last year* pagellae aliquot *of his edition had been seen, he and the book were censured.* Auctorem ajunt esse hominem haereticum, puta F. S. Senensem, aut alium non dissimilem... testor, quo tempore procurata fuit haec editio, auctorem mihi prorsus ignotum fuisse. Sed neque ipsi censores... praeter conjecturas aut suspiciones quidquam adferre potuerunt. Ita ut ne nunc quidem ex ipsis aliquid certi hac de re discere mihi licuit. *But even if such a one as they suppose be the author, still this his opuscule might be of use. From the fact that 1588 it was published under the name of* Dominicus Lopez, Soc. Jesu, *but the French translation* absque nomine auctoris, *he concludes that it was* incerti scriptoris, et nomen illud Dominici &c. fortassis idcirco tunc temporis vero auctori arrisisse ut eos tanto facilius ad lectionem sui libelli alliceret qui isto quam maxime opus habere videbantur. Certe a Jesuitico genio profectum non esse, satis ex re ipsa constare arbitramur. *The theologians of Basle found only three places to amend, Vorst repeats their censures* (Comba: non ristampa quali erano censurabili i tre passi, ma li stampa corretti). *On the nine objections made against the book by the opponents of Vorst and on his answers see the report of* Sigm. Jac. Baumgarten *in the* Nachrichten von merkwürdigen Büchern. Erster Band. Halle 1752, *p. 413 f. Lastly Vorst speaks of the additions and small omissions and some other changes he made in the text. He has not reprinted the preface of 1588 nor does he mention it.*

In the same year the booklet appeared at last with the name of its real author: De Sacrae Scripturae Auctoritate Libellus Fausti Socini Senensis. Cui addita est Summa Religionis Christianae, ejusdem Socini Utrumque ex Italico in Latinum conversum. Racoviae Typis Sebastiani Sternacii 1611. Sand 66 *and* Guicc. Cat. 323 : 8°. *Preface* Lectori Benevolo. Hunc libellum Auctor in gratiam magni cujusdam viri, ante annos quadraginta et aliquot conscripserat. Editus idem erat Hispali, ante annos viginti tres, sub nomine cujusdam Dominici Lopez Societatis Jesu. Sed dolus latere non potuit. Talis enim praefatio, libello huic praefixa erat, quae contrarium plane ejus, quod in eo disputatur, continebat. Affirmabat enim praefatio, dari naturalem Dei cognitionem, quod libellus prorsus negat... exemplaria ejusdem nulla amplius prostant, en denuo eum recudi... curavimus... Racoviae, Calend. April, Anno MIƆCXI. *The treatise has therefore been written some years before 1570 when Sozzino lived at the court of Florence.* Sand *writes p.* 66: Italice circa a. 1570, conscriptus in gratiam viri cujusdam magni, et editus non praefixo auctoris nomine. Idem Latine, ab auctore conversus: editus Hispali a. 1588. Sand *evidently takes something from this preface of 1611, where, however, it is neither said that the Italian original has been printed, nor that it was translated by its author, and both assertions must remain uncertain,* Sand *not being a sufficient authority.*

In the first folio-volume of the Bibliotheca Fratrum Polonorum, *after the special title-leaf:* De Sacrae Scripturae Autoritate Libellus Fausti Socini Senensis. Cui addita est Summa Religionis Christianæ, ejusdem Socini. Utrumque ex Italico in Latinum conversum. Irenopoli Post annum Domini 1656. *follows p.* 265—280 De Auctoritate Sacræ Scripturæ. With the *above preface* Lectori Benevolo, *dated* Racoviæ, Calend. April, Anno M. IOC. XI.

Auctoritas S. Scripturæ. Ad exemplar Steinfurtense. Apud Theophilum Caesarem anno 1656, 8° picc. *So registered p.* 324 *of the* Catalogo della collezione de' libri donata dal conte Piero Guicciardini alla Città di Firenze. Firenze 1877. Comba: La prefazione dell' ediz. 1656 in 8° piccolo concorda con quella dell' ediz. in folio. Ma la ediz. 1656 non ha prefazione affatto, solo il sommario dei capitoli in principio.

Dutch translation. Sand 67: van de Authoriteyt der H. Schriftuur, door Dirck Raphelsen Kamphuysen uyt het Latijn vertaalt, en met geleerde auteeckeningen verciert. 1623. 4°. Ejusdem secunda editio. Van de geloofwaardigheyd der H. Schriftuur: met Koenraad Vorstius verantwoordelijcke Voor-reden verrijckt. 1666. 4. Cloppenburg *in the* Dedicatio *of his* Anti-Smalcius 1652, *in the* Theologica opera omnia, 1684, Tomus alter, *p.* 502: anno MDCXXIII in linguam Belgicam translatus hic quem exhibemus Smalcii liber, conjunctus cum F. Socini Opusculo de Auctoritate Scripturæ sacræ.

An English translation, dedicated to queen Caroline in 1731, *I have found mentioned somewhere.*

That the preface-writer of 1588 *is not the author of the work edited by him, was first stated in the Racovian edition of* 1611. *As for the contradiction pointed out there between that preface and the work itself, the fact is that Socinus, although he says:* religio nequaquam res naturalis, sed, si vera est, patefactio quaedam divina (1588 *p.* 42), *still does not doubt that it can be effected* rationibus eo adigere ut dicant esse primum motorem primamque causam omnium rerum etc. (*p.* 44; *both places in the folio* 1656 *p.* 273ᵇ *where the* essentiam *of* 1588 *is corrected into* essentia), *and just this reasoning from the* naturae contemplatio *is meant by the editor of* 1588. *It is true, however, that* Psalm 19 *and* Rom. 1, *alleged by him are not admitted by Socinus as proofs for a natural knowledge of God, in the* Praelectiones theologicae cp. 2 (*in the same folio-vol. p.* 538. *The editor's preface is of* 1609. *The work was not printed before).*

The name of the editor of 1588 *and the author of the preface of that edition I do not find mentioned earlier than in the* Kerkelycke Geschiedenissen door Jacobum Triglandium. Leyden 1650. Trigland, *declaiming against the belauded moderation of Corro, says also, fol.* 156: Noch heeft zijne moderate Theologie soo verre gegaen, dat hy het boecken Fausti Socini, van de Authoriteyt der H. Schrifture, naderhandt uytgegeven onder den naem van een Spaensch Jesuyt ghenaemt Dominicus Lopez, het welcke hier te lande seer is bekendt geworden door het beroep Conradi Vorstii tot de Theologische Professie te Leyden, uyt het Italiaensch in 't Latijn heeft over gheset, ende met een voor-reden vereert. I. e.: *His moderate theology is gone so far that he translated from Italian into Latin and honored by a preface the opuscule of Fausto Sozzino on the authority of the Holy Scripture, afterwards edited under the name of a Spanish Jesuit Domingo Lopez, which in this country has become largely known in consequence of the appointment of Conrad Vorst to the theological professorship at Leiden.*

Sepp, Naspor. III 190 *says: I suspect Trigland cannot prove his assertion.*

I find a circumstance which supports the probability that Corro was connected with the publication of 1588. *The* Stationers' register *has on* March 4. 1587 (*i. e.* 1588 *mod. st.*): John Wolf. Receaved of him for his licence to prynte a booke intituled. De aucthoritate Sacre Scripture, vppon Condicon that yt maie be lycenced hereafter. vj (Arber II 485). *John Wolf was Corro's publisher. Corro's* Cohelet *published by him in* 1579 *has, however, other types; I have had no opportunity of comparing Corro's* Grammer, printed by John Wolfe 1590, *with the questionable impression.* Cloppenburg *in the* Præfatio ad Compendiolum Socianismi confutatum 1651, *reprinted in the* Theologica opera omnia 1684, T. alter, *p.* 331: Titulus præ se fert Autorem R. P. Dominicum Lopez Societatis Jesu: fingitur excusum Hispali, apud Lazarum Ferrerium, cum permissu superiorum. Memini fuisse, qui ex typorum indicio assererent Amstelredamensi Typographo, satis celebri olim Bibliopolæ, Cornelio Nicolai. (Sand 66 *refers to this passage of Cloppenburg without saying where to find it*). Frederik Muller *at* Amsterdam, *offering in his* Bibliotheca Rhynwykiana [1889] *a copy of the edition of* 1588 (*I bought it*), *says p.* 94: Cette éd. nous paraît sortir d'une presse hollandaise. *Possibly the license had been refused in England. In the paper is a watermark* B *in the outer margin of p.* 8. 32. 63 *of my copy*, D (*as it seems*) *in the outer margin of p.* 8. 32. 54.

I was convinced that Corro was the author of this preface, as soon as it struck me that God's scholae tres *in the preface of* 1588 *are the* trois classes en son escole *in the* Lettre *of* 1567 *to the king. I have reprinted above p.* 81*f.* and 105*f. the pages from both rare publications. Substantially the idea of the three kinds of knowing God is not new,* Valdés *had lately advanced it* (*cf. his* Considerationes 2 *and* 85), *but to call them schools or school-classes is peculiar.*

That Corro was the translator of Sozzino's Italian original (*which seems never to have been printed*) *is not probable. One would like to know how the Latin text came into his hands.*

It is noteworthy that, as Strype, *Annals* III 618, *writes, in the same year* 1588 *appeared at Cambridge* Disputatio de sacra scriptura contra hujus temporis papistas, imprimis Robertum Bellarminum, Jesuitam, pontificium in collegio Romano, et Thomam Stapletonum, regium in schola Duacena controversiarum professorem. Sex quaestionibus proposita et tractata a Gulielmo Whitakero, theologiae doctore ac professore regio et collegii S. Joannis in Cantabrigiensi academia magistro. *The third of the questions is* De authoritate scripturae. *Epistle dedicatory of the work to the Lord treasurer* Burghley, *chancellor of the University.*

The harmless Jesuits were so unsuspecting that they received the Reverend Father Dominicus Lopez *in the catalogues of their writers. It lasted nearly three centuries. till they publicly acknowledged that they had been mystified.*

Possevini Apparatus sacer. T. I. Venetiis 1603. 416: Dominicvs Lopez, Societatis Jesu, librum edidit De sacrę Scripturę auctoritate Hispali in Hispania apud Lazarum Ferrerium 1589. *The same in the* Apparatus ab ipso Auctore recognitus. T. I. Coloniæ Agripp. 1608. *p.* 483. *This Lopez figures also in* Justiniani Index universalis, Romae 1612. *To the two Italians* Alegambe, *born at Brussels, associates himself. In his* Bibliotheca scriptorum societatis Jesu, Antwerp 1643, *p.* 97 *he repeats* Possevino's *statement. A second edition of* Alegambe's Bibliotheca *appeared in Rome in* 1675 *by* Sotwell *who writes:* ... Ita Possevinus (qui fuit Secretarius Societatis, et vixit eodem tempore, potuitque illum nosse ex litteris, et catalogis mitti solitis ad Praepositum generalem) in apparata Sancto Tomo I. Meminit quoque illius Fabianus Justinianus in Indice Universali, verbo Scriptura Sacra. Unde mirum est, quo fundamento scripserit Valerius Andreas Taxander in Catalogo Scriptorum Hispaniae, et Nomen, et librum illum confictum fuisse ab Haereticis apud Allobrogas.

Even Sand 1684 *p.* 66 *believes the existence of that* Lopez, qui videtur opusculum hoc sibi vindicare voluisse: verum in praefatione contrarium laudatur his quae in ipso libro leguntur: itaque se ipse prodit. Baumgarten *l. c.* 407 *observes that no Jesuit in Spain durst write and publish sentences like that on p.* 5 *of the preface:* in caelis iam regnantem superstitioso cultu eum [Christum] demereri mundus vult.

Dominicus Lopez *reappears in the* Bibliothèque des écrivains de la Compagnie de Jésus, par Aug. et Al. de Backer. Première série. Liége 1853 *p.* 467. *They give the title of the edition of* 1588 *with the notice:* in-12, *pp.* 6—80, *the title of the Racovian edition of* 1611 (*which they ascribe to Vorstius*) *and the passage* Editus *till* negat *from the preface of this edition, and refer to* Sand, Bayle, Baumgarten, *but at the end they place* Sotwel's *judgment* (*which I have above reprinted from this* Bibliothèque) *without any further remark. They evidently won't venture to decide or to confess who is right.*

After all the candid Jesuits laudably retracted. Bibliothèque des écrivains de la Compagnie de Jésus par Aug. de Backer avec la collaboration d'Alois de Backer et de Charles Sommervogel. Nouvelle éd. refondue. T. deuxième. Liége Lyon 1872. *col.* 794: Les PP. Alegambe et Sotwel le donnent pour un Père espagnol, mais ils se trompent. Voici ce que le P. Alegambe dit de lui.... L'opinion du P. Alegambe fut bientôt ébranlée. Le P. Sotwel s'exprime en ces termes: — *see above, ending with* Allobrogas. Il est reconnu aujourd'hui que ce livre est du fameux Fauste Socin. *Follows reference to* Sand, Bayle, Baumgarten; *the title of* 1588 *with the notice* in-12, *pp.* 6 – 80; *the title of the ed.* „*by Vorstius*" Racoviae 1611 *with the important passage of the preface. The same in* Bibliothèque de la Compagnie de Jésus. Nouv. éd. par Sommervogel. Bibliographie t. IV. Bruxelles Paris 1893, *col.* 1941—2, *only instead of* Père esp. *is said* Jésuite esp., *and the injudicious sentence* L'opinion *to* ébranlée *has been cancelled.* —

Reference may be made yet to another place where Corro is named together with Socinus. To the same sentence which Corro's adversaries in 1576 *excerpt from his* Dialogus *of* 1574 *in* Thesis 106: Tres hominis ponit status, irrenati, renascentis et renati. Andr. Rivet *refers in the* Epistola ad fratrem *against* Mos. Amyraldus 1648, *reprinted in* T. III Operum 1660, *where p.* 885 *he avers that* Amyrant *said most of what* Socinus *and* Arminius *had said on* Rom. VII, *and adds:* Id post acceptum illum libellum literis ad te scriptis notavi, et quia putat se posse latere sub velo medii cujusdam status, praeter id quod ab eadem subtilitate non sunt illi alieni, monui te, Antonium Coranum Hispanum, olim Ecclesiarum Santonicarum [*he seems to be thinking of the decree of the synod of La Rochelle in Saintongef. here p.* 127] et postea Londinensis Ecclesiae turbatorem, edidisse Dialogum in Epist. ad Rom., in quo de illo capite agens distinguit inter irregenitos, renascantes, renatos, et mediis illis applicat luctam illam de qua in illo capite Paulus. *I copy this quotation from* Crenii de furibus librariis dissertatio, Lugd. Bat. 1705, *p.* 17*f.* Sepp, Naspor. III 184 *asserts that Rivet said there* (*misprint* Opera II *instead* of III) *Corro had taken it from Socinus, and that Crenius therefore placed him among the purloiners. But there is no reason to suppose that Rivet and Crenius did not know that Corro's Dialogue, where that distinction occurs, was printed long before Socin's explication of Rom.* 7, *which* (*according to Sand* 70) *has been written* circiter 1580 *and, together with a letter of the author dated* 1581 March 24., *has been printed* Cracoviae 1583.

Usóz *intended to reprint in his series of* Reformistas *writings of Corro; see vol.* XIII. 1857, *appendix p.* 35. *He has reprinted Corro's letter of* 1563 *to* Reina, Ref. XVIII. 1862. *He has got the* Acta *of* 1571, Cohelet 1579, *a ms. copy, made for him, of the two French publications of* 1567, *and of the then unprinted letter of* 1574 *to* Gualtherus, — *all these articles from his library are at present in the* Biblioteca Nacional *of Madrid; see* Menendez Pelayo II. *Usóz possessed also copy of the letter to* Atye; *see above p.* 136.

Only when my Life of Corro was already printing, did I receive many papers of Wiffen, *the existence of which was never before mentioned to me, and among them a collection of tracings and notices concerning Corro. Wiffen's extract about the burial I added p.* 76, *other useful items I incorporated with his name into the* List *p.* 110 *f.*

Wiffen *noticed the following editions of works of Corro and got a dozen title-tracings.* The two French publications of 1567, the Dutch translation of the epistle to the Augsburghians, the English of the same 1569 and 1570, and the English of both 1577. The Tableau of 1569 and 1570, the Tabula in the Lansdowne ms. and printed 1570 *(the existence of the* Tabula *of* 1584 *he learned from the* Biblioth. Heinsiana 1682, pars I, *p.* 88; *on* 1588 *he read in* Basse *and* Draudius). Acta 1571. Usóz's reprint of the letter to Reina. Dialogus on Romans 1574. 1587 (Basse and Draudius 1588), English 1575, new Latin 1581. The letters to Parker Jan. 16. 1568 (he got a tracing of Corro's signature), to Bullinger 1574, to Atye 1579. Cohelet 1579. (Draudius 1581), 1619, English 1586. Grammar 1590. *He probably knew also* the letter to Gualtherus. *He knew* Beza's letters, Strype's Grindal, the Grindal Remains, Wood's Ath. Ox., Brandt's und Uytenbogaert's works on Netherlandish church-history, also the passage from the Doc. inéd. quoted here *p.* 5.

For my article on Corro I had the advantage of using, besides other libraries already registered in my former volumes, the library of my dear friend Johannes Merck *at Hamburg, which will be mentioned still many times in the continuation of this work.*

The first to publish a life of Corro in the light of the monumental work of Hessels *was* Dr. M. F. van Lennep *whose judicious sketch is contained in his work* De hervorming in Spanje in de zestiende eeuw, Haarlem 1901.

It is strange that Nic. Antonio *has in his* Bibliotheca *no article on Corro, nor has* Bayer *supplied one in the second ed.*

CIPRIANO DE VALERA.

Cipriano de Valera was born in 1532 or 1531.¹ He mentions that Benito Arias, the editor of the Antwerp polyglot Bible, who was born not far from Seville, was his fellow-student in the High school of that city.² There, during six years, Valera studied dialectics and philosophy, and fulfilled all that was required to obtain a bachelor's degree.³ What he says of Arias, that he was a willing hearer of good sermons by such preachers as Dr. Constantino and Dr. Aegidius,⁴ is applicable also to himself; in fact, at that time few in Seville were opposed to those divines. He expressly states that he was on intimate terms with Juan Perez, Cassiodoro de Reina and Julian Hernandez.⁵ Like Reina he was a friar in the monastery of San Isidro, and with others he fled from it and from Spain in 1557.⁶ At the Sevillian auto of

---

1) *Exhortacion* prefixed to his Bible, fol. **: *en este año de* 1602 ... *soy de* 70 *años*. Pablo Besson in the Revista Cristiana, Madrid 1894 p. 41: *propriamente era natural de Valera la vieja (Herróbriga), no lejos de Frejenal de la Sierra, de suerte que era vecino de Benito Arias Montano. En* 1253 *el Rey don Alonso concedió á la catedral de Sevilla el castillo de Valera y sus dependencias* .... *Se puede decir de él lo que escribió de su condiscípulo:* (I transcribe the words textually from *Exhortacion* fol. *3) *su juventud passó en sus estudios en Sevilla: por lo qual, y porque su tierra Frexenal no es lexos, y es del territorio de Sevilla, se llamó Hispalensis. q. d. Sevillano*. Besson's conjecture is not improbable.

Burlamachi names him as *Cipriano Valleria di Siuiglia*. See above II 73. In Thomas Hyde's Catal. impressor. libror. bibloth. Bodlei., Oxoniae 1674 p. 219 he is called *Cyprian de Valera, seu de Valeriola;* the same entry occurs in the new Catal. vol. III p. 690.

2) Exhort. fol. *3.
3) See annot. 10.
4) Exhort. fol. *3.
5) ibd.
6) The narrative of the occurrences at Seville and the adventures of the fugitives, is reproduced in the second edition of his *Dos tratados*, reprint of Usóz p. 247, l. 7 a. i. to p. 252, l. 12, from the first ed. p. 205f. with the sole addition of the parenthetical notice on Julian p. 249, l. 4—5. Valera says twice in each edition that twelve fled and were saved; he does not mention the later capture of

April 26. 1562 ten fugitive Isidrians, among whom Reina and Valera, were condemned as Lutherans, and statues representing them were burned.[7]

On October 10. 1558 he was, together with seven Spaniards, admitted as a *habitant* of Geneva,[8] and in the same year he and other Spaniards were received into the Italian church there.[9] Thence he went like some of his countrymen to England after the accession of Queen Elizabeth. In February 1560 he was admitted to the bachelor's degree at Cambridge, on account of his studies and achievements at Seville.[10] He was also elected a fellow of Magdalen college.[11] The master's degree he took on June 12. 1563.[12] When at Christmas of the same year Corro invited Reina to come from England to the south of France, there to print the Spanish Bible, he suggested that Reina should bring Cipriano with him, to correct the proofs;[13] but they could not come. In 1565 Valera obtained letters from Cambridge

one of them. According to an official account, written before the auto of 1559, probably in 1558, eleven fled; one of them was caught and burned, ten were burned in effigy. Schäfer, Beiträge II 356.

7) Official relation in Schäfer's Beiträge I 454.
8) See below the appended note.
9) Above II 73.
10) Notice of Wiffen: „Copied from the registers of the University of Cambridge by Peter Lorimer: 9. Febr. 1559 [old style]. *Conceditur eodem die Cypriano Valera Hispano nato et educato in Academia Hispalensi ubi per sex annos dialecticis et philosophicis litteris operam dedit — peractis singulis in eadem academia quae ad Baccalaureatus gradum spectant ut possit hic cooptari in numerum Baccalaureorum in artibus, sic ut per examinatores hujus anni Ejus eruditio prius approbetur et ut stet et determinet cum reliquis quaestio natis.* 12. June 1563: A grace passed making him Master of Arts, his name appearing with many others."

Of course, the first sentence should not read: *Hispano, nato et educato in academia Hisp.*, but: *Hispano nato, et educato in ac. Hisp.* Cf. a Spaniard born, note 15. As to whether an Isidrian was allowed to accept a formal graduation, cf. above p. 67. At all events a Hieronymite must have been permitted to pursue literary studies. Helyot, Hist. des ordres religieux, nouv. éd., t. 3. Paris 1792, p. 452 mentions among the *droits* of the Prior of the Hieronymites of Seville: *Il est Protecteur de l'Université de cette ville.* I think he obtained this distinction only some time after the deserted monastery had been reorganized.

11) So Cooper, Ath. Cantabr. II 353, after mentioning that he was admitted to the degree of B. A. and before stating that he commenced M. A. in 1563. Cf. ibd. 560.

12) See annot. 10.
13) Above p. 79.

University testifying to his godly conversation.[14] On February 21. 1566 he was incorporated at Oxford.[15]

Valera acted as tutor to Mr. Walsh of Ireland who subsequently became a Bishop.[16]

Alfonso Baptista making his will at Geneva on July 14. 1573, two days before his death, named as his heirs Cassiodoro de Reina at Frankfort, Francisco Faries, Juan de Molino, and Cipriano [de Valera] schoolmaster, all three resident in London, bequeathing to each of them a fourth part of his estate. The testator and the heirs were fugitives from S. Isidro to Geneva and all were burned in effigy on April 26. 1562.[17]

In March 1579 we find Valera with Reina in London. Reina had returned to England some months previously, to obtain a final verdict on a long-standing accusation against his character. On his acquittal by the Archbishop of Canterbury, who had been appointed by the Privy Council to pronounce judgment, he presented himself before the French Consistory as he desired to be reconciled with them. Cipriano and Antonio Giustiniano accompanied him, and he

---

14) Cooper ibd.

15) Wood, Ath. Oxon., vol. 1, Fasti, 2ᵈ ed. 1721 col. 96: *Cyprian de Valera M. of A. of three years standing in the said University* [Cambridge] *was also then* [Febr. 21. 1565 old style] *incorporated. He was a Spaniard born, left his Country for Religion sake, spent all, or most of his time in England, and wrote* .... Without authority Pellicer says in his Ensayo de una biblioteca de traductores españoles 1778 p. 42: *Entre los Reformados era Valera Presbytero, y es regular lo fuese tambien en España.*

16) Leigh, Treatise of Religion & Learning (1656) *p.* 348: *Cyprian de Valera a Spaniard who was B. Welch of Ireland's Tutor, turned Protestant, and was here in England, and carried over into Spain the Bible translated into Spanish, and also Calvin's Institutions, and went and dispersed them there.* James Townley: Illustrations of biblical literature, London 1821. vol. III p. 385: *Valera, was tutor to Mr. (afterwards Bishop) Walsh in Ireland.* Townley quotes Leigh. Mr. George F. Warner of the British Museum writes to me: B. Welch is, I suppose, Nicholas Walsh, Bishop of Osson (murdered in 1585) who began a translation of the New Testament into Irish. There is no biography of him.

To Mr. Warner I am also indebted for the following information: Lansdowne MS. 60 art. 66 (f. 170) is a brief holograph certificate in Latin by Cypr. de Valera in favour of a Breton sailor who had been compelled by the Spaniards at Lisbon to take part in the naval expedition of 1588, shipwrecked in Ireland and imprisoned in Bridewell in London; *haec ex omnium qui cum eo sunt Hispanorum relatione habui eoque testificor* 13. *Septemb.* 1589 *Cyprianus de Valera.*

17) This note is appended p. 157.

expressed the wish that they might be present at the proceedings. This permission was refused, „as it was not customary to admit to the Consistory any but those who themselves have business there", and the result of the conference was likewise unsatisfactory to Reina.[18]

A theologian of Seville, Pedro de Fuentidueña, had said in a sermon which he delivered before the members of the Tridentine Council, that the protestant heretics sought to subvert the two pillars of the church, viz. the mass and the Pope.[19] Valera did his best to merit this reproach. In 1588 he printed in London his two Spanish treatises, the one upon the Pope and his authority, and the other upon the mass and its sanctity.[20] For the *chronique scandaleuse* of the Popes, Roman catholic writers afforded abundant facts and fables pêle-mêle. Valera praises the magnanimous and prudent Queen Elizabeth for having made her country an asylum of so very many who were persecuted on account of religion, and he prays God to bless England with spiritual and temporal riches.[21] In 1599 he brought out a second edition, likewise published in London, and in 1600 there appeared an English translation. A part of this work of Valera, the Three Tables, has been published in French. One of these tables presents the contrasts between the old and the new doctrine, the latter being that of Rome; Valera evidently made free use of Juan Perez's translation of the treatise of Regius.[22]

18) Archives of the London French Church. Schickler has printed almost the whole document I 232 f. I use the copy of it, made for Wiffen. The first 17 lines are traced on transparent paper; there appears the passage on *Ciprian et Anthoine Justinian quj laccōpaignoient*, but no mention of *trois témoins* whom Schickler mentions. The conference took place on *dimanche 22. de mars appres le catechisme*. On Ant. Giustiniano see above p. 48. 97. 98.

19) Valera's *epist. al lector* before the *Dos tratados*. This sermon, preached on the last day of September, as is stated by Valera, who omits the date of the year, must be the sermon which, according to Nic. Antonio, Bibl. t. 2. 1788 p. 195, was delivered by that theologian on S. Jerome's day 1562, and which was printed.

20) Wiffen: „The design and plan of the work is clearly taken from Barnes' and Bale's Vitis Pontificum Romanorum, known in English as John Studley's Pageant of Popes, London 1574; varied and accommodated for the perusal of his countrymen by Valera". Cf. Usóz p. [4] and [5] in the preface of his reprint of the second ed.

21) p. 198 f. Second ed. 240.

22) Compare for instance Valera's nos 14 and 17 with Perez, Rf. Esp. t. 7. p. 302. 108. Cf. Sp. Rf. II 92 f. — The Table on the Lord's Supper and the mass (enlarged in the second edition, see Usóz in his ed. in the Nota to p. 538) has in

In 1594 he printed a treatise addressed to the Spanish prisoners in Berbery, among whom there had been an evangelical revival. Valera wishing to strengthen their faith against Popery and Mahometanism, expounds to them the doctrine of the Bible, and also refers to the three oecumenical symbols. He exhorts them to show a model life to the heathens. And pray for Spain, he says at the end.[23]

Together with this work was published the history of the false miracles of a nun at Lisbon; it was reprinted in 1599. The English translation of 1600 gives the additional information that this Maria de la Visitacion was the person whom Philip called to bless the standard of his Invincible Armada.

In 1596 Valera reedited the Spanish translation of the Geneva catechism according to the Spanish edition of 1559. From the same work he had already in the Two Treatises of 1588 extracted the agenda of the Lord's Supper, which he repeated in the edition of 1599 of those Treatises.[24]

In 1596 likewise he reproduced with some retouches the New Testament of Reina (who had died in 1594).

In the succeeding year appeared Valera's Spanish translation of Calvin's Institutes.[25]

---

both editions 12 articles on the Lord's Supper and as many against the mass. I do not know the work: *André Epicime: Traité de la Cêne et de la Messe, Lyon* 1564, registered by du Verdier who states: *contenant vingt-quatre argumens: assavoir douze soutenants la Messe être la Cêne de Jesus-Christ, avec douze réponses, à la fin d'un chacun d'iceux: & douze autres argumens au contraire.* See *Les bibliotheques françoises de La Croix du Maine et de du Verdier. Par Rigolet de Juvigny.* T. 3. *Paris* 1772. P. 67. There is added La Monnoye's note that Epicime is Epitimus, the pseudonym of the Lutheran Hartmann Beyer, according to Melchior Adam. Adam writes in his *Vitae Germanorum theologorum, Haidelbergae* 1620, p. 517: *Sub nomine Andreae Epitimi quaedam de Missa edidit contra Sidonium Episcopum.* The City library of Frankfort o. M., where Beyer was born, and where he died in 1577, does not possess this work of his, nor have I been able to meet with a copy in other libraries.

23) Menendez Pelayo II 493: *Este tratado es la mejor escrita de las obras de Valera: no carece de cierto fervor y elocuencia; se conoce que quiso imitar la Epistola Consolatoria de Juan Perez.*

24) Cf. above II p. 46f.

25) In the preface he says: Years ago the Institutio has been translated into different languages. *Ahora sale a luz por la misericordia de Dios en lengua Española, en la qual yo la he trasladado.* He evidently means to say that his Spanish translation is the first which has been made, and that this is the first edition

In the preface he again expresses his thanks to Queen Elizabeth, the patroness of so many thousands of evangelical fugitives.

In 1599 he wrote a preface to the *Catholico Reformado,* a Spanish translation made by William Massan of the Reformed Catholic of Perkins, Professor in Cambridge, a Calvinistic Puritan.

The pamphlet published in 1600 on the jubilee proclaimed by the Pope does not bear Valera's name, but the internal evidence points strongly to his being the author of it.[26]

When seventy years of age, Valera edited in 1602 the whole Spanish Bible. In the exhortation prefixed to it he speaks, with the satisfaction to which a Spaniard is entitled, of the two polyglot Bibles: of the first, that had ever been compiled, the product of Spanish learning and of Spanish funds, the Complutensian, undertaken and carried out by Cardinal Ximenez, and of the second, the Antwerp polyglot, brought out by Valera's fellow-student Benito Arias at the expense of King Philip. He mentions the Spanish version of the Old Testament, published by the Jews at Ferrara, and the New Testament of Enzinas and that of Juan Perez. Reina was the first to publish the whole Bible in Spanish. His edition of 1569 was repeatedly re-read by Valera who, besides enriching it with fresh annotations, occasionally varied the text after consultation with learned and pious men. This process of revision extended over a period of twenty years before Valera committed the work to the press.[27] There was, he says, scarcely a copy of Reina's Bible to be found by a person desirous of purchasing one.[28] When he calls his Bible a second edition,[29] he wishes thereby to state that the translation is on the whole the same in both editions, the second being a revision of the first. And he repeatedly calls Reina the first translator of the

---

of it. Therefore the *ahora nuevamente traduzida* in the title does not refer to a former translation, nor did Valera know of one alleged to be printed at Saragossa (cf. above II p. 78), the very existence of which is more than doubtful.

26) That this *Aviso* is written by Valera is also the opinion of Ad. de Castro, Hist. de los Protest. Esp. 1851 p. 305, of Usóz Rf. ant. esp. t. VIII. 1854 p. XXXIIf., and of Menendez Pelayo II 495.

27) *Siendo de 50 años comencé esta obra.* Exhortacion fol. **.

28) Exhortacion fol. *6.

29) ib. and in the title-page.

Bible into Spanish,[30] not to claim for himself the honour of being a second translator of equal merit, but to extol the merit of Reina's work. It is not clear why Valera or rather the publisher did not name Reina in the title-page where, however, the second edition alone is attributed to Valera. In relation to the order of the sacred books Valera introduced an improvement into Reina's Bible, for he distributed them again into two parts, those which had been translated from the Hebrew, and the apocryphal books, which had been translated out of Greek or Latin; whilst Reina following the Septuagint and the Vulgate had mingled the protocanonical with the deuterocanonical books (only Esdras 3 and 4 he expressly called *apochrypho*). Nor did Valera admit marginal references to the apocrypha. Reina's wish to get a royal authorization for the version of the Bible[31] was reiterated by Valera. May it please God, he says, to inspire the King to command that at his expense pious and learned men assemble to revise thoroughly this translation upon the Hebrew and the Greek, and then may that version be authorized and read by king and people.[32] The reading, the writing, the correcting, all the literary labour which was needed to prepare and to finish this edition, Valera did himself, unsupported by any countryman, although he had finally reached an age at which, as he says, strength fails, memory flags and the eyes grow dim.[33] The work of many years was printed by Lorenz Jacobi at Amsterdam, where Valera himself lived when the printing was going on. To some copies a leaf was added with a dedication to the States of the United Provinces of the Netherlands and to their Governor Prince Maurice of Orange. Valera gratefully acknowledges in it, that by their Excellencies he has been treated not as a poor stranger, but like a father.[34] They kindly took care of him, and the

30) Exhort. fol. *6 and in the superscription of Reina's *Amonestacion*, which he reprinted there.
31) See above II 174f.
32) Exhort. fol. *4.
33) Exhort. fol. **.
34) On Valera's Bible cf. above II 247f. and 175f.
Wiffen in the Noticia prévia to the Epistola consolatoria por Juan Perez speaking of Reina's Bible says p. XXIIf.: *Valera la revisó y corrijió, con mucho cuidado, restituyendo, ademas, omisiones notables, que por descuido de impresores, se hallan en la edicion de la Biblia de Casiodoro de Reyna.*

printing-expenses were paid by Prince Christian I. of Anhalt Bernburg.[35] Arminius, the leader of the Remonstrants, wrote on October 30. 1602 (from Amsterdam) to John Uytenbogard (at the Hague), subsequently one of the leaders of that denomination (we have previously mentioned his praise of Corro): „Cipriano de Valera and Jacobus Laurentius are going to you in order to present to the Count [Maurice, the Governor] and to the States some copies of the Bible in Spanish which by God's grace has been brought to a conclusion. There is a disagreement[36] between them to settle which I beg you to compose, for they both wish you to arbitrate. It is but a small matter and will be easily arranged, especially since they are both good men and friends who have hitherto, in best friendship and one spirit, promoted that work, and are resolved that this their friendship shall not in any way relax its bonds. You will make the kindest provision you can, that Cipriano do not return to England to his wife without a liberal viaticum; I have done here whatever I could. In fact, this good man deserves to pass the short rest of his life under the least pressure possible."[37] On November 3. Valera was still at Antwerp.[38] We do not know when and where he died.[39]

35) See my article Protestantische Propaganda in Spanien im Anfange des 17. Jahrhunderts in 'der Zeitschrift für Kirchengesch. XVIII. 1897. Valera himself only says in the Exhortacion fol. **: *Esta biblia fue imprimida con la ayuda y assistencia de pia gente.* Perhaps Christian's brother Ludwig contributed, and they had expressed a wish not to be named.

36) *Sin duda por cuestion de maravedises,* says Menendez Pelayo II 497.

37) Praestantium ac eruditorum virorum epistolae. Amsterdam 1660 p. 134. Second ed. 1684. Third ed. 1704. Spanish translation of the respective part of that letter in Pellicer's Ensayo p. 42f.; it is reprinted by Ad. de Castro l. c. p. 305f.

38) Wiffen noticed on a separate leaf: „Autograph inscriptions in a book entitled ΣΟΦΙΑ ΣΕΙΡΑΧ siue Ecclesiasticus, Graece ad exemplar Romanum, & Latine ex interpretatione J. Drusii, Cum castigationibus siue notis eiusdem, Ad Reuerendissimum in Christo patrem D. Johannem Whitgiftvm archiepiscopum Cantuariensem. &c. Franekerae [a town in Holland] excudebat Ægidius Radæus, Ordinum Frisiæ Typographus CIƆ.IƆ.XCVI. 4 to. The first is at the beginning. Matthew Slade gives the book to Cypriano de Valera, returning to England, in token of eternal memory at Amsterdam 14th of October 1601. The second is at the end. Cypriano de Valera of Seville records his friendship to Matthew Slade and his gratitude for having completed his Spanish Bible this 3. of November 1602 at Amsterdam." Wiffen does not say where the book with these autographs was to be found. I should think that Slade's inscription was also written in 1602.

39) That he should have returned to Spain, as Leigh tells (above note 16), is most unlikely.

Valera draws a flattering picture when he writes in the Exhortation [40] addressed to the reader of his Bible: „There is no city nor is there, so to speak, any borough or any mansion in Spain that has not had, and has not even now, one or more persons whom God in his infinite mercy has enlightened with the light of his gospel. It has become proverbial in Spain when they speak of a learned man, to say: he is so learned that there is danger of his becoming a Lutheran. Our adversaries have done all that they could, to quench this light of the gospel, and then they have outraged many in Spain by the loss of property, of life and of honour. And it is to be observed that the more they outrage, the more they scourge, expose in sanbenitos, send to the galleys or to perpetual imprisonment and into the flames, so much the more do the evangelicals multiply, for the blood of the martyrs is the seed of the church." And in 1677 Diodati, the translator of the Bible into Italian, asserted that Valera's Bible had produced incredible effects in Spain, no less than three thousand copies having penetrated by secret ways into the very bowels of that kingdom.[41] It is, however, notorious that the tyranny not only prevented an organization of the evangelicals, but also suppressed clandestine conventicles. And what Nicolas Antonio wrote in his Bibliotheca Hispana in 1672 (the same in the second edition 1783) on Valera: „to us always an infamous name",[42] remains the feeling of the ruling Romanists still to-day. Nevertheless they are constrained by political circumstances to permit countless thousands of revised Reina-Valera Bibles being circulated over the length and breadth of Spain.

40) fol. *3.
41) See above II p. 248f. — Spanish Bibles in America about 1623 and 1650, Medina: Historia del Tribunal del Santo Oficio de la Inquisicion de Cartagena de las Indias. Santiago de Chile 1899. p. 156. 294.
42) . . . . *lenguaje poco digno de un hombre de su clase é instruccion,* says Pedro Salvá y Mallen in the Catálogo de la biblioteca de Salvá, Valencia 1872, t. II. p. 777.

---

17) *Noms des Espagnols reçus habitans le lundy* 10e *d'octobre* 1558. *Jehan Purius. Jehan de Viria. Joseph Cortois. Jehan Moreno. Jehan de Moline. Jehan de Lion. Allonso Baptiste. Cyprian de Valer.* Copied for me by Mr. Louis Dufour-Vernes. archiviste d'État, from the Registre des habitants. On the same day the Spaniards were allowed henceforward to have the gospel preached to them in the temple S. Germain, in their own language, as there was an aged man of good conduct,

willing to preach (above II 74). This man was Juan Perez, and he must be that Jehan *Purius*, write *Pierius*. He had stayed there already for some time. In 1558 we find as members of the Italian church (ib. 73 – 74): *Gio: di Viuares di Vagliadoli* = Jean Vivarte ou Vivarès, who is perhaps the *Jehan de Viria* of those eight. *Lopes Cortis di Castiglia* = *Cortes, de Seville ou Castilian, Jope ou Lope* = Lope Cortes (read *Cortés*), Isidrian monk, burned 1562 in effigy (Schäfer I 454. II 313), is *Joseph Cortois* of the above list (cf. Franc. Courtois above p. 34). *Jean Moreno. Giouanni di Mollina, di Varracina d'Arragona,* = *Juan de Molino*, vicario of S. Isidro, burned in effigy 1562 (Schäfer ibid. — Nicolaus Molinus above II 171). *Jean de Leon*, burned 1560. *Allonso Battista di Canaria* = *Alonso Baptista, natural de la ysla de Tenerife*, monk in S. Isidro, burned in effigy 1562 (Schäfer ibid.), bourgeois at Geneva 1569, July 22 (Galiffe VII 332). *Valera*.

I have had Baptista's whole testament copied from the Minutes et protocolles de Pierre Delarue, notaire, volume 7, f. 24 in the Archives d'Etat de Genève, by M. Louis Dufour-Vernes, who in his article Baptista in Galiffe's Notices généalogiques sur les familles genévoises, Tome cinquième, Genève 1884. p. 333 had given the names of the four heirs, of the two executors and of the seven witnesses.

Baptista left some legacies: to his wife 150 *escuz soleil* [écus d'or with a sun] *avecq tous ses meubles* [she may have had some property of her own], to the poor of the Italian church at Geneva 100 florins, to Camilie *qui demeure avecq luy* 20 florins, to a certain Marthe 3 *escuz soleil*, to a goddaughter the same; ... *ses aultres bien, droitz, noms, actions, successions et aultrement de quelle aultre quallité et quantité qu'ilz soyent, il y faict, crée et institue ses héritiers et successeurs généraulx et universelx* ... follow the names. They are charged to pay his debts [amount not mentioned] and without delay the legacies. The seigneurs Paul Arnulphini and Franc. Taruffe are requested to be executors, and the seigneurs de Justice to confirm them. On Faries see above p. 7.

Among the witnesses to the testament is a Spaniard: *Francisco Massuelo*. Fils de Francisco Fernandez Massuelo, né à Seville (Galiffe VII 357). He is mentioned in 1564 as member of the Italian church of Geneva (Sp. Rf. II 76). He married in 1565 a daughter of *Jean-Antoine Sterpino, de Lucques*) [Sterpin is wrongly called a Spaniard in the document Sp. Rf. II 75], he was received July 11. 1578 as bourgeois there, living as *marchant passementier;* he died, 60 years old, Nov. 23 1596 (Galiffe VII 357f.). *Francisco de Maçuelo*, Schäfer I 356. 397. II 409—11. A son of Francisco Maçuelo married a sister of Jean Hotman (cf. above p. 73f.) 8 août 1585 (Galiffe VII p. 359).

Baptista died July 16. 1573. From the Registre des décès copied by Dufour-Vernes. As to the amount of his estate nothing can be made out at present. His widow, Marie Genevois(e) in her last will March 14. 1605 *lègue divers meubles à Priscille Santa qui la gouverne à present et l'a assisté longtemps; heritiers universels les diacres de la Bourse des pauvres italiens qui l'ont assistée dès longtemps, n'ayant aucun parent.* Isaac Donzel, notaire, vol. VIII. f. 206. Copy by Dufour-Vernes.

The article on Valera which *La Aurora de Gracia* 28 *Agosto* 1875 *[B—r]* reproduces from her *colega Madrileña La Bandera de la Reforma* is taken from *Ad. de Castro, Hist. de los Protest. español.* p. 302—7. This is not said in the Aurora, I do not know whether in the Bandera. De Castro's article is copied nearly verbotenus, but without the letter of Arminius and the notes, and without any additions.

BIBLIOGRAPHY.

Index Sandoval y Rojas 1612, Palermo reprint 1628, Prohib. *in the third class p.* 35 *and* 86 *without naming the author:* Dos tratados. El primero del Papa *etc. and* Un Enxambre de los falsos milagros con que Maria de la Visitacion *etc.*

Index Juxta Exemplar excusum Madriti M. DC. LXVII *p.* 229. Cypriano de Valera. Llamado vulgarmente el Herege Español, traduxo en Castellano el libro intitulado Institucion de la Religion Christiana, que corre en varias lenguas, cuyo Autor fue Calvino. Iten, et Cathecismo Heretico, intitulado el Catholico Reformado. Iten, la Biblia, lo qual se prohibe con todo lo demas que escrivio, o traduxo, en qualquier lengua, y de qualquier impression.

1588 *f. Two treatises: on the pope and on the mass.*

1588 Dos Tratados. | El primero es del | Papa y de su autoridad colegi- | do de su vida y dotrina, y de lo | *que los Dotores y Concilios* | antiguos y la misma | *sagrada Escritura* | enseñan. | El segvndo es de | la Missa recopilado de los | Dotores y Concilios y | *de la sagrada Escritura.* | Toda planta, que no plantó my Padre | celestial, será desarraygada. | *Mat.* 15. 13. | Cayda es, Cayda es Babylonia aquella | gran ciudad, porque ella ha dado | à bever à todas las gentes | del vino de la yra de su | fornicacion. *A-* | *poc.* 14. 8. | *En casa de Arnoldo Hatfildo. Año de.* | 1588. | *On the reverse of the title* Dos Sonetos en loor d'esta obra *followed by* 7 *leaves* Epistola al Christiano Letor *dated* 15 de Iunio de. 1588, *signed* C. D. V. *which means Cipriano de Valera. The work* 1—488 *p., and an alphabetical index of the bishop's of Rome* 4 *leaves; on the reverse of the fourth leaf* Q. d. significan: Quiere dezir. *and Faltas de la Impression. Sm. octavo.*

OXFORD *Wadham, Wiffen's copy.* FRANKFURT *o. M. City.* GOETTINGEN *Univ.* HAMBURG *City. The copy of Usóz is at present probably in* MADRID *National.*

De la Serna Santander *in his* Catalogue des livres de la bibliotheque de M. C. de la Serna Santander, t. 1, Bruxelles, an XI (1803), *p.* 245: Traité fort rare, attribué à Cypriano de Valera. Voyez la bibliogr. instruct. num. 714 et le catalogue de M. Gaignat, num. 537, où il fut vendu 31 liv. o.

Tratado Del Papa y de sua autoridad, vnder the arch Bishop of Canterbury and master warden Coldockes handes *licensed by the London Stationers on* 24 *April* 1588 *to* Edmonde Bolifant, Arnold Hatfeild, John Jackson. Arber II, 488, *cf.* 140.

The Dos tratados *of* 1588 *are registered in* Willer's Catal. vern. 1589 *fol.* I. *In the* Elenchus *of* Cless 1602 *p.* 561 *with the years* 1587 & 1589, *and the same years are copied from this* Elenchus *in the* Bibliotheca Exotica Frankfovrt 1610 *p.* 211.

In the auction-catalogue, Bibliotheca Hulsiana, Hagae-Comitum 1730, t. 1, *p.* 312, *nº* 4867, *among the* Ms. theologica in Folio: Cyprianus de Valera van den Paus en van syne autoriteyt, mitsgaders van de Misse. *This title is given in Gothic letters. Then the notice:* „Ms. op papier, l. g." — *Wiffen sent to Usóz* a folio manuscript of 276 pages, closely written, bought from Frederik Muller, bookseller at

Amsterdam, *n° 5380 of his catalogue of* April 1857: Twee tractaten: van den Paus en van seyn autoriteyt, en van de Misse, overgeset uyt de Spanse in de Duytsche tale, door T. H. P. int jaer 1627. *Wiffen remarks:* It is a translation of Valera's Dos tratados, edition of 1588. This is shown by the list of the popes, Agathon being put before Adrian, and by not having the table of Antichrist, the Enjambre de falsos milagros, nor the table of La doctrina antigua y nueva, all which are added in the Spanish of 1599.

1599 Dos Tratados, | el primero es | del papa y de sv av- | toridad, colegido de | su vida y dotrina. | El segvndo es de la | Missa: el uno y el otro re- | *copilado de lo que los Doctores y Con-* | cilios antiguos, y la sagrada | Escritura enseñan. |

Iten, un Enxambre de los falsos Mi- | *lagros con que Maria de la Visitacion, Prio-* | ra de la Anunciada de Lisbra engañó à muy | *muchos: y de como fue descubierta* | *y condenada.*

Revelacion 17. 1. | *Ven, y mostrarte he la condenacion de la gran Ramera,* | *la qual está sentada sobre muchas aguas.* Y vers. 15. | *Las aguas que has visto donde la Ramera se sienta, son pueblos, compañas, gentes, y lenguas.* |

Segunda edicion, augmentada | por el mismo Autor. |
En Casa de Ricardo del Campo. | Año de 1599. |

Sm. octavo. Title and epistola 8 *leaves, the work p.* 1 — 610, *alphabetical index of the popes* 4 *leaves, on the last of which also* Faltas. *After p.* 352 *which is* [Z 8], *a folding sheet:* Tabla en la qual se declara quien sea el Antichristo, *replacing p.* 353 *and* 354, *after which on p.* 355 *begins* Tratado segundo. *In this between p.* 538 *and* 539 *another folding sheet, a* Tabla *contrasting the* Lord's Supper *with the* Mass; *in the first edition it runs from p.* 467 *to* 473. *Additions of the second edition are the* Enxambre de los falsos milagros of Maria de la Visitacion *p.* 554—594, *and the* Tabla *of the* dotrina antigua de Dios *and the* dotrina nueva de los hombres *p.* 594 — 610.

BODLEIAN. OXFORD *Wadham, Wiffen's copy.* VIENNA *Court.* WOLFENBÜTTEL. ZURICH *City.*

De la Serna Santander, *l. c. p.* 245: Cette édition, sans être moins rare que la précédente, a l'avantage d'être augmentée. — Vincent Salvá, catalogue of Spanish and Portuguese books, London 1826, *p.* 211 f., *n°* 2156 *a copy for* 16 sh. — *Two copies of this edition in* Morante's library, Catalogus, t. VI, Matriti 1859, *n°* 9701 — 2; *the price of the one* rs 190, *of the other* rs 500. — Livres, Estampes, Manuscrits du magasin de Frederik Muller à Amsterdam, N° 2, 1870, *p.* 30, *n°* 530: ₤ 15 [= £ 1. 5 sh.]. — *A copy for* 120 francs *in* Tross *at* Paris Catalogue de livres anciens 1870, n° VI, *p.* 248. — Superbe exemplaire, *with the two* tablas, mar. vert, fil., riche dent., tr. dor. (Derome), *for* 250 francs *in* Bachelin-Defloreune's Catalogue, Paris 1872, *p.* 186, *n°* 2440.

In Simler ms. 173, *Zurich City, a printed copy of the* Tabla *on the Antichrist (without paging and signature) is bound among mss.*

Cless, Elenchus 1602 p. 561 *registers the ed. of* 1599, *adding:* Antwerp. Nutius. Hence repeated *in* Biblioth. exotica 1610 p. 211. *But no copy of an Antwerp edition is found. No doubt Nutius is only the bookseller who offered the book in the fair. Such inexact entries are not unfrequent in the fair-catalogues.*

1851 Los dos tratados | del Papa, i de la Misa. | Escritos | por Cipriano D. Valera; | i por él publicados | primero el a. 1588, luego el a. 1599: | i | ahora fielmente reimpresos. | «Totius injustitiæ nulla capita- | lior est, quam eorum, qui cum | maxime fallunt, id agunt, ut viri | boni esse videantur.» | Cic., *de Offic.*, Lib. 1, cap. XIII. | Año de MDCCCLI. |

Octavo. Editor's preface 6 leaves. The titles of the two former editions 2 leaves (with the two sonetos of the first which had been omitted in the second). Epístola al Christiano lector 7 *leaves.* Tratados, Enjambre, Tabla *p.* 1—610, *corresponding page for page with the ed. of* 1599; *another* Tabla *with independent numeration, p.* 1—11, *inserted after p.* 538. *Catalogue of Popes* 4 *leaves.* Notas *by the editor* 31 *leaves, likewise unnumbered.* Errata 1 *leaf.*
Edited by Usóz.
Not all copies have the series-title. The copy which, when in Madrid, I bought from the editor, had not got it. My other copy has it: Obras antiguas | de los | Españoles reformados. | Tomo *without number, but on the back of the leaf in the list of the* Obras *hitherto published, the* Tratados *are number 6, the last number.*
With this copy is bound Wiffen's autograph English translation of Usóz's preface.

1895—99 Tratado de la misa y de su santidad escrito por Cipriano de Valera, y por él publicado, primero el año 1588, luego el año 1599. Fielmente reimpreso por d. Luis Usoz y Rio. 1851.

Reprinted in Revista Cristiana periódico científico religioso. Madrid. N° 374. 31 de Julio de 1895 *to* N° 408. 31 de Diciembre de 1896.

Tratado del papa y de su autoridad colegido de su vida y doctrina y recopilado de lo que los doctores y concilios antiguos y la sagrada escritura enseñan, por Cipriano de Valera. Ven, y te mostraré... Apoc. 17, 15. Segunda edicion, aumentada por el autor, en casa de Ricardo de Campo, Año de 1599. Epistola al Cristiano Lector.

In the same Revista N° 409. 15 de Enero de 1897 *to* N° 476. 31 de Octubre de 1899. *Likewise from the ed. of* 1551.
The alphabetical table of the Popes and the preceding remarks p. [610]*f. are not reprinted.*
The orthography of Usóz has been changed into the usual one. I have not verified whether there are or are not any other changes.

1600 Two Treatises: | *The first,* | of the lives of | the Popes, and | their doctrine. | *The second,* | of the Masse: the one | and the other collected of that, which the | *Doctors, and ancient Councels and* | *the* *sacred Scripture do teach.* | *Also,* | A Swarme of false Miracles wherewith *Marie de* | la Visitacion, *Prioresse* de la Annuntiada *of Lisbon*, | deceiued very many: and how she was dis- | couered, and condemned. | Reuelation 17. 1. | *Come, and I will shew thee the condemnation of the great Whore, which sitteth | vpon many waters.* And vers. 15. *The waters which thou sawest, where | the Whore sitteth, are people, and multitudes, and nations, and tongues.* | The second edition in Spanish augmented by the | *Author himselfe, M. Cyprian Valera, and translated | into English by John Golburne.* 1600. | *[Ornament.]* Printed at London by *John Harison,* and are to be | *sold at the Grey-hound in Pater noster row.* 1600. | 6 *leaves* A, *and Octavo p.* 1—446.

A·2, *ending* A 3 *recto* Epistle Dedicatorie *to* sir Thomas Egerton, lord keeper of the great Seale, *signed* Fleete my miserable prison this 24. of October. 1600 … Golburne. A 3 *verso and* A 4 *recto* The Translator to the Reader. A 4 *verso to* [A 6] *verso* Valera's Epistle to the Christian Reader 1588. *The work* B *foll. At the end of it, p.* 438 An Addition *to the original on* Maria de la Visitacion.

Cf the preface of Usóz to his edition of the original 1851. *The cipher* 558 *for the pages of the translation is a misprint instead of* 458, *total sum. Usóz says there that Golburne was then already at least six years in prison, for, according to a notice afforded by Wiffen, he petitioned June* 14. 1594 *to be released. He may, however, have been discharged and afterwards imprisoned again. Usóz calls the translation* mui fiel. *On Golburne's above mentioned* Addition *see Usóz, who translated it into Spanish, in the* Notas *appended to his edition of* 1851.

BODLEIAN. OXFORD *Wadham, Wiffens's copy.* MERCK. B—r.

Licensed on July 14. 1600 *by the London Stationers to* John Harrison son of master John Harrison th[e] eldest: Two treatises the one of the Pope and his aucthoritie &c. th[e]other of the masse &c. translated into English by John Golbourne Arber III 167.

1704 A Full view of | popery, | In a Satyrical Account of the | lives | of the | popes, *&c.* | From the Pretended Succession of | St. *Peter,* | To the Present | Pope *Clement* XI. | Wherein | All the Impostures and Innovations of the Church | of *Rome* appear in their true Colours, and all their | Objections, Cavils, *&c.* are fully Answer'd and | confuted. The whole being Interspers'd with se- | veral Pasquils. | To this is added, | a confutation of the Mass, | and a vindication of Re- | form'd Devotion. | In two Parts. | Written by a Learned *Spanish* Convert, and Address'd to his | Countrymen: Now faithfully Translated from the Second and | best Edition of the Original. | *London:* Printed for *Bernard Lintott,* at the | Middle-Temple-Gate in *Fleetstreet.* 1704. | *Below between the two lines by which the title is framed:* Price 6 s. Octavo. Title-

leaf, dedication to the R. Hon. Robert Harley *signed* J. Savage, *and Index of Popes, together* 3 *leaves, and p.* 1—488.

Wiffen's copy which I used is at present probably at Wadham college. He says: This is a garbled translation with additions and omissions.

Compare p. 7 *of Usóz's preface to his edition of the original.*

1724 *f.* Wiffen: „The lives and Transactions of the several Bishops of Rome *in* Gavin's Master-key to Popery *vol. II p.* 1—195 *and* Of the Mass and the holiness thereof *vol. III p.* 1—117 *are taken from* Golburne's *translation of the* Dos Tratados, *merely abbreviated in parts, without any reference to the source whence they are derived. The account of* Maria de la Visitacion, Gavin *vol. III p.* 165—195 *is taken from the same.*"

Gavin's Master-key *has been translated into French and Dutch and German. See below the article on him.*

1719 *The* Tabla de la contrariedad entre la dotrina antigua de Dios i la dotrina nueva de los hombres *is reprinted from the edition of* 1599 *of the* Dos tratados *in* Alvarado's Dialogos 1719 *p.* 545—571 *and translated into English. See below under* Alvarado.

1601 Trois | tables | Espagnol- | francoises. | La I. | De l'ancienne doctrine de | Dieu, & de la nouvelle des | hommes. | La II. | De la S. Cene, & de la Messe. | La III. | De l'Antichrist, & de ses mar- | ques. | *[Ornament.]* | A Savmvr. | Par Thomas Portav. | CIƆ.IƆCI. | *Sm.* 8*vo.*

These Trois Tables *are a reprint of those in* Dos Tratados 1599 *with a French translation.*

Inscription on the title of the copy from which this is taken: Domus Prof. Paris.is soc. Jesu.

I take this from a tracing in Wiffen's papers and from his remarks. It seems he sent the Trois tables *to Usóz.*

I noticed that they are registered in the Catal. de la Bibl. du Roi. Théol. t. III *p.* 162. *I cannot verify it at present.*

1594 *f.*   ***Epistle to the captives of Berbery.***

1594 Tratado | Para confirmar los pobres ca- | tivos de Berueria en la catolica y an- | tigua fe, y religion Christiana, y para | los consolar con la Palabra de Dios | en las afliciones que padecen | por el Evangelio de | Iesu Christo. | Por tu causa, O Señor, nos | matan cada dia: somos tenidos co- | mo ovejas para el degolladero. Despierta, | porque duermes Señor? Despierta, | no te alexes para siempre. | psalmo 44, 23. | Al fin deste tratado hallareys un en- | xambre de los falsos milagros, y ilusiones | del Demonio con que Maria de la visitaci- | on priora de la Anunciada de Lisboa en- | gaño à muy muchos: y de como fue | descubierta, y condenada al fin | del año de .1588. | *En casa de Pedro Shorto,* | *Año de .1594.* |

Sm. 8*vo.* [A]—K [2]; *title-leaf and* 145 *pages.*
Peter Short *printed in London. Cf. Usóz p.* II *of the preface of his edition.*
BRITISH MUS. *MERCK's copy is stamped:* Musevm Britannicvum. Duplicate for sale 1769, *and has on the binding in gold-letters:* Biblioteca de Salvá. Catálogo Salvá 1872 t. II *p.* 822: Este libro es quizas el más raro que existe de los que dieron á luz los protestantes españoles del siglo XVI: solo conozco, de él otro ejemplar que debe existir en el Museo británico.

1854 Tratado | para | confirmar en la fe Cristiana | a los cautivos de Berbería. | Compuesto por Zipriano d. Valera. | i por él publicado el a. 1594. |

Aviso a los de la iglesia Romana, | sobre jubileos. | Compuesto por el mismo, i publicado el a. 1600. |

El Español reformado | publicado el año 1621. |

Ahora fielmente reimpresos, con un Apéndize. | A. de 1854. |

Edited by Usóz, with his orthography. Printed at San Sebastian *by* Ignazio Ramon Baroja, 200 *copies, according to Wiffen.*

Prefixed a blank leaf and a leaf with the series-title Reformistas antiguos españoles. Tomo VIII. *and on the back the titles of the 7 other* Obras ya reimpresas.

Follow sheets [a], b, c, d *in octavo, and two leaves* e, [a 1] *the above title, verso a quotation.* [a 2] *recto the preface by Usóz, paged* II *on* [a 2] *verso to* LXVI *on* [e 2] *verso. Then the sheets in octavo* [A], B, C, D, E, F, G, H, I, J, K, L, M, *and again* I, J, K, L, M, N, *and two leaves* [O].

Tratado para los de Berbería. *Old title on* [A 1], *verso blank. Text* [A 2], *verso paged* 2, *ends p.* 137 *on* [I 6].

Aviso sobre la indiccion del jubileo. *Old title* [I 7], *verso blank. Text* [I 8], *verso paged* 2, *ends p.* 64 *on* [M 7].

El Español reformado. *Title* [M 8], *verso blank. Usoz's preface* I [1]. *Text* [I 2], *verso paged* 2, *ends p.* 47 *on* L [1].

Vozes, que se hallarán en este volumen, ahora ya anticuadas. [L 2—5] *page* [1]—7. [L 5] *verso blank.*

Algunas cosas notables en el tratado para los cautivos. [L 6. 7].

Tabla de algunas cosas notables en el aviso sobre el jubileo. [L 8]. M [1. 2]. *Verso blank.*

Apéndize N°. 1.° [M 3]. *Verso blank.* Copia de la sentenzia contra Maria de la Visitazion. [M 4—N 7]. *Paged* [1] *on* [M 4] *recto to* 23 *on* [N 7] *recto. Verso blank. Wiffen's ms. copy, mentioned p.* 22—23, *from the printed copy in the British Museum is bound into a copy, mentioned above p.* 161 *of the* Dos tratados *of* 1851, *at present in my possession.*

N.° 2.° Induljenzias. [N 8—O 1], *paged* [1]—3. *Verso blank.* Fe de erratas. [O 2], *two pages.*

Wiffen's copy, at present in Wadham college, OXFORD, contains a lithographed additional leaf to p. LI *of Usóz's preface with some passages on the Purgatory, concluding:* El purgatorio es, pues, el zentro de la relijión papal: como le ejemplificó, con el diagrama siguiente, N. Roussel. *The diagram is somewhat vary-*

ing in the two copies of the leaf which are found in Wiffen's copy of this volume of the Reformistas.

I got the leaf copied for my copy of that volume.

With the same copy in Wadham is bound Wiffen's manuscript English translation of the title, of the quotation on the reverse of the title-leaf, and of p. I—LXVI of Usóz's preface.

1872 Tratado | para confirmar | los pobres cautivos de Berbería | en la católica y antigua fé y religion Cristiana | y para consolarlos con la polabra de Dios | en las aflicciones que padecen por | el evangelio de Jesu Cristo. | Compuesto | por | Cypriano de Valera, | y por él publicado el año 1594. | Fielmente reimpreso. | Madrid 1872. | Librería de C. Bailly-Bailliere, | Plaza de Topete 10. |

Octavo, 106 *pages*, *title included*. *P*. 3: Basten como prólogo algunas palabras de Don Luis de Usoz y Rio, el cual tanto ha servido á su patria, reimprimiendo esta obra y ostras muchas de los antiguos reformadores españoles, las cuales sin él tal vez hubieran quedado olvidadas para siempre. *Text p.* 7—106. *Reprinted by F. Fliedner from* Ref. ant. t. VIII.

1594 f. *The false miracles of Maria de la Visitacion.*

1594 Enxambre *appended to the* Tratado para los cativos de Berberia.
1599 *appended to the second edition of the* Dos tratados.
1851 *reprinted with the third edition of those tratados.*
1896 *reprinted from* 1851 *in the* Revista Cristiana Nº 402 *to* 407.
1600 *with* Golburne's *English translation of the* Two treatises.
1704 *in* Savage's *translation of them?*
1724 f. *in* Gavin's Master-key *and its translations.*

1596 *Calvin's catechism.*

Valera was no doubt the revisor and editor of the Spanish translation of Calvin's catechism published London 1596. *See above vol.* II *p.* 47 f.

1597 f. *Calvin's Institution.*

1597 Institvcion | de la religion Chri- | stiana; compvesta en qvatro | libros, y dividida en | capitvlos. | *Por Juan Calvino.* | Y ahora nuevamente traduzida en Romance | Castellano. Por Cypriano | De Valera. | *Richard Field's device with* Anchora spei. | En Casa de Ricardo del Campo. | 1597. |

Large octavo. First leaf blank (in the Zurich copy, not in the Strassburg one, nor in mine nor in Merck's both). Title-leaf. 13 *unnumbered pages* A todos los fieles de la nacion Española que dessean el adelantamiento del reyno de Jesu Christo. *Begins fol.* *iij, *signed on* A [1] *recto* 20. de Septiembre. 1597 ... C. D. V. *Two pages*, A *verso and* A 2: Juan Calvino al lector ... Agosto. 1559. 13 *pages*

Al Christianissimo rey de Francia... Juan Calvino... 1536. *The text, beginning on* B [1] *is paged* 1 *to* 1032. *Then follows a list of the heads of the chapters, two leaves.* Tabla o svmario de las principales materias 25 *leaves and one page. On the back of this* 26*th leaf* faltas de la impression.

BRITISH MUS. BODLEIAN. PARIS *Nationale.* ZURICH *City.* STRASSBURG *Univ.* GOETTINGEN *Univ.* MERCK, *two copies.* **B—r**, *a present from* Merck.

In the Bibliotheca Hulsiana, Hagae Comitum 1730, t. IV *p.* 318 n° 1337 *among quarto volumes:* Institucion de la Religion Christiana, por Juan Calvino, 1577. *Not quarto, but large octavo,* 1577 *is a mistake for* 1597.

De la Serna Santander *says in his* Catalogue des livres de la bibliotheque de M. C. de la Serna Santander, t. 1, Bruxelles, an XI (1803), *p.* 18: ouvrage qu'on peut compter comme le plus rare, qui existe en fait de traductions castillanes, *and p.* 244: Peu de livres existent dans la république des lettres, d'une rareté égale à celui-ci.

Vincent Salvá, catalogue of Spanish and Portuguese books, London 1826, *p.* 24, *n°* 293 *offered a fine copy, without fixing a price. In the* Catalogo de los libros antiguos ó escasos, castellanos... que se hallan de venta en la librería española de los SS. D. Vicente Salvá é hijo... Paris 1836, *p.* 14, *n°* 193, Buen ejemplar *offered for* 150 francs.

Catálogo Salvá 1872 *n°* 3864, *speaking of* La Serna Santander: no valieron estos encarecimientos para que esta joya bibliográfica produjese mas de dos francos en la venta de los libros de aquel distinguido colector, siendo así que si alguno desea adquirir la edicion-original dificilmente la logrará ni aún centuplicando esta cantidad.

In Quaritch's catalogue n 295 1875 p. 273 n 3266 for £ 7. 10 s, excessively rare.

In Catalogue de livres rares et précieux appartenant a M. H. Tross ancien libraire. 1879. N° V. Paris *p.* 215 *n.* 1677 veau br. (Première reliure) *for* 180 *francs.* Volume d'une rareté excessive dont nous ne connaissons en Espagne que l'exemplaire Salvá. On en connaît plusieurs autres en Angleterre et en France.

In Bär's Antiquarischer Anzeiger 435. Frankfurt a. M. 1894. *n°* 3314 Bel ex. M. 80. *The same in* 437 *of the same year* n° 3842.

1858 *Fore-title.* Reformistas antiguos Españoles. | Núm. XIV. | *On the back, list of* 13 Obras ya reimpresas.

Instituzion religiosa. | escrita por | Juan Calvino, | el año 1536; | y traduzida al Castellano | por Zipriano de Valera. | Segundo vez fielmente impresa, en el mismo número de páginas. | *Sunt bona, sunt quædam mediocria, sunt mala,* | *quæ legis hic:* | Martial epigr. | „Cuando a cada uno le plazen sus proprios con- | zeptos, los combates no tienen número: lo mas ex- | pediente es, que en el entretanto que peregrinamos | aquí bajo, nos contentemos con ver en espejo y es- | curamente, las cosas que á la fin veremos cara á cara | sin impedimento ninguno." [Véase la pájina 696]. | „El Profeta (dize) que tiene sueño, cuente su sueño: y el que | tiene mi palabra, habla mi verdadera palabra.

Zierto, á todos | en jeneral les pone Lei: „la qual es esta: que Él no permite, que | alguno enseñe otra doctrina, sino la que le fuere mandada pre- | dicar. I despues llama paja, á todo cuanto Él no ha mandado que | se predique." [Véase pájina 789.] | Madrid: | imprenta de José Lopez Cuesta. | 1858. | *On the following leaf:*

Instituzion | de la relijion Cristiana; | compuesta en cuatro libros, i dividida en capitulos. | Por Juan Calvino. | I ahora nuevamente traduzida en Romanze Castellano, | por Zipriano de Valera. | [Device] | En casa de Ricardo del Campo. | 1597.

Translator's preface f. III *foll.*, 13 *pages. Author's prefaces* 17 *pages. The work p.* 1—1032. *Index of the chapters two leaves. Alphabetical* Tabla 26 *leaves, last page blank.* Erratas 6 *leaves. Closing remarks signed* 1859. Luis de Usóz i Rio, *who was the editor, three leaves, last page blank. Total* 1142 *pages. Large octavo.*

Betts translated from a letter of Usóx July 27. 1859 *to Wiffen the notice:* In the new title-page of Calvin by Valera you will observe: printed by José Lopez Cuesta whilst in point of fact the printer was only known by the surnames José (Martin) Lopez (Alegria) — the name is not therefore a feigned one. *And from a letter of the same to the same July* 28. 1858: Alegria, the printer of the Bible, negotiated the sale of the printing press employed by Alton which was purchased by the funds of B. & F. B. S.

As so big a volume on strong paper is really too inconvenient, there was printed a special title for a second volume, to be inserted before p. 521. *It repeats the new title described above, beginning:* Instituzion religiosa, *but instead of the quotations between* pajinas *and* Madrid *it has the words* Parte segunda; *the lines are divided as above; the letters differ from those of the general title;* pajinas *and* Jose *have no accents. This special title is found in the copy bound in two volumes, which belonged to Wiffen and is now in Wadham College, OXFORD. My copy is bound as one vol. which was presented by Luis Usóz's widow to John Betts and by him to me; I have joined to it the title-leaf for the second half (several copies of that title were found among the papers left by Wiffen).*

I do not recollect whether the copies in the BODLEIAN and in the BRITISH Museum (which I saw in 1868) *have the title for this second part.*

The Wadham copy contains Wiffen's autograph English translation of Usóz's closing remarks.

1599 f. *Epistle to the readers of the Spanish translation of the Reformed Catholic of Perkins.*

1599 Catholico Reformado. | O | vna declara- | cion qve mvestra | qvanto nos podamos con- | formar con la Iglesia Romana, tal, qual | es el dia de hoy, en diversos puntos de la Re- | ligion: y en que puntos devamos nunca | jamas convenir, sino para siempre | apartarnos della. | Yten, Vn aviso à los afficionados | à la Iglesia Romana, que

muestra la dicha | Religion Romana ser contra los Catholicos | rudimentos y fundamentos del Catecismo. | Compuesto por Guillermo Perquino Licen- | ciado en sancta Theologia, y trasladado en | Romance Castellano por Guillermo | Massan Gentil-hombre, y à | su costa imprimido. | [Ornament.] | En casa de Ricardo del campo. | 1599. |
Title and prefaces 4 leaves, the work, p. 1—326. *Sm.* 8*vo.*

„Otra Epistola al Christiano Lector" . . . 4do Julio de 1599 Vuestro afficionadissimo hermano en el Señor C. D. V. *that is Cipriano de Valera, 4 pages. In this address he says:* En este numero *(of true Christians)* se deve contar un gentilhombre llamado Guillermo Massan, el qual auiēdo leydo y releydo un libro pio y docto, que Guillermo Perquino Licenciado en sagrada Theologia compuso, en que se tratan los principales puntos de la religion Christiana . . . y pareciendole muy bien (como de veras el libro es muy bueno) ha tomado la pena de trasladar lo en Español, y a su costa imprimirlo.

BODLEIAN. MADRID *Nacional, from Usóz.*

Dr. M. Spirgatis informed me that Lamberg's Leipzig reprint of the Frankfort Michael-mess catalogue of 1599 *contains fol.* E 4^a *the entry:* Cathalico [*sic*] Reformado, O' vna Declaratione quae [*sic*] muestra quanto nos podamus conformar con Iglesia Romana; yten, un auiso à los afficionados à la Iglesia Romana, Antuerp, in 8° apud Nutium. — *Cless in his* Elenchus *of 1602:* Cathalico reformado, ovna declaratione que muestra, quanto nos podamos conformar con jglesia Romana; iten, vn auiso à los afficionados à la jglesia Romana. Antuerp. 1599 in 8. *He mentions only an Antwerp copy of the* Catholico reformado, *as also of the* Dos tratados *of 1599, see above p.* 161. *What I have said there on Nucius, is likewise to be applied here.* — [*Draudius*]. Bibliotheca. Exotica. Frankfovrt. MDCX *p.* 211: Catholico Reformado, o vna declaratione que muestra, quanto nospodamos conformar con Iglesia Romana: iten, vn Auiso à los afficionados à la Iglesia Romana, Antuerp. 1599. 8. *This, according to Spirgatis, is reprinted in the edition of Draudius,* Frankf. 1624, *p.* 273.

1624 Catholico Reformado, | o una | declaration | *Que* | *Muestra quanto nos podamos conformar* | *con la Iglesia Romana, tal, qual es el dia de hoy, en* | *diversos puntos de la Religion: y en que pun-* | *tos devamos nunca jamas convenir, sino para* | *siempre apartarnos della.* | Yten, | Un Aviso à los afficionados à la Iglesia Ro- | mana, que muestra la dicha Religion Romana | ser contra los Catholicos rudimentos y | fundamentos del Catecismo. | *Compuesto por Guillermo Perquino Licenciado en* | *sancta Theologia, y trasladado en Romance* | *Castellano por Guillermo Massan Gentil-hom-* | *bre, y à su costa imprimido.* | Ornament. | En Amsterdam, | En casa de *Iacob Wachter.* | 1624. *Duodecimo.*

Verso of the title: Los Puntos que se tratan en este Libro. A 2: El Autor al Christiano Lector. A 3: Otra epistola *al Christiano Lector, signed* A 5 *verso* C. D. V.

Text of the Cath. Ref. *and the* Aviso *p*. 1—401. *P*. [402] *Al Lector an explanation of what had been said that* Christo obedecio à la Ley por si mismo.
HAMBURG City.
The English original, A Reformed Catholike, *appeared in* 1597 *at* Cambridge *registered by the Stationers* August 1. *of that year*, Arber III 88. *A second ed.* 1598, *title-copy by Wiffen. I know an ed.* A Reformed Catholike, Cambr. 1604, 8vo, *Wiffen's copy. The* Catal. libr. impress. biblioth. Bodleianae. III 1843 p. 86 *has under* Perkins *the following four titles:* A reformation of a catholike deformed. 4°, n. p. 1604. The 2nd part of the reformation of a catholic deformed, 4°. n. p. 1607. His theological works. Cambr. 1603. His works, 3 vls. Cambr. 1608.

A defence of M. Perkins booke, called a reformed catholike: ... By Antony Wotton. At London Imprinted by Felix Kyngston. 1606. *(Merck has got a copy.) It treats the first nine controversies of which the English text by Perkins is inserted there. Entered in the Stationers' register* 16. January 1605 (= 1606 *n. st.*), Arber III 310.

On the controversy excited by Perkin's powerful treatise see the literary notices of Lowndes ed. Bohn *vol* 7 *p.* 1832.

After the Spanish translation appeared a Latin one: Catholicvs | reformatvs: |[Addita est breuis quædam Admonitio ad | eos qui dediti sunt Rom. Ecclesiæ, in qua demon- | stratur Rom. doctrinam pugnare cum fundamentis & articulis fidei, ab omnibus Christianis confessæ. | Omnia primo conscripta et edita lingua Anglica à V. Cl. D. Gvilielmo Perkinso, | Cantabrigiensi Anglo, S. S. Theologiæ Licentiato: deinde vero in | Hispanicam linguam translata à D. Gvilielmo Massa- | no Nobili Anglo: nunc verò demum à quodam lingua | rum & veritatis studioso in Latinum | sermonem conuersa. | X | Hanoviæ | Apud Guilielmum Antonium. | *[Under a stroke:]* MDCI. | *Five leaves* Epistola dedicatoria, *three pages* Avctor Lectori, *one page* Index, *the work p.* 1—446, *at last one page errata. Octavo.*

COLMAR Consistorial library. B—r.

Burgersdijk & Niermans, Catalogue N°. 48. Leyde 1900 *p.* 478: Perkins, G. Catholicus reformatus; h. e. expositio et declaratio praecipuar. aliquot religion. controvers. Han. 1603. Catholicus reformatus. Ed. III. Hanov. 1608. *in* Ludwig Rosenthal's *at Munich* Catal. 70 *p.* 1143 *n°.* 18000.

The translator says in the dedication fol. 4. 5: Hunc porrò librum non multo pòst in Hispanicum sermonem conuertit verè nobilis D. Gvilielmus Massanus Anglus, si forte his armis Hispanica quoq; gens expugnari, atque ad Christum reduci posset. Quia verò omninò dignus est hic liber, qui non angustiis istarum duarum linguarum cōstringeretur, ... eum in Latinum sermonem converti. In quo tamen labore præcipuè curæ mihi fuit, non tam verba, quam sensum dictorū quam fidelissimè reddere. Illud enim, nec faciendum vbique fuit, cum (meo iudicio) Hispanicus interpres incommodius quædam reddidisse videatur: nec, si debuit, facile à quoquam præstari potuit: cum sua cuique linguæ sit proprietas & singularis verborum ac phrasium emphasis: quæ nusquam aut rarissime in alia aliqua reperitur. Addam & hoc, (ne fraudem aliquam subesse Lector existimet) quædam S. S. Patrum loca, quę ita allegari debuissent, vt apud ipsos authores legūtur, à nobis aut ob defectum codicum desiderata, aut certè ob numerorū marginalium vitium non inuenta, nostris verbis ex Hispanico reddita esse. *This preface of the translator is dated* Francofurto ad Mœnum, 9. Aprilis, Anno MDCI. *The Latin* Catholicus Reformatus *is incorporated in* Guilielmi Perkinsi opera theologica t. 1, Genevae 1611, *(Bodleian) col.* 357—482, *where the translator's words copied above are read col.* 358f., *not without changements.*

Bibliotheca Exotica. Frankfovrt. MDCX: *p.* 9:

Guil. Perkins, Le Catholique reformé c'est á dire vne exposition & declaration de certains points des quels les Eglises Reformees sont en different auec ceux de l'Eglise Romaine, Lion pour Francois le Februe, 8. 1607.

Théologie Catalogue *of* Frederik Muller & Co., Amsterdam 1899 *p.* 80:

Alle de werken van Mr. Wilhelm Perkins. Amsterdam 1659—62.

Sandoval y Rojas Index Madrid 1612, Palermo reprint 1628, Prohib. *p.* 27 *third class:* Catolico reformado, ò vna declaraciō, que muestra quanto nos podamos cōformar con la Iglesia Romana. &c. Item, Otro tratado que anda con el, intitulado, Auiso à los aficionados à la Iglesia Romana, de qualquier manera que ande, sin nombre de autor, ò con el. Vea se deste tratado en la segunda Classe, Auiso à los aficionados, &c. *In the place referred to, p.* 12, *is read:* Auiso a los aficionados a la Iglesia Romana, que muestra la dicha Religion Romana, &c. compuesto por Guillermo Perquino, trasladado en Romance Castellano por Guillermo Massan, Auctores condenados. *P.* 23: *second class:* Catolico Reformado, &c. compuesto por Guillermo Perquino, y trasladado en Romāce Castellano por Guillermo Massan, autores condenados. *They are both named p.* 40 *among the first class prohibited ones.*

1600f. *Advice on the jubilee proclaimed by the pope.*

1600 Aviso a los de | la iglesia Romana | sobre la indiccion del Jubileo por | *la Bulla del Papa Clemente* | *octavo*. *Richard Field's device with the words* Anchora spei. | En casa de Ricardo del | Campo | 1600. | 8vo. Diiij, *paged* to 53. *No preface.*

BRITISH *Museum. When I asked there for the volume, it was not available; the above is given according to a tracing found in Wiffen's papers and to his remarks. The* Bibliothèque de la société de l'histoire du protestantisme français *at PARIS is in possession of a printed copy of this edition, as the librarian Mr. N. Weiss informs me.*

In Bachelin-Deflorenne's catalogue nº 2438 *a copy for* 50 francs. *A copy in* Morante's Catal. t. VI. Matriti 1859 *nº* 10941.

1624 Aviso á los | *De la* | iglesia Romana, | Sobre la indiccion del jubileo, | por | *La Bulla del Papa Clemente* | *Octavo.* | *Ornament.* | En Amsterdam, | En casa *de Iacob VVachter.* | 1624.

Title-leaf and, paged 1—66, *the text, Duodecimo. It is appended to the* Catholico Reformado *of that year, described above, with continuation of the signature, the first text-page being signed* S 3. *The last leaf* [V 12] *is blank.*

HAMBURG City. The Aviso *of* 1624 *and the* Catholico Reformado *of the same year are the only editions of works by Valera which remained unknown to Wiffen. Nor have I found them mentioned anywhere, except in an auction-catalogue of* 1890 *the* Cath. Ref.

1854 Aviso | a los de la | iglesia Romana | sobre la | indiccion del jubileo | por la bulla del papa | Clemente, octavo. | En casa de Ricardo del Campo. | 1600. | *Reprinted from the London copy as the second part of the described above p.* 164 T. VIII *of the* Reformistas antiguos españoles. *In the preface and in the appendix Usóz treats also of the* Aviso.

Sandoval y Rojas Index *1612, reprint Palermo* 1628, Prohib. *p.* 14: Auisos a los de la Iglesia Romana sobre la Indiccion del Iubileo por la Bula del Papa Clemente VIII. Impresso en casa de Ricardo del Campo, año de 1600.

1600 An answere | or admonition | to those of the Church of Rome, | touching the Jubile, proclaimed by the Bull, *made and set foorth by* Pope Clement | *the eyght, for the yeare of our* | Lord. 1600. |

Translated out of French. *[Ornament.]* London, | Printed by E *Allde for John VVolfe.* | 4*to* 16 *leaves, incl. title.*

OXFORD Wadham, *Wiffen's copy.*

The French was not known to Wiffen and to Usóz, nor have I obtained any information concerning it.

Usóz *thought that the French was translated from the Spanish* Aviso, *and that the translators had omitted a passage on pope Alexander* VI (*see the introduction to the reprint of* 1854 *p.* XLVII). *Wiffen left the notice:* The Spanish is amplified in some passages and has an addition of about four pages at the end. Probably the English is the original of the Spanish.

Bible.

Cf. II *p.* 247*f.*

1690 *Some passages of Valera's Preface to the* N. T. 1596 *(cf. above* II n° 355) *in* Hist. crit. des versions du n. t. Par Richard Simon. Rotterdam. *P.* 503*f.*

1708 *The same preface with omissions: in* Enzina's N. T. (*cf. l. c.* n° 356). *In the passage:* Quando los Godos se apoderaron de España (que ha ya como 1200. años) *the number is changed into* 1320.

Valera's autograph dedication of his Bible.

In 1891 Joseph Baer & Co. Francfort s. M. Catalogue No. 276 *p.* 31 n° 589 *offered Valera's Bible of* 1602 *for* 60 *marks with the notice:* Précieux exemplaire avec dédicace autographe de l'éditeur aux Etats Généraux de Hollande: Amplissimis *and so on, the whole dedication which I append literally:*

    Amplissimis, eisdemq3 prudentissimis viris Pro-
    vincię Hollandicę à rationibus hoc Bibli-
    corum Hispanicorum exemplar dicat ac
    vovet   Cyprianus de Valera p

The *sign after the name I take for a* p, *meaning* propria manu. Biblicorum *instead of* Bibliorum *is a slip caused by* Hispanicorum. *The copy is dedicated not to the* États Généraux, *but to the Chamber of accounts.*

In the cover, opposite the title where this is written, there is above pasted in a label with the printed name of the possessor: Dr. A. M. Ledeboer, *known by his works on Netherlandish typography. On the same page below:* Zie over deze Bybel uitgave en dit exemplaar de: Bibliograph. Adversaria 's Gravenh. Mart. Nijhoff 1876 N 5 en 6 bl. 67. *This is written by the same hand which wrote on a letter-cover lying in the Bible:* Brieven behoorende by den Spaanschen protestantischen Bybel van de Valera., *no doubt by the hand of Ledeboer, to whom one of those papers is directed.*

The Bibliographische Adversaria. Derde deel. N° 5 en 6. 's Gravenhage, Martinus Nijhoff. 1876. *contain a* Catalogus van boeken, voorhanden in het magazijn van Mart. Nijhoff te 's Gravenhage, en voor de bijgestelde prijzen te bekomen. *Where p.* 67—68 N° 663 Biblia. Por Cypr. de Valera... 1602. fol. veau. Av. fermoir. f. 18,—. Spaansche Protestantsche bijbel. Hoogst zelzaam. Wat dit ex. bijzonder merkwaardig maakt is de oude lederen band waarop aan beide zijden in goud is gestempeld een gezicht op Amsterdam, waarboven twee figuren met de opschriften „Fides" en „Justitia". De stempels zijn uitstekend bewaard; het overige van den band *[the binding]* heeft een weinig geleden. *The* Catalogus *does not mention the autograph dedication of the translator.*

A reference to Kortholt, Le Long, Clement Bthq, curieuse [1752], *written under Valera's dedication and preceding Ledeboer's words, makes it very probable that the copy had belonged to some private library before Nijhoff acquired it.*

I bought this Bible from Baer. *To a letter of mine* Professor J. van Toorenenbergen *at Amsterdam answered in* 1891: Uw vortreffelijk exemplaar van den Spaanschen Bybel van de Valera kunt Gy ohne Gewissensbisse behouden: er is hier geene bibliotheek waarin het te huis behoort. Gewis is het een geschenk, dat door den Voorzitter der Rekenkamer van Holland als zijn privaateigendom is aangemerkt. Nu is het in uwe collectie op de rechte plaats.

I have already spoken of this my copy of Valera's Bible on p. 385 *of my article quoted above p.* 156 *note* 35.

This copy contains the printed dedication to the States and Prince Maurice (*cf. above* II *p.* 247).

The reprint of this dedication (*cf. ibid.*) *has at the end the notice:* De un ejemplar de la Biblia por Zipriano de Valera, e impresa el a. 1602, que posee Luis de Usoz i Rio, se reimprime esta hoja, este año de 1858. El mismo costeó la reimpresión reduziéndola a solos zincuenta ejemplares numerados. *Usóz writes to Wiffen,* Rf. Esp. t. XVIII. 1862, Sumario de induljenzias, *p.* VI: reimprimió ud. haze tiempo, i a mi costa, la rarísima Dedicatoria que Zipriano de Valera prepuso a várias ejemplares de su version de las Escrituras, de la cual remití a ud. un facsimile. *My copy which I joined with my other copy of the Valera Bible, and some others which Wiffen left are not numbered.*

Valera's Exhortacion, *prefixed to the Bible. See above* II *p.* 293 *f.*

Some passages in Latin.

1709 *in* Le Long Bibliotheca sacra. Parisiis. Pars altera. P. 121—122.
1709 *The same in the edition* Lipsiis. Pars altera. P. 148—149.

1723 *The same in the edition* Parisiis. Pars II. *P.* 363.

1781 *An analysis of this* Exhortacion *with extracts is given by* José Rodriguez de Castro *in his* Bibliotheca Española, t. 1, Madrid 1781, *p.* 469—470.

1864 Mrs. Tregelles *sent me a small leaf with the notice that she* had a number of these Extracts printed to fix into the commencement of the reprints of Valera's Bibles and Testaments. *It is entitled*:

Un extracto desde la Exhortacion al Lector, la cual precede la edicion revisada de la santa Biblia, por Cipriano de Valera.

About 1880 *I received* From American Tract Society. New York. *the following tract, lately printed. On the cover, in a frame:*

La Biblia para Todos: | ensayo preliminar | por Cipriano de Valera | en su | Biblia Española, | impresa en 1602. | 13 | Nueva York: | Sociedad Americana de tratados. | 150 calle de Nassau. | Sp. | *Title-leaf:* La biblia para todos: | ensayo preliminar | por Cipriano de Valera | en su | biblia Española, | impresa en 1602. | *[emblem]* | Nueva York: | Sociedad Americana de tratados | no. 150, calle de Nassau. *At the end of the same line: Sp.* 13. *Second leaf [p.* 3]: la biblia para todos. *Follows* Valera's *text:* Nuestro buen Dios *&c., abridged in some places which are either marked by a series of full stops or by specific words. The words* Asi sea *are put thrice p.* 38, *in the original twice, p.* 40 *twice, in the original once. Column-title on each page:* La biblia para todos. *Height of the column (title excluded) about* 110 *millim. One larger of* 40 *pages.*

B—r.

Additional note.

In the Enxambre de los falsos milagros, *appended to the* Conforto para los cativos, *Valera says p.* 106 *on the unmasking of the prioress* Maria de la visitacion *at Lisbon:* no ha sino quatro años que acontecio en nuestra España, año 1588. *At that time Portugal was united to the crown of Spain. The sentence of condemnation on this woman was passed in* December 1588. *Therefore Valera wrote those words in* 1592. *The title of the book in which they occur has, however, the year* 1594. *In the reprint of this* Enxambre *with the* Dos tratados *of* 1599 *Valera has cancelled the words* no ha sino quatro años que.

Half a page later he continues p. 106. 107: adverti mis Españoles en un libro, que al principio del año de 1588. escrevi, que no creyessen de ligero lo que desta Monja se dezia. Mis palabras son estas. p. 419. Otra Frantiscana [*sic*] (avia de dezir, Dominicana) se ha pocos años ha levantado en Lisboa, que dizen que tiene las cinco llagas de Christo, como las tuvo S. Francisco: y otras muchas cosas dizen della. Peró al tiempo doy por testigo. Ella descubrira su hypocresia, como las demas. En el entre tanto no creays de ligero á todo espiritu: mas como nos avisa S. Iuan cap. 4. ver. 1. de su primera epistola, provad los espiritus, si son de Dios. Porque muchos falsos prophetas (como el mismo nos avisa) son salidos en el mundo, &c. *This passage, quoted from the book of* 1588, *viz. the* Dos tratados, *is reprinted in the second edition of them p.* 486 *where it, however, begins* Otra Dominicana. *All I have transcribed here from the* Enxambre *of* 1592—94 *is repeated in the* Enxambre *of* 1599, *only the* escrevi *in the opening sentence is changed into* publiqué, *inadvertently, for the preliminary* Epistola *of the* Dos tratados *of* 1588 *is dated June* 15. 1588, *so that the book cannot be said to have been published in the beginning of that year.*

Immediately after that quotation from the Dos tratados *Valera continues:* Dios quiso que yo escriviesse esto, y que lo imprimiesse à costa de dos Christianos mercaderes Flamencos, los quales por el gran zelo que tienen de que la nacion Española participasse del beneficio del Evangelio reformado de que Dios ha hecho misericordia á otras naciones, no perdonaron ni à costa ni à trabajo. El Señor los enriquezca con sus dones espirituales, y les augmente la fe. Imprimiose pues esto por dos causas: la una para advertir aquellos que eran de Dios, que no se dexassen engañar con falsos milagros: la otra, para hazer inescusables à todos aquellos que aun con toda la luz del Evangelio, que Dios por su gran bondad ha revelado en estos nuestros ultimos tiēpos, creen à la mentira confirmada con sueños, y con falsos milagros: y no al Evangelio escrito en la sagrada escritura. *All this is repeated in the edition of* 1599. *As the words* Imprimiose esto *in the last sentence evidently refer to the* Enxambre, *I think that* esto .. imprimiesse *in the first sentence, points to the same, and that the two Dutch merchants paid the printing-expenses of the* Enxambre.

PEDRO GALÉS.

Pedro Galés was a Catalonian, born in Uldecona, most likely in 1533. When studying at Saragossa, he assiduously attended the lectures of the professor of philosophy Pedro Juan Nuñez; in 1554 he wrote some verses on Nuñez, praising his love of liberty and wisdom. In 1556 Galés became convinced that one ought not to adore nor reverence images, and when, probably in the spring of 1559, he arrived in Rome, he was soon seized by the Inquisition, which flourished vigorously under Pope Paul IV. Because Galés had maintained that it was not necessary to abstain from meat on certain days and to confess to a priest, he was declared to be a *suspect* and was ordered to abjure; and the youth did so. He may have witnessed the sack of the Inquisitionary buildings after the Pope's death in August of the same year. He went to Bologna and, after a stay at Paris, returned to Italy where he lived at Turin and Asti, freely expressing his religious views. In Turin he conversed with the renowned French jurist Cujas who was professor there in 1566—7.[1] In a work published in 1570, and often reprinted, Cujas calls Galés *doctissimus et acutissimus*. After a stay in Rome Galés sailed, perhaps early in 1580, from Naples to Spain, where he remained about two years. Juan Idiaquez, afterwards Minister of State, wished to have him as tutor to his son; the count de Chinchon, treasurer general of the crown of Aragon, invited him to remain with him; the city of

---

[1] The passage quoted in the *Journal des Savants* 1902, p. 477, I can only take to mean that Galés remained at Turin while Cujas made his excursion in Italy. Cujas, lately arrived at Turin, began his lectures in November 1566. Shortly before returning to France where he had accepted a professorship at Valence, he made a journey in Italy during June and the greater part of July 1567. See *Histoire du droit romain, suivie de l'histoire de Cujas; Par M. Berriat-Saint-Prix. Paris* 1821. I presume he first went to Florence in order to see the most important of all mss. of the Pandects, and thence by way of Bologna and Padua to Venice; on his return to Turin he probably visited Pavia. It may be questioned whether Cujas sent those inscriptions in 1567 to Turin (whither he was to return very soon), or sent them to Galés at a later period in France.

Valencia offered him a professorship. These offers were made to him as being „one of the greatest scholars in Greek and Latin, in Spain and also abroad." But he declined them all, having made up his mind to return to Italy. The Valencian scholar Baptist Cardona who relates this in a letter of April 21. 1581, adds the remark: literary men are retiring *(encogidos)*, and he is very much so. In a letter of July 14. Cardona asks Antonio Agustin, who had been nominated to the see of Tarragona in 1576, to detain Galés and not let him go.

Agustin makes an epoch in the history of canonical law, as in certain respects does Cujas for ancient Roman civil law. The Archbishop inaugurates modern scientific study of those ecclesiastical documents.[2] By both these eminent authorities Galés was highly appreciated on account of his profound knowledge and fine judgment. As early as 1543 Agostin had begun to work on a new edition of the so called *decretum Gratiani* which, collected about the middle of the 12. century, had taken root in general use; and when in 1566 Pope Paul V. named correctors of that code, Agostin was invited to collaborate. He did not go to Rome, but sent contributions. The Roman work proceeded by very slow degrees. When Galés, who had had free intercourse with the correctors in Rome, arrived in Spain, the Archbishop eagerly received from him reports of what they had done and were doing, and both thoroughly debated the interesting questions. In Agustin's work on the emended Gratian the first book is a series of 20 dialogues which he had with Galés, a third interlocutor being someone of the Archbishop's relations who had studied Gratian, but wished to get more instruction from the two others, whose dicta, with his own remarks thrown in, he consigned to a kind of protocol. Galés exhorts Agustin to abstain from emending Gratian and to edit a better collection of the decrees. The Archbishop answers: You seem to me by your pre-eminent power of speech to annihilate great things and to extol to the skies smaller ones. As for a new collection, you jest with your usual abundant urbanity; let us think of that afterwards.[3]

---

2) See p. 184.

3) Dial. 1: *Ludis tu quidem, ut soles, perurbane, et mihi videris pro tua praeclara dicendi facultate magnas res contemnere et pro nihilo ducere, minores vero in caelum tollere atque augere dicendo.* On a new collection *facis tu quidem ludos, ut dixi, sed hac de re posterius cogitabimus.*

Yet Galés is ready to prove that Gratian was a stupid fellow.[4] The second book of Agustin's work consists likewise of 20 dialogues, held after Galés had left;[5] the last one contains the notice that the Roman edition of Gratian had appeared. This took place in 1582. Agustin then enriched his work with additions, where he also points to blemishes in the new Roman text. The forty dialogues were published in 1587[6] a year after the author's death at the age of 70. Galés is supposed to be also the learned friend mentioned in the Archbishop's Spanish dialogues „on medals, inscriptions and other antiquities", likewise published in 1587.

The principal reason why nothing could prevail upon Galés to remain in his native country, was no doubt that he felt stifled by the Inquisitorial air which pervaded all Spain; there were places even in Italy where he could breathe more freely. From Barcelona he writes Sept. 27. 1581 to the Archbishop that he intends to go to France by land. From Marseille, where he stayed more than two months, he wrote to the Archbishop and to the prelate's secretary in April 1582, and to both from Padua on Sept. 2. His letters turn particularly on points of classical philology. Nothing in them foreshadowes the step which he unexpectedly took soon after the last letter.

In this same year 1582 he was inscribed as member of the evangelical Italian church at Geneva. He must have paid a visit to Beza and have expressed his wish to teach in the academy; but, as there was no opening at the moment, he returned to Italy. In February 1583, however, Beza and Trembley proposed to the *Conseil* of the

4) Dial. 17: *ostendam hominem stupidum fuisse.*
5) Lib. 2, dial. 1. one of the interlocutors, Martinus Augustinus Ioannis filius says to the Archbishop: *Cum ad te venirem, Ilerdae apud Vincentium fratrem consobrinum meum commoratus, intellexi ab eo te cum Petro Galesio de Gratiani emendatione aliquot diebus egisse ipso praesente; cujus sermonis summam fuerat is scriptis complexus quam ab eo accepi. Sed ajebat, cum aliquot distinctiones percurrere coepisset Galesius, classis cujusdam nuntio interpellatum, Barcinonem profectum, ut in ea, si posset, in Italiam perveniret, ipsum autem Ilerdam paullo post rediisse ad studia intermissa....*
6) It appeared at Tarragona. Baluze in the preface to his edition of the same, Paris 1672, is inclined to think that the first editor was the Jesuit Andreas Schott, who also delivered a funeral oration on the Archbishop. When Schott in 1608 in his *Hispaniae bibliotheca* had occasion to mention Galés, he passed in silence over the fact that the disciple of Nuñez and collaborator of the great Archbishop had turned Protestant.

University to call Galés, a *savant* in literature and all departments of philosophy, an *homme de bien* with good testimonials; and the *Conseil* agreed. On May 10. 1583 a letter from Orthez to Mr. Rotan at Turin says: *me suis emploié pour Mr. Galesii suyvant la charge que m'en aviez donnée et le desir aussi que j'ay qu'il soit pardeça tellement que l'affaire a esté mesme jusqu'à ce point que j'ay charge de vous prier qu'il vous plaise faire en sorte qu'il s'en viene au plustot s'il veut servir au college car on a faute d'hommes. Je pense que pour quelque temps il sera employé à la premiere classe, mais qu'il s'asseure que ce ne sera pour longtemps s'il veult faire profession de la Philosophie ou de la langue grecque il jouira tousjours de quatre cens livres par an et son voyage deffrayé.*[7] Galés had been highly recommended by Casaubon, professor at Geneva, in his work on the history of Greek philosophy by Diogenes Laertius; this work of the Genevan professor appeared in 1583 at Geneva and Morges with a preface dated February 20. of that year. Casaubon applies to Galés the same epithets which had been bestowed on him by Cujas; he calls him also *Galesius meus* and *carissimus*, and adopts many emendations proposed by him. Also on later occasions he gives thanks to his learned friend. Galés married at Geneva August 4. 1583 Lavinia Buci from Vicenza.[8] He was in office at Geneva from 1583 to the end of 1586, when the city, owing to financial difficulties, dismissed the professors, except two theologians who seemed to be indispensable; however he continued his lectures privately in 1587.[9] In this year September 4. his son died at Geneva.[10] Afterwards he lectured for some months at Nimes. Called to Orange, he lectured there for about three years; the following two years he continued lecturing at

---

7) Bibliothèque de Genève, Mhg. 197. ā ā II. *Main italienne*. The name of the writer is not clear, perhaps only *Louis*. According to a transcript sent to Mr. Morel-Fatio and not yet used for the essay in the Journal des Savants.

8) *A di 4 Agosto 1583 si sposo il signore Pietro Galesio spagnuolo, lectore di filosofia, con Lavinia Buci, Vicentina.* Found upon my inquiry by professor Eug. Ritter in the *Registre des mariages de l'Eglise Italienne* and copied for me by Mr. l'archiviste Louis Dufour-Vernes.

9) To Saravia he said that he lived at Geneva *cinco años leyendo filosofia*, and also in the first audience before the Inquisitors of Saragossa, that he had there *leido cinco años*.

10) *Décès le 4 septembre 1587 de Théodore, fils de Pierre Galésy, habitant, environ 18 mois, rue St. Léger.* Notice sent to me by M. Louis Dufour-Vernes.

Castres, where he had likewise been called. But as he had arrived at convictions diverging on some points from Calvinism, he gave offence. A conference of 35—40 ministers held a discussion with him at Montauban[11] and reproved his doctrine as in many things contrary to that of Calvin. We do not know any particulars, but may be sure that the principal difference was about predestination, in the sense which Beza incessantly proclaimed. Galés therefore set out for Bordeaux with his wife and their two little daughters. He intended to lecture there if possible and to wait till the next national synod should give him the opportunity to explain his opinions, although he was prepared for a failure, as the assembly would be both party to the suit and judge.

When he arrived with his family at Marmande on August 8. 1593, — then the headquarters of the catholic leaguists under the marquis de Villars, — they suspected him of being a Huguenot and brought him before captain Saravia, whom king Philip of Spain had sent with a detachment to assist the marquis. Galés openly avowed his protestant views and was arrested. His ten bales of books and manuscripts were opened. From letters written to him they learned that he was considered to be one of the chief authorities in philosophy and Greek. There were also found memoranda on his opinions and mischances, and on his discussions with ministers. Saravia wished him to be delivered to Spain, but the marquis having scruples against the extradition, which would be a novelty, liberally offered to hang him or to drown him. Saravia, however, thought it preferable to burn him, and did not give up hope of bringing this about, notwithstanding all difficulties. On August 19. he writes: The heretic's wife is very busy, recurring to influential sympathizers, and inventing a hundred thousand devices to liberate her husband; I greatly fear that she may succeed. And two days later: I apprehend, in consequence of this truce (concluded on the last of July for three months, and afterwards prolonged), that they will not deliver to me this Spanish Huguenot; to secure him and to depart I want money. From the documents of the Inquisition, we learn that Saravia triumphed.

When they arrived (it must have been about the end of 1593) at Saragossa, where Galés had been a student and where his Archbishop

11) It must be the provincial synod of May 1593.

Agustin had been born, he was denounced to the Inquisition by two witnesses (most likely Saravia and the sergeant Baños) who declared that they had heard him admit having been a teacher in heretical schools, and that, when they had entered Aragon and one of them had admonished him to abandon his errors, he had answered he would do so if it were clearly shown that he misunderstood the words of Christ, for he followed Christ and not men; they added that while travelling through this kingdom he did not reverence images nor crosses. He was arrested by the Inquisition. The first audience always began with binding the prisoners by oath to speak the truth. Galés refused, swearing being contrary to the gospel. Such a refusal was unheard of, and the instructions for Inquisitors did not prescribe what should be done in this unforeseen case. Should they send him back to prison and wait till he changed his mind? But the fellow might prefer to live there quietly instead of being tortured and burned. They thought it wiser to make him speak unsworn. And they were certainly satisfied to find him as openhearted and communicative as they could desire. He declared himself against the adoration of images, the prohibition of meat on certain days, the invocation and intercession of saints, the presence of the body of Christ in the sacrament of the altar, the confession to a priest (he had not confessed in this manner for 26 years), the clergy being superseded by Christ. He disapproved religious orders, monastic life and disciplining oneself (by flagellation etc.). There was no purgatory. One ought not to adore the cross. The Roman church does not always follow the apostolic one. One cannot hear mass with a good conscience. He did not cross himself. Nor did he believe in the intercession of Mary who could not be called *mater misericordiae*, because God is the sole father of mercy. Keeping the Lord's day is not catholic, but politic, and so it is not a duty to keep the feasts. He did not acknowledge the commandments of the church nor the sacraments of confirmation, ordination, matrimony and extreme unction, nor the necessity of baptism of children. The pope ought not to be called papa or pontifex, Christ being the true pontifex. Confessing to have read and possessed prohibited books, he expressly mentioned Peter Martyr. He confirmed what he had professed by swearing in conformity with the custom of his sect (so the Inquisitors write, who were very glad to have got something like an oath): I say with Christ on whatever I have said and has been read to me: yes yes, because it is true, and if need be I say it again; and on what I may henceforth say, it being truth, I shall say and I say now: yes yes, and to what is not such: no no; and I sign with my name. And when he had confessed „these heresies and many others", he added that this faith availed to his salvation, and though he knew and knows that all these opinions are and have been contrary to the Roman catholic church and her traditions, still, because they conform more to the word of Christ and the apostolic church, he follows them and has followed, believed and kept them for 37 years, even as he at different times had studied and perceived each several one; and at present he persevered with them as true and useful for his salvation, and intends to maintain them always, unless confuted by reasoning and words of Christ and the adhering apostolic church, or that God revealed to him that he was not on the right path. The beginning of his aversion from Romanism was that, when still in Spain, he understood that to adore and reverence images was wrong. In the second audience he related his adventures in the Inquisition at Rome, and in the third he acknowledged as his own the papers which contained the said heresies. When the procedure had reached this stage, he fell dangerously ill. Two theologians endeavoured twice to win him back to the Roman church, but in vain. He died pertinacious. Three terms were fixed for his brothers (we do not find them mentioned anywhere else) to defend him. As no one had appeared, a defender was named by the Inquisition, and finally the buried man was condemned to be exhumed and burned together with a statue representing him. The general counsel of the Spanish Inquisition agreed. The sentence was executed April 17. 1595 (it was the next *auto* at Saragossa to that of Dec. 1. 1593).

On Dec. 7. 1598 at Montpellier Casaubon writes in his journal: The widow of my old friend Galés came to us. I loved him on account of his supreme erudition while he lived, at present I reverence the name of the deceased and I should like to be serviceable to her in every way. On the next day he notes that the guest had left. Not a word as to her children.

Galés seems never to have published anything, nor have we any of his writings beyond some letters.

The great scholar's and teacher's noble confession before his stern judges remained unknown during three centuries, till it lately emerged from the archives of Simancas to his honour and to our edification.

2) In funere Ant. Augustini Andreae Schotti Oratio. Reprinted in Augustini opera, vol. I. Lucae 1765 ... nemo fortasse ad jus sacrum profanumque illustrandum, ad artemque redigendum, et dispersa melius colligenda, aut majores animos aut plura literarum subsidia, cum ab Antonio discessero, Cujacium semper excipio, attulisse videatur.

In the same vol. p. XXIII Basilius Zanchus canonicus ordinis Lateranensis, speaking to him calls him jurisperitorum eloquentissimus et eloquentium jurisperitissimus.

J. F. von Schulte (Professor of jurisprudence, a leader of the Old-catholics): Die Geschichte der Quellen und Literatur des Canonischen Rechts. Dritter Band. Erster Theil. 1880. P. 728: Es ist schon oft und mit Recht hervorgehoben worden, dass Ant. Augustinus auf dem Gebiete des canonischen Rechts eine Stellung einnehme wie Alciat und Cujas für das römische. Er ist der Erste, welcher in wirklich wissenschaftlicher Weise vorging ... er ging auf die Quellen zurück. Indem er aber diese selbst kritisch prüft, ist er der eigentliche Begründer der äusseren Geschichte des canonischen Rechts geworden. Man darf sagen, dass mit ihm das Mittelalter auf diesem Gebiete prinzipiell abgethan ist und die Neuzeit begann ... Aber nicht bloss durch seine Methode ist er epochemachend, sondern auch dadurch, dass er seine historischen Studien dem römischen Rechte zuwandte, damit im vollen Zusammenhange blieb mit der geistigen Operation seiner Zeit auf den Rechtsgebieten. Schliesslich muss die Eleganz seiner Sprache und Darstellung noch ganz besonders hervorgehoben werden.

For further details concerning Galés see the essay: *L'humaniste hétérodoxe catalan Pedro Galés par Ed. Boehmer et A. Morel-Fatio* in the *Journal des Savants*, Paris 1902, July, August, September. Some copies have been printed separately, 37 pages in 4° and a special title-leaf.

My article on Galés in the *Revista Cristiana*, Madrid, April 15. 1903, of which I saw no proofs, is disfigured by misprints and other mistakes; even my remark that I had added something new to the extract from the Journal des Savants, has been omitted. This Spanish article may henceforth be neglected, as the additions which it contained are more fully repeated here.

Mr. Paul Besson, the discoverer of the Saravia letters, has written in the journal *L'Eglise libre*, Montpellier, Decembre 11. 1903, a short review of the essay of Morel-Fatio and myself, without giving new data on Galés.

MELCHIOR ROMAN.

1600 Conversion dv | sievr Melchior Roman, | Espagnol, iadis procvrevr | de l'ordre des Iacobis a | Rome: povr la province de | Tholose: lequel à protesté publiquemēt | en l'Eglise Reformée de Bragerac, | le Dimanche vint-septiesme | d'Aoust, mil six cens. | *⁎* | [A tree] | A Bragerac, | Par Gabriel Decourtaneue. | M. DC.

In the repetition of the title on the next leaf is printed Jacobins.
Title-leaf. Text paged 3—32, *signature* Aij *to* H 2. *Eight single leaves, each folded so as to form two. Height of the title column about* 15 *centimeter, breadth about* 9.
In the auction of the Bibliothek Lobris *at Munich in* 1895 (Ludwig Rosenthal's *catalogue of it, p.* 37) *bought by MERCK*.

... Qui est ce Laban trompeur, traistre & ingrat, lequel tant de fois trompa Iacob: Qui est-ce meschant, lequel n'a que l'apparence de bon, & n'a chose solide, n'y constante? Cest ceste papauté & sophisterie, que nous voyons par ses tromperies de richesses, & soubs titre de Saincteté, d'obeissance, de pauureté, de jeusnes, & disciplines feintes, mener vn chacun à desespoir... s'il falloit croire que les oeuures fussent suffisantes, il faudroit totalement nier Iesus Christ, & dire que sa Passion fut sans fruict, Ce qui seroit vn peché contre le Sainct Esprit... Qui seroit si fol, & abruti de vouloir attacher à ceste corruption le Prince d'immortalité, veu que l'hostie consacrée sera souuent rongée des rats, & subjecte à se moysir. Ie puis alleguer en tesmoignage de verité, ce que i'ay veu à Lymoges au cōuent des Iacobins: Le Prouincial y estant arriué trouua vne infinité de formes, ou bien hosties consacrées: en partie mangées des rats & vers, enveloppées de toilles d'araignées. Dauantage audit lieu, le Dimenche de l'octaue du corps (pretendu de Dieu) le Soubsprieur jetta la custode contre terre, accussant fausemēt ceux de la vraye Religion reformée: pour les faire massacrer, comme à confessé vn seruiteur domestique dudict Conuent, qui fut foyté en ladicte Ville & bany d'icelle. (En Leride Ville celebre d'Espaigne, dans l'Eglise du Cōuent de S. Dominique: en ma presence le Procureur du Conuent, estant venu de lauille dit messe, & consacra beaucoup de formes pour donner aux communians: Desquelles en resta plusieurs, dont retornant à la Sacristie, luy en tomba & marcha sur vne: attachée à ses pieds mouillez, sans la pouuoir retirer aucunement: mais fut meslée auec de la boüe, sans la pouuoir retirer d'icelle. Quatre moines Augustins furent pendus en Ciuilhe, pour auoir dit Messe sans auoir intention de consacrer, faisant idolatrer le peuple apres le pain & le Calice. Molon Inquisiteur de Barselone, apres la consecration, coupa l'ostie auec des ciseaux ... les signes demeurent en leur naturelle & essentielle proprieté: Non en leur vsage, qui represente, comme vne viue image, & presente reallement, comme instrument de la grace Diuine, la nourriture Spirituelle, refection viuifiante, gage d'immortalité à l'ame fidelle & penitente, estant le pain la communion du corps, & le Calice benit la communion du sang de vie, connu, receu, apprehendé & appliqué: tant par la secrete operation de l'esprit és esleus, que par l'efficace de la foy, qui est vne presence des choses absentes, vision des inuisibles, hypostase des misteres du salut eternel... Ie ne veux donc estre plus captif en Babilone... Nonobstant les aduersitez, qui nous lauent de toutes imaginations vitieuses, de toutes superstitions & idolatries pour adorer vn seul Dieu, & croire en son Euangile... Ie puis bien dire cecy que i'ay experimenté, mesmes ces iours passés, ausquels i'estois tourmēté de pensees infinies, causees de l'absence de mes parés, & de me voir en vn pays estrange, comme aussi des fascheries de ce que ordinairemēt des papistes parlent de moy, auec beaucoup de menaces & fausetés. Mais quoy qu'il soit ie prieray le Seigneur pour ceux qui me persecutent, & pour ma consolatiō: Car c'est le vray moyen pour me fortifier dauantage en la verité de l'Euangile, comme pour le present ie voy oculairement nóuuelles consolations, nouueaux effects du Sainct Esprit en mon ame, pour mieux perseuerer en l'obeissance de la parole de vie... Par la bouche du Prophete Osée, dit le vray Dieu, en leurs tribulatiōs se leueront & me recognoistront: Par Ezechiel, mon zele sera osté de toy, & ie reposeray, & ne m'indigneray plus contre toy: Dieu nous dōne à entendre clairemēt en ce passage qu'il est irrité d'auantage contre nous, quand il ne nous punit & chastie... ie recognoy que quand i'ay esté en tranquilité & repos il m'auoit cōme oublié: mais si tost qu'il ma fait porter la croix, i'ay recognu que i'estois sa Creature rachetee par son propre Sang... Pourtant Seigneur ie te prieray auiourd'huy me mōstrer ce chemin pour ne faillir: Car ie croy que Iesus-Christ viuant en moy, abolit la malediction de la Loy, condamne le peché, mortifie la mort, luy seul est la paix, cōsolation, iustice, & vie eternelle de mon esprit. Or il faut qu' auiourd'huy l'estonnement face place à toutes ces choses, il faut que toute tristesse, l'enfer s'en aillent: Iesus-Christ demeurāt & viuant en moy, engloutist toutes sortes de maux qui m'affligent. Parquoy ceste vnion & conionction fait que ie suis deliuré des frayeurs, separé de la chair, transporté en Iesus-Christ, & dans son Royaume, qui est le Royaume de grace-iustice, paix, ioye, vie, salut, & gloire eternelle... Mais qu'elle recompence veux-tu auoir, me diront les mondains, puis que tu as quitté ta Patrie, tes parens, moyens que tu pouuois auoir pour viure à ton plaisir: Tu as quitté ta vocation, tu l'as abandonnée au meilleur de ton aage. Ie leur respondray ce que dit S. Bernard en ses meditations, que s'il est fort difficile à l'vn des plus iustes en la Loy se sauuer à l'heure de la mort, il sera plus difficile & cōme impossible que celuy soit sauué, lequel en sa mort fait present à Dieu de ses os, lesquels les chiens ne voudroient, ayās donné leur chair au diable, comme ils font, employant le temps en vaine gloire, & superbe ambition, se delectans auec la chair, guidés & conduits par le malin: Mais ils me diront qu'à l'heure de la mort par la bulle du Pape, disant Sainct Pierre, Sainct Iean, Sainct Paul, Sainct Chrespas, & S. Machere, aydés moy, ils seront sauués. Or attendans ce temps là, ils verrōt manifestement cōme Dieu les ouïra, ou attribuans à la creature la gloire de l'Eternel, mettans leur esperance en la Bulle de la Crusade, fort estimée en Espaigne, & achetée dix solz par chacun an, pour pouuoir manger des oeufs, laict, beurre, fromage en quaresme, chose bien ridicule, & sur tout estre absous, ou auoir remission des pechés, tant de la coulpe, que de la peine vne fois en la vie, vne autre fois, (ce qui esteint le purgatoire) en l'article de la mort, Outre cela il y a vne autre Bulle nommée delos finados: C'est à dire des morts, par laquelle, bien payée tous les ans, le viuant peut retirer pour autant de bulles, autant d'ames de ses amis ou parens des peines: **Bref il s'amasse force argent, & gros reuenu des indulgences, ou bien pardons du Pontife Romain, se disant tenir & garder le tresor du Sang de Christ, & des Martyrs.** Abus & piperie auaritieuse, contraires aux sainctes lettres, qui certifient que la misericorde du Pere des compassions, presente aux fidelles la remission des pechés à salut, par la vertu de son Esprit, appliquée & receüe de la foy viue & iustifiante, d'vn chacun croyant en Christ, donné pour nostre iustice, sanctification, & redemption, mort pour nos pechés, & resuscité pour nostre iustification. C'est la toute mon esperance, le fondement de ma foy, pour vaincre les terreurs du peché & de la mort, afin de viure eternellement. De mesme farine puante que les bulles susdictes, est la Canonization des Sainets & Sainetes deifiées, apres lesquelles les ignorans paillardent spirituellement, & idolatrēt follement auec impieté & infidelité contre Dieu, seul puissant à sauuer & viuifier. De la viennent tant de pelerinages és païs estranges, sous pretexte desquels plusieurs adulteres, fornications, sodomies, incestes, yurongneries, & autres malefices execrables se commettēt ordinairement, Et les corps de ceux sont adorés & honorés par superstitions en terre, desquels souuent les ames sont tourmentées en Enfer. La procedure que tient le Pontife Romain à Canonizer plusieurs Saincts pour la pluspart pretendus, le rend tout notoire. Car l'on à mis & met en ce ranc depuis le regne du Papisme, ceux dōt il ne reste aucune memoire ny tesmoignage de leur vie & conuersatiō: afin que par la longueur du temps, & flux des siecles soit enfantée l'oubliance de leurs vices, & crimes enormes qu'ils pourroient auoir perpetrées. Puis apres si quelqu'vn ose parler contre telles personnes, afin d'empescher qu'on ne leur attribue la sainteté à faux titre, l'Inquisition scait bien remedier par cruelles peines, & fermer la bouche auec torment. D'auantage ne manquent en ses affaires les dorures, odeurs aromatiques, paremens precieux, pierreries, impostures, illusions de signes & prodiges, tant és tombeaux on les reliques sont posées, qu'és statues erigées, ausquelles des larmes souuent sont attribuées, des mouuemens artificiels, afin de tromper par semblables spectacles les yeux des spectateurs. Chose assés familiere, & mesmes que la iustice à recognuë, punissant tels pipeurs. Bref sans entrer plus profond en cet abisme de matiere si deplorable, ie diray seulement que l'or, l'argent, les faueurs, les largesses enuers le Pape, seruent aussi à esleuer en cette reputatiō de Sainctété, & edification prouenante, non de l'esprit de sanctification, mais de l'authorité d'vn homme pecheur & mortel. Tesmoin en sera le bruit esclattant dans Rome, en plusieurs Royaumes, & dans les Conuens des Moynes, touchant l'inuention des Iesuistes, qui ont offert cinquante mil' escus, Employé le credit des Potentats & Princes diuers, afin de faire canonizer Ignace leur Patron, & premier fondateur. Mais sa mal'heureuse memoire est si ressēte qu'il n'a peu encores passer, ny aucun de ses disciples. Sur ce propos des impostures en ce fait, ie n'oubliray les traicts de la Nonain de Portugal, tant renommée, à cause des effects du diable en sa personne. Elle priant se haussoit en l'air, sans appuy visible, Elle portoit en sa teste les espines, & playes de Iesus-Christ, és autres parties du corps semblablement. Pourtant plusieurs Princes, Ducs, Seigneurs, & vn nōbre innombrable de peuple couroit de païs treslointain, pour la voir & adorer. Or le Seigneur de verité en fin descouurit ce mensonge diabolique, & l'inquisition, forcée de la lumiere estincelante de ceste verité, le reprima. Ce sont l'a des Saincts & des Sainctes leur enfantement & qualité, ou les Papistes esperent, attendent secours en vie & en la mort. Pourquoy ie renonce à cela, & pose toute ma fiance à mon Createur. Quant à l'absence de mes parentés, & de ma patrie, ie dois rendre graces infinies à Dieu tout puissant, de ce qu'il ne m'a point mis au rang vniuersel: mais au rang particulier, m'ayant retiré de la seruitude du diable, de l'adoration des Idoles, de l'inuention & erreurs des hommes, pour me communiquer les dons & graces de son Sainct Euangile... L'eunuque de Candace[a] cheminoit au Royaume d'Ethiopie. Quand venant de Ierusalem Sainct Philippe luy apparut, lequel luy declara l'Escriture Saincte, le Baptiza, & l'instruit és choses de la foy, comme dit S. Luc aux Actes 8.[b] Plus il apprint en vne heure, esloigné de sa patrie, qu'en toute sa vie demeurant en sa maison. Ie puis bien dire cecy en verité: car tandis que i'ay conuersé en ma patrie, ie n'ay iamais cognu que traditions & fatras infinis, lesquels au jour du jugement m'eussent jetté en desespoir & perditiō: mais si tost que ie me suis retiré à l'Euangile, soubs les ailes de la grace diuine, esloigné des miens, i'ay apprins en vn iour plus qu' en tout le temps passé de ma vie... Au reste si quelqu'vn est desireux de sçauoir quels sont mes parens, & les charges publiques que i'ay exercées entre les Papistes, auant ma Conuersion, ie le diray briefuement, non pour me glorifier en cela: mais afin de repousser toute calomnie, qui pourroit suruenir, comme les fidelles y sont fort sujets. Mon pere s'appelle Melchior Roman Fidalgo, & la mere de mon pere Ferrer, des Villes de Frague, Caspe, au Royaume d'aragō. Ma mere s'appelloit Isabeau Ramon,[c] de les Baillies d'Aragon, assés bien renommés & connus.[d] Car d'iceux sont sortis S. Roman Martir & soldat. Vn Cardinal nōmé Romain, & Sainct Vincēt Ferrer, le corps duquel est venere superstiticusement en Bretaigne:[e] Derechef S. Raymō Euesque de Balbastre,[f] ou il est adoré par jdolatrie. Telles Canonizations declarent assés ma race, n'estant besoin d'en parlé d'auantage.[g] Quant à ma charge accompagnant l'Inquisiteur Samora, ie vis brusler à Saragousse vn vertueux personnage, pour la querelle de la Religion, lequel tant par sa viue voix & doctrine, que constance du Martire, me persuada de quitter les erreurs du Papisme. Ceste cause me transporta en France, estant arriué en la Prouince de Toulouse, ie fus reçeu assés humainement dans le Conuent d'Agen, puis apres suruenant le Chapitre tenu en l'Isle en Dodon, president Pierre Capdeuile Prouincial, d'vn consentement tous m'esturent Procureur Prouincial, pour aller à Rome, comme appert par la lettre, qui commence. Nos infra signati, &c. Retourné de Rome, mes affaires expediés, le Prouincial me fit son visiteur & vicaire Prouincial, cōme il appert par la lettre qui commence. Nos qui infra, &c. En fin voyant ma conuersation honneste & vertueuse, ils me feirent Confesseur des Dames du Chapellet d'Agen. Or loüé soit le Pere des lumieres, m'ayant par la grace de son S. Esprit, en faueur de son fils, desbandé les yeux, manifesté les corruptions du Papisme, declaré ou ie trouuerois la tranquillité de ma conscience, la verité du salut de mō ame: Ie luy en rens actiōs de graces eternelles, sur tous les autres benefices de sa liberalité enuers moy, protestāt d'employer les graces & dons qu'il m'a distribués à la glorieuse loüange de sa Majesté, edification de son Eglise, la ou sa parolle est purement preschée, les Saincts Sacremens sincerement administrés, selon l'institution du Seigneur. Pro-

---

a) *The original has* Le nuque de Candaces.
b) *The original has* 6.
c) sic Ramon *in the original.*
d) *The German translates* I. R., in den Vogteien oder Ämtern in Aragonien berühmte und wohlbekannte Leute.
e) *where he died in* 1419.
f) Barbastro *in Aragon.*
g) *From the difference between* s'apelle *and* s'appelloit *one must conclude that his mother had died, but his father was still living.*

testant que ie renonce à la Papauté, Messe erreurs & autres superstitions, disposé d'espendre mon propre sang & vie, pour la parolle de Dieu, qui m'enseigne parfaictement mon salut. Parquoy à mō exemple, j'exhorte toutes sortes d'ames, desireuses de leur salut, s'adonner à l'intelligence de verité, mespriser le mōde, ne craindre aduersité, preferer de ioye excellente l'eternité, gloire de l'heritage celeste, à toutes cōmodités, & vanités mondaines, craignans que s'ils mesprisent la voix du Sauueur, s'endurcissant en leur mal, il ny ait plus de lien de repentance, ains pleurs & grincement de dents en la gehenne espouuentable, au lieu de leurs ris, passetemps, & voluptés brieues. Or ie supplie le tout puissant, que nous faisant à tous bien connoistre la brieueté, incertitude, & calamité ds la vie presente, nous cerchions d'auancer sa gloire en la voye droicte, nous conduisant en son Royaume. Ainsi soit il.

In diæ mandauit dominus misericordiam suam,
Et nocte canticum eius. Psal. 41.
Manus supra globum.
O
Dextra tenet coelū, manus altera sustinet orbē,
Vt me sancta leuat, sic grauis ista premit.
Sidera perlegerem semper, diuumque cohortes,
Me nisi notorum solicitaret amor.
H
Lux vera Ioan. I.
Illumina tenebras meas. Pseau. 29.
Splendor eius. Abachu. 5.
De ti depende mi ser:
de tu luz, mi resplandor:
Mi valor, de tu valor.
R I A.
MELCHIOR ROMAN.

1600 Conversion | dv sievr Melchior | Roman Espgnol *[sic]*, ia- | dis Procureur de l'Ordre des | Jacobins à Rome: pour | la Prouince de | Tholose. | *Leqvel a proteste publi- | quement en l'Eglise Reformée de Bergerac, le Di- | menche vint-septiesme d'Aoust, mil six cens.* | A Pontorson. | De l'Imprimerie de Jean de Féure. [*or* -ro?] | 1600. |

Q. 4 sheets, paged to 31. *CAMBRIDGE Trinity.*
Wiffen's tracing from the same copy has Féurs.

1601 Conversion de plusieurs personnages notables de l'église romaine au protestantisme. Sedan, 1601. 12⁰.

GENEVA Bibliothèque Publique.

So registered in the Catalogue de la Bibliothèque Publique de Genève, rédigé par Louis Vaucher. Genève 1834. *P.* 178. *The librarian, Mr. Gas, informed me:* Cet opuscule de 64 pages renferme 7 pièces dont la 3ᵉᵐᵉ p. 23—44 est signé Melchior Roman.

— *Same in* Diverses Revocations *etc.*, du Papisme publiquement faites *etc.* A la Haye 1601. 4 *to. Wiffen's note.*

German from French.

1600 or **1601** there appeared at *Zweybruck* a *German tract containing the conversion of three persons in France to Protestantism, one of them being* Melchior Roman. *See below here the passage from the* Gedenckwürdige Historien 1601.

1601 Gedenckwürdige Hi- | storien vnd Exempla etlicher fürnemer hohes | vnd nidrigen Stands Personen, So in Teutsch- | land, Franckreich vnd Italien, von dem Ab- | göttischen Bapstthumb abgetretten, demselben | offenlich renuncirt, vnd sich zu der Evangeli- | schen Religion begeben haben, deren | Namen auff der andern seitten ver- | zeichnet sind. [*Small ornament*] | Ausz vnderschiedlichen Sprachen ins | Teutsch gebracht. | [*Ornament.*] | Getruckt zu Zweybruck durch Caspar Witteln. | Anno Christi. 1601. |

Q. *Leaf* 2—4 *Preface* An den Christlichen Leser. *Leaf* 5 *is signed* Aij, *with the page-numbers* 3 *and* 4; *the preface has not been taken into account.*

P. 7: Christliche Bekerung Herrn Melchiors Ro- | mans, eines fürnemmen Hispaniers, so etwan von wegen | der Landschafft Tholose, des Jacobiter Ordens Procurator vnd Sachen Verwalter | zu Rom gewesen, vnd sich offenlich in der reformirten Kirchen zu Bra- | gerac, zu der wahren Religion bekennet hat, Sontags den | 27. Augusti. Anno 1600. *Ends p.* 32.

ULM City.

I have ascertained that Roman's autobiographical notices p. 30—32 *agree with the French.*

The preface begins: Wir haben newlichen (Christlicher Leser) treier fürnemer Männer in Franckreich, darunder ein Hispanier, Melchior Roman genannt, gewesē, Bekehrung zu der Christlichen Religion, allhie in truck gegeben, welche Männer (vñ bevorab gedachter Hispanier eines fürnemmen Geschlechts) mit hohem Christlichen eifer begabet vnd erleuchtet worden, — *now in this new edition the lives of four other persons are added (the last of them* Galeazzo Caracciolo).

1601 *The following notice has been copied for me from Wiffen's papers.*

„Von dem leben und sterben eines Margraven von Vico in Italia: welcher ein ungewönlich und verwunderlich exempel einer sehr eifferigen Beständigkeit des einmal angenommenen und bekanten wahren Christlichen Glaubens, allen Christen zur nachrechtung an den tag gegeben wird.

Christliche bekerung Herrn Melchiors Romans, eines furnemen Hispaniers, so etwan von wegen der Landschafft Tholose etc. cum alia." *Sic, perhaps* aliis. Zweyruck 1601. 4 to."

Galeazzo Caracciolo, who appears here in the first place, cannot be one of the three persons in France of whom the above mentioned publication was treating (his conversion took place at Naples and he afterwards lived and died at Geneva); in the Gedenckwürdige Historien *his life is the last one.*

English from French.

1601 Eight learned personages lately couverted (in the Realme of France) from papistrie to the Churches reformed: having aduisedly and holily set downe the reasons that moued them thereunto. The names and degrees of the Conuerts. Melchior Roman, a Spaniard, Proctor for the Jacobins at Rome. 2 John Norman, Subprior of Marestay, a Preacher. 3 Father Abraham, Prior of Carmes in Arles. 4 Anthony Ginestet, a Confessor, of the order of S. Francis. 5 Signeur Lewis of Caransy, a Priest. 6 Father Edmon, a Jesuite Preacher in Burbon, Doctor of Divinity. 7 John Colleij, a Capuchin and a Preacher, Guardian of S. Omer. 8 Symon Palory, Pryor of the Order of the Holy-Crosse. Translated out of the French printed Copies, By W. B. Printed at London for J. B. and are to be solde at the signe of the Bible in Panles Church-yard 1601. 4*to, pages* 95

Copied for me from Wiffen's papers. MADRID National possesses Usox's printed copy according to Menendez Pelayo II *505.*

Licensed on April 20. 1601 *in the Stationers' register (Arber* III 183) *for* mistres Brome *(this name is therefore meant by* J. B. *in the above title-copy):* The conuersion of Eight learned personnages within the kingdom of Ffraunce from properye (*write* poperye) to the true churche Reformed wherein they haue learnedly set Downe the reasons that haue moved them thereunto Translated out of Frenche by W. B. *The names of the* personnages *are given in this entry in the following order:* 1 *Ginestet.* 2 *Caransey.* 3 *Norman.* 4 *Beauval.* 5 Melchior Roman a Spanyard. 6 *Abraham.* 7 *Colleij.* 8 *Pallory.*

On August 23. *of the same year are entered (ib. p.* 191) *for* George Potter *some books* whiche belonged to mystres Brome Lately Deceased, *and among them:* 10. Conuertes. *Arber refers to p.* 183, *viz. to the article just transcribed here; perhaps he means that a new edition enlarged by two other lives had been undertaken.*

„*Another edition* Thirteen learned persons." *Wiffen.*

The voluntary Conuersion and seuerall recantations of ffoure great learned men professed frieres in sundry monasteries of Ffraunce from the errours of Idolatry and popery to the true Religion established in the reformed churche.

Licensed for William Jones *on* March 27. 1604 *in the Stationers' register (Arber* III 257). *It is not probable that Roman is one of the four.*

Errata.

Write p. 7, note 14, l. 17: last; p. 28, note 90 l. 7: ended; p. 89, l. 7 from below: F. instead of J.; p. 160, l. 13: Lisboa.

www.ingramcontent.com/pod-product-compliance
Lightning Source LLC
Chambersburg PA
CBHW051054160426
43193CB00010B/1178